CLOSE KIN AND DISTANT RELATIVES

Close Kin and Distant Relatives

The Paradox of Respectability in Black Women's Literature

SUSANA M. MORRIS

University of Virginia Press

CHARLOTTESVILLE AND LONDON

University of Virginia Press

First published 2014

9 8 7 6 5 4 3 2 1

LIBRARY OF CONGRESS CATALOGING-IN-PUBLICATION DATA

Morris, Susana M., 1980–
    Close kin and distant relatives : the paradox of respectability in Black women's
literature / Susana M. Morris.
    pages   cm
    Includes bibliographical references and index.
    ISBN 978-0-8139-3549-2 (cloth : alk. paper)
    ISBN 978-0-8139-3550-8 (pbk. : alk. paper)
    ISBN 978-0-8139-3551-5 (e-book)
    1. American fiction—African American authors—History and criticism. 2. American
fiction—Women authors—History and criticism. 3. Women and literature—United
States—History—20th century. 4. Families in literature. 5. Politics and literature—
United States—History—20th century. 6. African Americans—Intellectual life.
7. African Americans in literature. I. Title.
PS374.N4M67 2014
813'.54099287—dc23

                                                                    2013023501

A book in the American Literatures Initiative (ALI), a collaborative
publishing project of NYU Press, Fordham University Press, Rutgers
University Press, Temple University Press, and the University of Virginia
Press. The Initiative is supported by The Andrew W. Mellon Foundation.
For more information, please visit www.americanliteratures.org.

To my mother,
Ethlyn Morris,
my first and best teacher

Contents

Acknowledgments

Not only does it take a village to raise a child, it also takes a village to write a book. And I am both beyond blessed and grateful to have a village that has truly illuminated an ethic of community support and accountability in my own life. I thank Lois A. Brown, Amy E. Martin, Michelle Stephens, and Lucas B. Wilson, professors I had as an undergraduate at Mount Holyoke College, for lighting my path toward graduate school and for continuing to inspire me.

My time as a graduate student at Emory University has also been invaluable in this journey. I am eternally grateful to my dissertation chair, Frances Smith Foster, for her generosity and honesty throughout the years. I thank Kharen Fulton for her continuing kindness and encouragement. I offer special thanks to Berky Abreu and Rudolph P. Byrd for providing stellar examples of grace and charity. May you both rest in peace and in power.

Support from Auburn University's Department of English, College of Liberal Arts, and Office of Diversity and Multicultural Affairs allowed me time to devote to my research. I thank my current and former Auburn colleagues for the generous support they have shown in a number of ways, especially Chantel Acevedo, Jean Joiner, Tracey K. Parker, Cheryl Seals, Patricia Serviss, L. Octavia Tripp, Victor Villanueva, and Hilary Wyss. Special thanks go to Paula R. Backscheider for her devoted mentorship and kindness, and for always having an open door.

Thank you to DoVeanna S. Fulton for generously reading a very rough draft of the manuscript. This project would not have come to fruition without her keen eye, sharp questions, great advice, and steadfast encouragement. I am also grateful to everyone at the University of Virginia Press who worked on this book. The experience has strengthened my research in profound ways.

Very special thanks go to my phenomenal chosen family. I appreciate the unselfish giving of your time, intellectual energy, and support. The phone calls, G-chatting, and Skyping kept me tethered to reality, gave me something to smile about, and nourished me so that I could keep going. Words really are inadequate to express the full measure of my gratitude. I appreciate all the love and support from my folks over at the Crunk Feminist Collective. Thanks to Brittney Cooper and Robert J. Patterson for reading and critiquing early drafts of this work. You two are not only great friends and comrades but ideal readers who helped me step up my game and built up my confidence too. Eesha Pandit, thank you so much for your listening ear, your wit, and your kindness. You're the best.

Thanks to my sisters, Rose Marie Rick and Carine George, for your love and examples as voracious readers. Much love to my girls, Alexa Encarnacion, Belissa Alvarez, and Heidy Gonzalez. Thank you for your unconditional love and support. You ladies are the best sister-friends anyone could ask for.

Many thanks to Lola Maye, whose not-so-silent feline companionship was a welcome distraction and a frequent source of comfort, laughter, and delight.

This book is dedicated to my mother, Ethlyn Morris. You recognized my love for books early on and did everything in your power to nurture my desire to learn. I would not be where I am today without you. Thank you for your unwavering support and love.

CLOSE KIN AND DISTANT RELATIVES

Introduction: Family Matters

Tensions around marriage and family provide perhaps some of the most compelling examples of the ambivalence around respectability politics for many Blacks in the United States and the Caribbean. Take, for instance, the issue of marriage. In a recent article entitled "When Having Babies Beats Marriage," *Harvard Magazine* writer Kevin Harnett provides persuasive evidence that "the decoupling of marriage from childbearing among lower-income Americans is arguably the most profound social trend in American life today and has sparked intense political debate" (11–12). While "When Having Babies Beats Marriage" is focused generally on low-income families of all stripes, it is important to note that, more often than not, the term *low-income family* and its attendant characteristics—female-headed, poverty-stricken, undereducated—have been code for the (mis)perceptions of Black families generally in the public imaginary.[1] Given the significance of marriage and family in public discourse during the last decades of the twentieth century, Harnett's claim is certainly not without merit.[2] Harnett outlines the trends concerning marriage, noting that "in 1960 it didn't matter if you were rich or poor, college-educated or a high-school dropout—almost all American women waited until they were married to have kids. Now 57 percent of women with high-school degrees or less education are unmarried when they bear their first child" (11). However, citing the research of public policy scholar Kathryn Edin, Harnett also suggests that "even as low-income Americans view marriage as out of reach . . . they continue to see bearing and raising children as the most meaningful activity in their lives" (12).[3] That is, even without legal marriage the low-income Americans featured in the article routinely form strong attachments to one another through child rearing. Although "When Having Babies Beats Marriage" foreground's Edin's desire to "[reestablish] the link between childbearing and marriage in low-income communities," the article clearly outlines major shifts in values in contemporary society; many Americans have rejected the idea of a necessary link between marriage and childbearing, a decision that reveals the ongoing significance of raising children in family units that may or may not be connected by formal marriage (12).

Similar ideological shifts are also occurring throughout the Caribbean.[4] In nations such as Barbados, Jamaica, and Trinidad and Tobago, cohabitation and out-of-wedlock births among the working class of African descent are not uncommon.[5] What is changing, however, is the reaction to such circumstances when they occur among the middle classes. The scholar of Caribbean family studies Raymond T. Smith asserts that "fortunately, and not a little ironically, 'mainstream' family practice is beginning to approximate, in some respects at least, the previously despised patterns of poor [Blacks] so that the pejorative expressions such as 'born out of wedlock' are losing their capacity to injure" (2–3). Indeed, Smith uncouples deviance from family practices that do not affirm "traditional" ideals of respectable family life, noting that "unstable marriage, separate residences of spouses, or even the complete whittling away of the marriage relationship . . . is not necessarily a sign of social instability or of pathological development" (24). These shifts in notions of respectability and family underscore both the dynamic nature of contemporary families and an increasing recognition that functional family life is not a one-size-fits-all proposition.

Nevertheless, even as the numbers of those pursuing legal marriage decrease in the United States and the Caribbean, the notion that marriage is both an ideal worth pursuing and an example of highly respectable behavior has not gone out of fashion—a circumstance that has, at times, yielded problematic results. Indeed, marriage not only has continued to be an ideal for many Blacks in the United States and the Caribbean but in some cases has also been ascribed an elevated, almost mythical, status.[6] To be clear, I am not dismissing marriage as a viable social practice or institution. However, I do want to underscore the ways in which heterosexual marriage is often discussed not only as a panacea for the problems of working-class Blacks but also as a marker of social responsibility and respectability.

Thus the ongoing significance of marriage, for example, as an ideal, even as Black folk make serious commitments to one another in other forms of intimate family practices, is critical to recognize, for it reveals important tensions in Black communities in both the Caribbean and the United States.[7] The reality of fluid family practices has not completely eliminated the continuing ideological importance of structures such as the nuclear family and legal marriage in the forefront of public and private discourses on African American and Black Caribbean families and respectability. While adhering to the ideals of respectability politics, such as those that underscore marriage as a major pathway to mainstream social acceptance, respect, and legitimacy, can certainly raise one's cultural currency and perhaps even afford an individual, or a family, a certain degree of stability, power, and privilege, it is difficult for many and impossible for some. Furthermore, as Raymond T. Smith suggests, while notions of what constitutes a respectable family may be expanding in the public imaginary more generally, poor or working-class Blacks who deviate from the patterns of normative respectability are often stigmatized.[8] So what does it mean when what is touted as a primary way to secure honor and respect in one's community or in society at large is connected to practices that can be alienating, difficult, or even exclusionary? Yet not adhering to the practices that reflect mainstream notions of respectability may also result in the possibility of alienation and social stigma. The result is a sort of paradox of respectability, by which I mean simultaneously desiring to be respectable according to the ideals of respectability politics and finding this difficult, if not impossible. Thus respectability, at least as imagined through the current manifestation of the politics of respectability, is largely out of reach for many Blacks, which makes being judged by or internalizing a rubric informed by the politics unfair at best and cruel at worst.

Conversations around the pitfalls of respectability politics are occurring on multiple fronts, such as criticism, film, history, sociology, and even social media; however, in *Close Kin and Distant Relatives: The Paradox of Respectability in Black Women's Literature* my interest lies primarily in the ways in which Black women writers from the Caribbean and the United States make sense of and challenge the prevailing links between normative notions of respectability and family in literature of the last decades of the twentieth century. This project's attention to the Diasporic manifestations of respectability politics both draws attention to aspects of respectability politics that are obscured by singular analyses and reveals aspects of the operations of Diaspora that are often underanalyzed.[9] I contend that there is a discernable tradition in Black women's literature from the Caribbean and the United States written in the last decades of the twentieth century that challenges many popular discourses around the concepts of family and respectability and that advocates for radical understandings of community support and accountability, especially as these relate to women's roles within families. Writers such as Erna Brodber, Michelle Cliff, Gloria Naylor, and Alice Walker depict Black families that are ravaged by respectability politics and have ambivalent intimate relationships as a result.[10] These writers invoke a hermeneutics of suspicion that challenges the ideals of respectability politics, using ambivalent familial bonds among characters not to highlight "Black pathology" but to underscore the paradox of respectability.

The ambivalent familial connections in these works are marked not by hesitancy or indecision but by a set of seeming contradictions—a strong sense of duty and, simultaneously, an active harboring of resentment toward duty, for example—that the paradox of respectability begets. Black women writers in this tradition do not dismiss the possibility of sustaining and affirming family systems. However, they do illustrate that it is most often rooted in an ethic of community support and accountability that rejects repressive sexual and social mores and class hierarchies. Furthermore, Black women writers advocate a fundamental reimagining of kinship to include examples of extended and fictive kin (as opposed to making the nuclear family the only legitimate model), platonic unions (such as Boston marriages), and queer families (such as same-sex unions and polyamory).[11] Also at the core of these family systems is a connection to affirming African Diasporic cultural rites—such as music, dance, storytelling, and writing—that prompt and/or assist characters in (re)negotiating transgressive forms of community. Black women writers in this tradition call for an understanding of family that includes all of these elements and thus moves beyond the narrow confines of respectability politics' ideology about the Black family.

This project specifically profiles the work of Paule Marshall, Jamaica Kincaid, Edwidge Danticat, and Sapphire as representative examples of late twentieth-century Black women's writing about family, ambivalence, and notions of respectability. The novels I have chosen to discuss in the project are connected not simply because they are written by Black women since 1970 but because they are representative of a literary tradition that illuminates the impact of respectability politics and grapples with the paradox of respectability in distinct but interrelated ways.

* * *

Close Kin and Distant Relatives illuminates the complexities of respectability politics and its depiction in African American and Black Caribbean women's literature published in the last decades of the twentieth century.[12] This project's Diasporic focus underscores respectability politics' complicated political history across several regions, revealing that grappling with this strategy is often a central aspect of modern Black life in the Caribbean and the United States. At its core, respectability politics is a strategy for navigating a hostile society that characterizes Blackness as the definition of deviance—animalistic, hypersexual, ignorant, uncivilized; it makes bettering one's life chances depend on adhering to a set of mainstream ideals regarding behavior, and it takes place where the public sphere meets the private.

There are some subtle differences in the manifestation of respectability politics in the Caribbean and its U.S. American counterpart. Evelyn Brooks Higginbotham coined the term to describe, in the United States, the political machinations that arose out of African American women's participation in the Black Baptist Church. The ideology these women employed about honor, self-respect, piety, and propriety as a path to full citizenship in American society reflected a social strategy that reverberated, and continues to reverberate, across Black communities.[13] Peter J. Wilson uses the concepts of respectability and reputation to describe the organizing principles of Caribbean family life.[14] Respectability denotes a set of behaviors largely dedicated to a public image that reflects piety, sexual modesty, and strict notions of dignity and honor, particularly for women.[15] Conversely, reputation is in some ways respectability's symbiotic nemesis: a set of behaviors, like licentiousness and irresponsibility, that are reactions to respectability's constraints. Yet although they are seemingly antithetical to traditional notions of respectability, they are not only tolerated but, in some cases, applauded.[16] Whereas in the United States respectability politics evolved as a political group strategy with the aim of improving conditions for Blacks dealing with de facto and de jure segregation, in the Caribbean it evolved as a set of cultural practices that were the offspring of class hierarchies and color caste systems developing after the "end" of slavery and persisting into the period of independence from colonial powers.[17]

Nevertheless, despite these distinctions, there are important points of convergence in the role of respectability politics in the United States and the Caribbean. Both regions have distinct but interrelated racial histories, and respectability politics is a tie that binds, albeit in ways particularly connected to the social landscape of each region. In the United States, for example, respectability politics is a group strategy with interracial and intraracial ramifications, used in a society where Blacks are marginalized and yet under intense public surveillance. In Caribbean nations where there is a Black majority (even if white or mixed-race elites still maintain a modicum of political and economic power), respectability politics is an intraracial social strategy that not only helps differentiate the Black middle class from the working class but also operates as a social climbing strategy for the working class to (attempt or aspire to) enter the upper echelons.[18] Moreover, regional distinctions can be blurred further, especially given the extensive migration between the two regions, which has often allowed the influence of multiple types of respectability politics to coalesce. Ultimately, my analysis of Black women's literature reveals that in the Caribbean and the United States the politics of respectability is a strategy for dealing with various iterations of imperial power, however distinctly manifested in each region.[19] In both the Caribbean and the United States it is aligned with what Inderpal Grewal and Caren Kaplan have called a network of "scattered hegemonies" that work in tandem across regions to reify dominant structures of power.[20] Thus my comparative approach underscores respectability to be not just a strategy for navigating the operations of racism within the United States but part of a larger Diasporic, anticolonial framework that Diasporic Black peoples have used to both navigate and resist the operations of racial politics in their respective cultural and national contexts. Although there are some key differences in the respectability politics of the United States and the Caribbean, there are also significant similarities that make the two regions worth considering together.

This book both enters a vibrant conversation in critical discourse and makes a significant contribution to the discussion of ambivalence, respectability, and family life in recent African American and Black Caribbean women's literature.[21] The analysis in the following chapters is a comparative study that enacts a paradigm shift in literary studies, foregrounding the role of ambivalence in Black women's literature in order to illuminate the ways in which Black women craft antiracist feminist narratives about family amid hegemonic pressures to do otherwise. As respectability is a long-standing, though differently iterated, facet of Diasporic Black subjectivity, ambivalence is a critical feature of Black communities in the Caribbean and the United States. This critical intervention seeks to expand the ways in which we recognize the purposes of respectability politics in Black family dynamics through a comparative analysis of the complicated familial negotiations Black women writers portray and, ultimately, calls for a new understanding of the ways in which Black women writers write themselves into and against prevailing narratives of family.

* * *

In the 1970s, at the start of what some critics have called the Black women's literary renaissance, Black women writers in the Caribbean and the United States such as Sylvia Wynter, Merle Hodge, Toni Morrison, Alice Walker, and Gayl Jones published texts in which characters often wrestled with the connection between respectability politics and family. With characters such as Tee in Merle Hodge's *Crick Crack Monkey* and Nel in Toni Morrison's *Sula*, writers repeatedly illustrated the heavy burden and cost that the paradox of respectability can be for many Black women. In both texts, young Black women eschew non-normative family politics in favor of the seeming security and safety of traditional notions of familial respectability, Tee in aligning herself with Aunt Becca's family and Nel in losing her identity first to Jude and then in an all-encompassing motherhood. However, both characters' ambivalent sense of self and family underscores how ultimately isolating and destructive these choices can be for these Black women and their peers.

Likewise, Gayl Jones's 1975 novel *Corregidora* is another poignant early example within this renaissance of writings exploring the violence of respectability politics, and a brief look at the text underscores the issues at the center of this tradition in late twentieth-century Black women's literature. In the novel, a family of Afro-Brazilian women living in rural Kentucky honor the horrific memory of their ancestors by defiantly refusing to be silenced. However, the Corregidora women not only pay homage to their ancestral memory as a defense against a history of injustice but also fall prey to the paradox of respectability, becoming mired in parochial ideals, fostered in both Brazil and the United States, that incite ambivalence toward and even disconnection from their family members. Nevertheless, the novel also draws attention to the possibility of the Corregidoras counteracting this repressive ideology with an alternative ethic of family. In *Corregidora*, Ursa uses the blues to reconfigure her identity and her notion of family without falling back on inflexible and reactionary notions of respectability. Ultimately, the novel illuminates that reclaiming Diasporic modes of expression (such as the blues) is helpful but not wholly effective in combating familial violence and dysfunction. This suggests that for Black women supportive community where kinship ventures beyond the stultifying borders of respectability on the one hand and isolation on the other is of vital importance.

Crick Crack Monkey, *Sula*, and *Corregidora* are not unique in their illustration of the Diasporic ramifications of the paradox of respectability and their call for a more transgressive ethos of family. Indeed, these novels reflect a pervasive motif concerning ambivalence, family, and respectability politics seen throughout African American and Black Caribbean women's literature in the last forty years. These novels chart a turn toward hegemonic notions of respectability as a political strategy often called on by Blacks (under both inter- and intraracial pressure). However, these novels reject the oft-repeated narratives that blame Black pathology, repeatedly insisting that adhering to respectability politics not only is potentially damaging, but can, in fact, lead to the dissolution of some families. Indeed, novelists suggest that (re)assessing the range of family constructs that Blacks have employed during slavery, colonialism, and their wake rather than believing that respectability politics is the only way to configure family is key to improving conditions for Black people. Furthermore, literature in this tradition insists that healthy expressions of family are also tied to a type of Diasporic cultural connection; for Ursa it is the blues, for Sophie in Danticat's *Breath, Eyes, Memory* it is storytelling. Alternatively, those who become estranged from these forms of creative expression are often eventually estranged from their families and communities as well. Lastly, works in this tradition insist that these lessons are important not simply for their characters but for Black women across the Diaspora.

While the novels explored in this book show diverse manifestations of respectability and family dynamics, they also show commonalities in their depictions of respectability politics and the paradox of respectability. In late twentieth-century literature by African American and Black Caribbean writers, the ideals of the respectability politics include but are not limited to a steadfast sense of duty to family and community; emphasis on self-respect and honor; rigid gender roles and identities; strict adherence to the notion that the nuclear family is the ideal family model; investment in a middle- or upper-middle-class identity; narrow notions of propriety, sexual and otherwise; a commitment to policing the behavior of members within the family and community; and attitudes of detachment, rejection, or hostility toward a range of Black cultural practices not considered appropriately mainstream. All of these characteristics are interconnected and serve not only to strengthen one another but also to reify the hegemony of dominant power structures, such as class and gender inequities, more generally. Respectability politics, then, grows out of a complicated and intertwined set of political histories and prerogatives that are concerned with improving conditions for Blacks but that also employ tactics such as surveillance, control, and repression; that provide insufficient political gains; and that ultimately secure the hegemony of ruling social structures.

In this book, I am most interested in how writers depict women's roles in families and how the paradox of respectability affects their familial connections, largely through the effects of ambivalence. To that end, my analysis uses feminist theologian Elisabeth Schüssler Fiorenza's notion of "kyriarchy" to describe the structures of domination at work in the paradox of respectability. Kyriarchy is a "socio-cultural and religious system of domination constituted by intersecting multiplicative structures of oppression," a notion that is particularly suited to foregrounding how women participate in domination, insubordination, support, and a whole host of other interactions within society. The term *kyriarchy*, as opposed to *patriarchy*, allows for a more nuanced understanding of power dynamics that is particularly helpful in understanding the ways in which women relate to one another in a misogynistic society (118). My analysis of Black women's writing contends that these novels illustrate a concurrent investment in and wariness of kyriocentric social systems that ultimately creates ambivalent relationships within individuals and families. There are key features to this ambivalence as depicted in Black women's writing. For example, duty to family is prized but is, at the same time, often considered a burden because of the high price it exacts. Similarly, Black women's writing also depicts the strains of family relationships beneath the facade of stability and respectability. Novels frequently portray female characters who question or struggle with adherence to the ideals of respectability politics, yet persist in policing others' behavior under the same rubric. Likewise, these writers emphasize characters who project blame onto others for their own perceived failings in living up to the ideals of respectability politics. Through these recurring themes, Black women writers insist that because of the paradox of respectability, a family under the sway of respectability politics cannot be functional, even if its adherents gain or attempt to gain social privilege.

Thus my analysis of the role of ambivalence in Black women's literature in this book highlights its presence as an authorial strategy that foregrounds the potential dangers of respectability politics for Blacks throughout the Diaspora. Black women writers repeatedly reveal that those who adhere to such repressive politics can do their families more harm than good, and they use ambivalence as a marker of this intimate disruption. This ambivalence is a generative construct, a set of behaviors used to navigate hostile and confusing political social terrain and not an attempt to opt out of decision making. Black women writers configure ambivalence in a variety of ways, perhaps most notably through portrayals of familial relationships marked by intense notions of duty, honor, and respect coupled with thinly veiled enmity, indifference, estrangement, repression, and even outright domination and/or violence.

Alice Walker, for instance, uses ambivalence to foreground destructive family practices in *The Color Purple*. Harpo and Sofia's relationship is functional and perhaps even somewhat egalitarian at the start of their marriage, with the couple eschewing normative divisions of domestic labor. For example, in a gendered role reversal that rejects the norms of their community, Sofia fixes the roof while Harpo tidies the kitchen. It is not until Harpo becomes overly concerned with his status as a respectable man in his community, wanting Sofia to "mind," that ambivalence comes into play in Walker's depiction of their relationship and, subsequently, their family is divided. Thus Walker highlights the destructiveness of respectability politics, for, in Celie's words, if Harpo "hadn't tried to rule over Sofia the white folks never would have caught her" (200). Walker, then, aligns Harpo's desire for control with the violence of white supremacy.

Similarly, in *Me Dying Trial*, Patricia Powell profiles the tumultuous marriage of Gwennie and Walter, which produces six children and a family life racked with violence and repression. While Gwennie revels in her role as a respectable Jamaican woman and schoolteacher, the constant threat of physical and emotional violence that she endures from her husband leaves her resentful and ambivalent about their relationship and their family unit, particularly their ever-increasing brood of children. Powell describes Gwennie's affair with Luther and her move to the States as a result of this ambivalence. Thus, although Gwennie has a socially sanctioned position based on her family status, Powell uses her ambivalence to expose the facade of the "protective" nuclear family system, as idealized in respectability politics.

Some Black women writers' depictions of ambivalent relationships in families can also be understood as manifestations of what Gay Wilentz has identified as "dis-ease," or socially constructed illness (*Healing Narratives* 21). This dis-ease, such as Avey Johnson's mysterious illness in Paule Marshall's *Praisesong for the Widow* and Annie John's adolescent malaise in Jamaica Kincaid's titular novel, is a mental and physical illness brought on by the pressures of the paradox of respectability, which manifests in order for the individual to seek healing. Time and again, Black women writers use ambivalence to underscore the potential destructiveness of respectability politics. Thus my analysis insists that it is crucial to understand the pivotal role of ambivalence in Black women's literature from the Caribbean and the United States written in the last decades of the twentieth century.

In addition to using ambivalence to cast doubt on respectability politics, Black women writers in this tradition respond to discourses of respectability with what I have termed an ethic of community support and accountability, an ethos of family that emphasizes mutually observed affection, affirmation, loyalty, and respect without the repressive aspects of respectability politics.[22] This ethic includes fluid gender roles, expansive notions of sex and sexualities, elastic notions of propriety and dignity, rootedness in a variety of Diasporic cultural practices without romance or nostalgia, and an emphasis on familial accountability rather than policing or surveillance. It is not a political strategy in the way that respectability politics has been (in the United States, at least) but a diverse range of cultural practices that, like respectability politics, is intent on improving Black people's lived experiences. What I have termed an ethic of community support and accountability is a set of practices and thus is invoked in a whole range of ways throughout Black women's writings. Therefore, while some novels are more centered on complicating class dynamics (*Praisesong for the Widow*), some are more interested in unpacking conflicts between mothers and daughters (*Annie John*). Likewise, while some novels are more engaged in challenging state-sanctioned violence and its domestic counterpart (*Breath, Eyes, Memory*), others are rejecting the kyriarchy in Black nationalism and homophobia in favor of truly Diasporic connections (*Push*). Nonetheless, all of these works foreground a similar set of ideals. Like respectability politics, this ethic of community support and accountability emphasizes self-respect, honor, and duty to loved ones. But unlike respectability politics, this ethic is not primarily connected to improving one's social standing in the larger society; instead, it is concerned with maintaining and strengthening bonds within families and communities.

A large part of my analysis of Black women writers' depictions of an ethic of community support and accountability foregrounds the importance of Diasporic cultural practices, such as dance, healing arts, music, poetry, spirituality, and storytelling. Writers depict these practices as possible forms of validation and vehicles to heal dis-ease, with women embracing them as ways to affirm themselves and connect to others. As we know, family life is often sustained or reified through tradition and ritual.[23] Such rites and rules largely serve to affirm the primacy of repressive race and class relations, in addition to centering heterosexuality as a dominant paradigm. Black women writers who invoke an ethic of community support and accountability, however, illustrate that family traditions can also actively decenter and even reject oppressive ideologies. To that end, they depict traditions and rituals that affirm Blacks, and Black women in particular, in ways that do not simply reinscribe kyriocentric power dynamics. Feminist practices of traditions such as art, music, poetry, sewing, storytelling, and syncretic religions, (obeah, *Santería, vodou*) become unifying experiences that honor both the collective and the individual. For example, in Gloria Naylor's *Mama Day* African-derived mystical and spiritual practices not only help provide individual identities for the characters but also strengthen relational bonds in the novel's African American sea island families. Likewise, in *Crick Crack Monkey*, Trinidadian author Merle Hodge uses storytelling both as a creative expression and as a way of remembering ancestors that also serves to form and maintain families. The significance of Diasporic rituals and traditions in Black women's writings underscores the understanding that resources for healing are often already present or potentially present in Black communities. Ultimately, Black women writers' depictions of Black family life unapologetically embrace Diasporic cultural resources that provide or offer the potential for resistance to oppression.

That is not to say that these novelistic depictions of an ethic of community support and accountability are utopian visions of domestic felicity. Since the ethic manifests in a varied set of practices, it has varied results.[24] It is less a rigid formula to create healthy families than a set of conversations that seeks to move the discourse around Black family life in the United States and the Caribbean to consider a wider range of viable family structures and experiences. In that way, Black women writers' portrayal of an ethic of community support and accountability is part of what Kimberly Nichelle Brown has identified as the "decolonizing properties and initiatives prevalent in the traditions of African American culture" (9). Thus the recurrent trope of Diasporic rituals recenters Black people's agency and ability to create and/or sustain kinship and community in the face of hostile societies, without falling back on conventional myths of self-help or meritocracy.[25]

To be clear, however, I am not arguing that Black women writers portray an ethic of community support and accountability as simply the opposite of dominant epistemologies of family or that this ethic is another set of monolithic ideals that seeks to supplant mainstream notions of family. I take seriously E. Frances White's warning in *Dark Continent of Our Bodies: Black Feminism and the Politics of Respectability* about invoking simple binaries, for, as she suggests, even "the site of counterdiscourse itself is contested terrain" (132). Thus I posit that Black women writers use a set of transgressive family practices to challenge Western ideals of family, foregrounding the complex negotiations at the center of family relations. Put another way, while hegemonic notions of family seek to collapse family and family practices into rigid, unyielding customs, Black women writers use an ethic of community support and accountability to illuminate the complicated and nuanced ways that Black family life is and can be experienced.

* * *

Although respectability politics and ambivalence do not look exactly the same in the Haiti of *Breath, Eyes, Memory* as in the Brooklyn, New York, of *Praisesong for the Widow,* some general unifying factors make a comparative analysis between African American and Black Caribbean texts viable, interesting, and necessary. Respectability politics reflects a marked, though often futile, desire for social mobility, and the notion that class advancement is based on cultural assimilation to the norm is at the heart of much public discourse in both the Caribbean and the United States. To that end, respectability politics often privileges Western mores and values to the extreme; likewise, repressive sexual practices and westernized notions of art, beauty, and conduct are held in high esteem. Above all, respectability politics advocates eschewing cultural family practices that reflect the African Diaspora and promotes a particularly rigid notion of family based on Western ideals that Kathleen Renk calls "the mythical family" (8).[26] Not only has this model been unrealistic for many Europeans and European Americans, but respectability politics has both generated ambivalence toward family and promoted an unattainable and often a toxic paradigm for Blacks convinced that conforming one's own family to this mythical family is necessary for combating the difficulties of life in the Caribbean and the United States. Contemporary Black women writers from the Caribbean and the United States routinely deplore this circumstance and should be placed in conversation with one another for fuller analysis of the continuities and discontinuities of family life across the Diaspora.

Thus my project has a Diasporic focus and compares literature by Black women from both the Caribbean and the United States. I was inspired to do a comparative analysis for several reasons. The first is personal. As someone who was born in the Caribbean and was raised in Caribbean immigrant communities in the United States, I certainly see the differences between experiences of Blacks in the Caribbean and the United States, but I do not find Caribbean and U.S. Black identities to be necessarily mutually exclusive. Indeed, given the regions' similar histories and the often parallel (mis)perceptions of Black families in both places, it is very productive to consider African American and Black Caribbean women's literature together. Another reason for the project's Diasporic focus arose organically out of the texts. African American and Black Caribbean women's writing often eschews rigid geographical boundaries. Take, for instance, Gayl Jones's *Corregidora*, which imagines a family of Afro-Brazilians living in Kentucky, or Michelle Cliff's Clare Savage novels, where the protagonists move in a triangular path from Jamaica to the United States and to England, and then back to the Caribbean. As Carole Boyce Davies contends, "The rigid compartmentalization into geography and national identity which academia forces on writers disintegrates when confronted by writers like Paule Marshall, or Claude McKay or even Olaudah Equiano" (*Out of the Kumbla* 70–71). Thus my approach in this project foregrounds the fluidity of Caribbean self-identification and experience and illuminates the connections between African American and Black Caribbean literary traditions, connections that often reflect the reality of the creators of the literature. Writers such as Paule Marshall and Edwidge Danticat, for example, who are discussed in my project, possess dual literary and cultural heritages. Since so many themes are paralleled, criticism would be remiss in erecting strict lines of demarcation within the North American Diaspora that disallow the study of African American and Black Caribbean texts together.

However, in my analyses I resist collapsing or conflating Black women's experiences across regions and enacting what Alison Donnell has called "the cutting and pasting of one historical experience into the place of another" that has occurred in some comparative frameworks (144). Indeed, I am well aware of the cultural and theoretical divides between those of African descent from the Caribbean and the United States.[27] Nevertheless, my contention in this project is that comparative study of texts from and about the Caribbean and the United States is not arbitrary but based on a recognition of both the fluid boundaries and the productive tension between these spaces. My goal in comparative analysis is to enact a transnational literary "feminism without borders." In Chandra Mohanty's words, such a feminism "is not the same as borderless feminism," for it "acknowledges the fault lines, conflicts, differences, fears, and containment that borders represent." It recognizes "that there is no one sense of a border, that the lines between and through nations, races, classes, sexualities, religions, and disabilities are real"—and "[envisions] change and social justice [working] across these lines of demarcation and division" (2). Thus, while the Caribbean and the United States have distinct cultures and politics, it is useful to discuss their literatures in tandem to consider both the productive sites of difference and valuable points of convergence. Ultimately, this book, like the persuasive comparative analyses in Carole Boyce Davies's *Black Women, Writing and Identity: Migrations of the Subject* and Caroline Rody's *The Daughter's Return: African-African and Caribbean Women's Fictions of History*, analyzes the connection between Black women's literature from the Caribbean and the United States as a vital and significant critical point of departure.

The chapters that follow trace the role of ambivalence, the paradox of respectability, and an ethic of community support and accountability in depictions of family in Black women's literature. Chapter 1, on Paule Marshall's *Praisesong for the Widow*, argues that although Marshall's depiction of the quest journey is one of the most celebratory pieces in recent literature, it is a text with ambivalence at the center. Marshall writes a warning against a type of fragmentation that eschews family tradition and cultural memory in exchange for the spoils of capitalism. Chapter 2 discusses Jamaica Kincaid's debut novel, *Annie John*. My reading rejects the notion that the novel is primarily a nostalgic take on childhood and instead argues that it is an ambivalent love letter to the politics of respectability. Chapter 3, on Edwidge Danticat's *Breath, Eyes, Memory*, argues that the women in the novel move between ambivalence toward one another and a transgressive ethic of family because of their belief in the self-effacing cult of virginity and their tradition of storytelling. My analysis of *Breath* contends that Danticat's portrayal of Sophie's spiritual emancipation is a cautionary tale, especially when juxtaposed to the marked marginalization of her female kin. Chapter 4 discusses the fictional memoir of Precious Jones in Sapphire's *Push*. Precious challenges the hegemony of respectability politics by creating a sustainable community of fictive kin with individuals from across the Diaspora who exist on the margins of society. I contend that Precious's coming to voice, an uneven and flawed process, reveals not a straightforward triumph of language but the difficulty of undermining prevailing narratives. Lastly, the epilogue takes a look at the continued importance of ambivalence, respectability, and family in Black women's literature and culture into the present. Together these chapters suggest a larger leitmotif in late twentieth-century Black women's literature, one that emphasizes the tensions of ambivalence and respectability Diasporically and the possibility of enacting a paradigm shift in thinking as a way of engaging popular discourses of "the Black family."

1 / A Wide Confraternity: Diaspora and Family
in Paule Marshall's *Praisesong for the Widow*

On November 2, 1983, President Ronald Reagan signed a bill to designate the third Monday of every January a federal holiday honoring the birth of slain civil rights leader Martin Luther King Jr. The next day, the Reverend Jesse Jackson, who had worked with King in the 1960s, declared his intent to run for president of the United States, becoming the second African American, after Shirley Chisholm, to launch a national campaign for the presidency. For some, these two events marked the culmination of decades of political activism and agitation and denoted a significant shift in the public perception of Blacks generally.[1] However, just one month prior, the United States and its allies had launched an attack on the small eastern Caribbean nation of Grenada, after the island experienced a coup by communist leaders. While this move had popular support within the United States, much of the international community decried the military maneuver as a flagrant act of imperialism, citing the incongruous juxtaposition of a massive Cold War superpower and a developing country with a modest population of one hundred thousand people, mostly of African descent.[2] Taken together, the creation of the King federal holiday, Jackson's (ultimately unsuccessful) presidential bid, and the invasion of Grenada reflect some of the complications and contradictions of the times for Blacks in the United States and the Caribbean. On the one hand, there had been significant gains for Blacks in both regions in the decade or so since the waning of the civil rights movement in the United States and the establishment of independent nations across the Caribbean, a confluence that reflects the symbiotic connection between the civil rights struggles and anticolonial resistance.[3] On the other hand, the mounting backlash to advances in civil rights beginning in the 1970s and continuing into the 1980s, alongside the instability and conflicts within the newly independent nation-states in the Caribbean during the same period, in conjunction with the United States' continued paternalism toward its neighbors in the global South, reflects a rather hostile political landscape for Blacks in these regions in the last decades of the twentieth century. Indeed, the rollback of civil rights in the United States was closely tied to the increase of U.S. imperialism in the Caribbean, as both circumstances emerged from political epistemology rooted in the suppression of peoples of African descent.

Paule Marshall published *Praisesong for the Widow* in 1983, and the novel reflects many of the concerns of this tumultuous era.[4] More specifically, *Praisesong* meditates on the complex and often dangerous social negotiations for Blacks that live in a world where seemingly momentous political strides (such as the King holiday, Jackson's presidential bid, and independence from colonial powers) are made alongside unmitigated expressions of violent dominance (such as the Grenada invasion and Reaganomics). *Praisesong* closely examines the particular survival strategies adopted by some African Americans during and in reaction to this time period, namely a politics of respectability aimed at assimilating into middle-class American society. Although it is in many ways a celebratory work, it is also a referendum on the contemporaneous manifestation of respectability politics that evolved alongside and in the wake of the major social upheaval of the 1970s and 1980s.

More specifically, Marshall's novel challenges the paradox of respectability, in which some Blacks simultaneously aspire to be respectable according to the ideals of respectability politics and find it difficult, if not impossible, to adhere to its tenets. *Praisesong* invokes a hermeneutics of suspicion toward respectability politics, countering the hegemony of the nuclear family and middle-class materialism as normative cultural symbols and calling into question kyriocentric models of power in which women are heavily invested in upholding dominant systems of power and inequity. Thus the novel illustrates that while respectability politics may assist Blacks in gaining some measure of social success, struggles with the paradox that it presents can also engender ambivalence and estrangement among family members, ultimately revealing that rigid, repressive constructions of family can actually do Black people more harm than good.

Praisesong, instead of advocating for narrow notions of respectability, repeatedly portrays characters living by an ethic of community support and accountability that involves honoring Diasporic cultural connections, recognizing the potential for supportive networks among extended and fictive kin, and rejecting bourgeois classism. In challenging respectability politics, the novel highlights characters' honoring of family relations and fictive kin and participation in enriching rituals grounded in Diasporic traditions that require a renegotiation, though certainly not a rejection, of concepts of success. The novel compels us to consider that it is pivotal for Black people, and for Black women in particular, to recognize the sustaining cultural practices that are already present or potentially present in Black communities, rather than succumbing to the "safety" of dominant standards. Ultimately, this chapter argues that *Praisesong for the Widow* not only engages and challenges some of the problematic assimilation strategies of the post–civil rights era and the paradox of respectability but advocates for a transgressive yet pragmatic ethic of community support and accountability that has implications not only for Marshall's troubled characters in the 1970s but also for her readers in the 1980s and beyond who are still grappling with the legacies of respectability politics.

Ring Shouts and Silken Threads

Praisesong illustrates that the most powerful example of an ethic of community support and accountability that Avey can draw from is actually already a part of her heritage, a circumstance that suggests that viable alternatives to respectability politics often already exist in Black communities. A native New Yorker, Avey spends childhood summers in Tatem, a fictional sea island off the coast of South Carolina, with her paternal great-aunt Cuney. Aunt Cuney is reminiscent of many ancestor figures seen across Black women's texts from the end of the twentieth century, such as Ma Chess in Jamaica Kincaid's *Annie John*, Baby Suggs in Toni Morrison's *Beloved*, Grandmè Ifé in Edwidge Danticat's *Breath, Eyes, Memory*, Nana Peazant in Julie Dash's *Daughters of the Dust*, Pilate in Toni Morrison's *Song of Solomon*, and even Da-Duh of Marshall's eponymous short story.[5] Aunt Cuney insists that Avey spend one month with her every summer in South Carolina. During this summer tutelage, Aunt Cuney nurtures, guides, and teaches Avey about her ancestry, repeating the legend of Ibo Landing to Avey and entreating her to bear witness to the memory.[6] Aunt Cuney is a maternal figure who is pivotal to Avey's development and remains emblazoned on her memory and consciousness. Even before Avey is born Cuney claims her, identifying Avey as a type of reincarnation of her grandmother, Avatara (42). In this way, Avey is born into a motherline in which she is ordained to carry on the legacy of her heritage. Keith A. Sandiford notes that, "in her single person, Cuney united the functions of materfamilias to her extended family, griot and mentor to her great-niece" (374). Cuney values the bond with her niece and seeks to connect her to a legacy far beyond that of her immediate family. In mentoring Avey, Aunt Cuney provides a positive link to ancestral memory. The depiction of Aunt Cuney, with its emphasis on the importance of history and political resistance, becomes a framing narrative for an ethic of community support and accountability in the novel. That is, Avey's memories of her great aunt become a lens for her own and the reader's understanding of her identity, her family history, and her connections to other Blacks across the Diaspora, providing an example of family dynamics not rooted in dominant systems of power and respectability.

This framing narrative is not only genealogical but also geographical. As a sea island, Tatem is a step removed from mainland African American culture, an environment where African retentions flourish without being undermined by the ubiquity of repressive cultural standards of society at large. It is thus a physical link to an ethic of community support and accountability, exemplifying a way of understanding the world that honors cultural practices that are often marginalized. Avey accompanies her aunt to the Landing, where Cuney retells the story of the Ibos to her eager niece; however, the walk toward the Landing becomes, in some respects, almost as important as the story that is the culmination of each trip.[7] In addition to passing aged locals like Gollah Mack and "Doctor" Benitha Grant, Avey and Aunt Cuney frequently pass Tatem's only church, an important site for both women. Although Cuney no longer attends church, she sometimes brings Avey to stand with her outside it while "through the open door the handful of elderly men and women still left, and who still held to the old ways, could be seen slowly circling the room in a loose ring" (34).[8] Sterling Stuckey has identified this ritual, the ring shout, as a mixture of African ritual and Afro-Protestant tradition (12).[9] While Aunt Cuney does not participate in the ring shouts, preferring to watch "unreconciled but nostalgic," the gesture of taking Avey along causes the ritual—a remnant from slave celebrations that retained African traditions—to become part of Avey's eventual ability to reject respectability politics and reclaim a type of Diasporic kinship (34).

The ring shout is more than a positive reminder of African heritage, however. It also signifies an aspect of an ethic of community support and accountability because of its purpose as both a subversive form of praise and worship and a celebration of heritage. The elders engaged in the ring shout represent a form of kinship and a community engaged in an act of affirming that is both personal and collective. They are part of the few "who still held to the old ways," and they come together both in spiritual worship and in communion. And because the ring shout is the result of the syncretism of Judeo-Christian religious prohibitions regarding dancing, African worship, and African musical practices with a transgression of those prohibitions, it also provides a model for identity and community that does not abandon tradition in the face of colonialism and racist repression; as Keith Cartwright asserts, "The shout dances with 'dancing,' much as *santería* and *vodou* devotees have managed to pray to *orishas* and *loas* in catholic whiteface. In this marvelous manner, creole forms have answered the needs of New World realities" (139). Young Avey's fascination with (and clandestine imitation of) the ring shout illustrates that although the ritual is losing popularity in Tatem, it still represents the possibility of creating oppositional strategies of care rooted in Diasporic tradition that Blacks can use to navigate dominant systems of power that aim to marginalize them. DoVeanna S. Fulton suggests, "The ring shout is a sacred oral and dance ritual that functions as a vehicle to collapse time and space dimensions so that participants experience and are sustained by history" (119). The intimation is that Avey can take the ethics embodied in the ring shout—namely a call to community and a recognition of tradition in the face of marginalizing social dictates—and use this epistemology not only in Tatem but also wherever she goes. In other words, cultural rites and rituals do not have to be idealized to be useful; even practices that may be almost forgotten can and should be recuperated or reimagined and used to support modern-day Blacks across the Diaspora. Furthermore, the ring shout exemplifies a sort of kinship practice that challenges the tenets of respectability politics; it is not a ritual that is recognized or approved of by mainstream society and cannot advance one's social standing in any normative sense. Instead, it offers community support through a pragmatic strategy for affirming notions of selfhood rooted in African Diasporic practices.

Another powerful example of an ethic of community support and accountability from Avey's childhood is connected to another family trip with Diasporic connections. This trip up the Hudson River, like the one south to Aunt Cuney, affects Avey profoundly and emphasizes the significance of connections to fictive kin from across the Diaspora without romanticizing or collapsing differences among various groups of Blacks. Avey feels such a connection to her fellow travelers that she imagines silken threads connecting them all: "She would feel what seemed to be hundreds of slender threads streaming out from her navel and from the place where her heart was to enter those around her. And the threads went out not only to people she recognized from the neighborhood but to those she didn't know as well, such as the roomers just up from the South and the small group of West Indians whose odd accent called to mind Gullah talk" (190).

The silken threads originate from two crucial parts of Avey's body. The navel is the geographic center of the body—scarified evidence that we were connected to our biological mothers via the umbilical cord. These silken threads originate as hereditary proof of a larger connectedness, that of motherlines—collective umbilical cords—linking the children of the Diaspora together as fictive kin.[10] Those linked by the threads become, in effect, kin, joined not only by their desire to enjoy a holiday but also by their shared experience as Blacks—northern, southern, Gullah-Geechee, and Caribbean—in the United States.[11] Even as a young girl, Avey feels kinship with both Blacks from the South (certainly because of her fondness for Tatem and her Aunt Cuney) and Caribbean folk who remind her of those cherished memories, marking her as a young woman with a Diasporic consciousness and a budding sense of transnational solidarity.[12]

This ethic of community support and accountability in the form of kinship to Diasporic communities does not come at the expense of Avey's individuality, however. We are told that "while the impression lasted she would cease being herself ... someone small, insignificant, outnumbered. . . . Instead, for those moments, she became part of, indeed the center of, a huge wide confraternity" (191). But rather than effacing her, membership in this community erases Avey's feelings of unimportance because of her age, gender, and relative lack of power, emboldening and empowering her. In that way, these threads, which stream out of people's hearts as well as their navels, signify an integral life force holding them both up and together and further linking the group as kin. Avey is literally the navel of a sort of collective consciousness in this moment, a sort of Diasporic everywoman whose feelings of worth and power are amplified by her connection to other Black people; the book suggests that the silken threads Avey envisions are the threads that link all people. The novel, then, depicts ascribing to an ethic of community support and accountability as a possible way not only to feel connected to others but to do so without being dominated or becoming subsumed by family and also without dominating others. *Praisesong*'s exemplification of an ethic of community support and accountability through the ring shout and the Hudson River trip underscores the significance of supportive Diasporic networks that prioritize both individual and collective Black experiences and suggests that Blacks do not necessarily have to be guided solely by normative models of family and respectability when they can harness the potentially already present resources in their communities for support and intimacy. The emphasis on Diasporic rituals and communities in *Praisesong* forces us to consider alternative social and communal strategies, besides respectability politics, that have the potential to improve Black people's lives but that do not compel Blacks to engage with one another in ways that provide a measure of individual political power while also damaging familial ties.

Praisesongs

Avey's childhood experiences of Diasporic community become touchstones that, for a time, help her transition into adulthood.[13] In fact, in the early years of her marriage on Halsey Street, before a momentous argument between Avey and her husband Jay that precipitates a relentless struggle for upward mobility, Avey and her family do their best to form a supportive network and resist the policing of their bodies. Initially, small rituals of love and affirmation mark Jay and Avey's life as a married couple. For example, after long days of working at thankless jobs, they kick off their shoes and, under the "ministrations" of Count Basie, Duke Ellington, Ella Fitzgerald, Billie Holiday, Ma Rainey, and Mamie Smith, relax and enjoy each other's company (94). Music like jazz and the blues act as a sort of therapy—not unlike the ritual of the ring shout on Tatem or the trip up the Hudson River—to combat their daily drudgery. It is no coincidence that these musical genres pointedly describe working-class Black life, with an emphasis on its trials and triumphs, in a way that directly speaks to Jay's and Avey's experiences. Thus Mamie Smith's song "You Can't Keep a Good Man Down" is more than a melodious tune: it is a poignant testimony to how the young Johnsons use music as a ritual to reaffirm themselves, their connection to one another, and their dignity in a hostile world.[14] *Praisesong*, then, illuminates the transgressive politics behind Black musical traditions such as the blues as having the potential to sustain equally transgressive family practices for Blacks in the civil rights era world of the novel, with implications as well for Blacks living in the post–civil rights era of the novel's publication, inviting us to consider what late twentieth-century cultural practices might serve as "ministrations" for modern-day upwardly mobile African Americans.

Listening to the unabashedly sensual music also encourages the already robust and open sexuality in the Johnsons' marriage, which is a rejection of the dissemblance so central to respectability politics. Egalitarian and loving, their intimacy bespeaks a partnership based on respect and desire: "He would lie within her like a man who has suddenly found himself inside a temple of some kind . . . sensing around him the invisible forms of the deities who reside there: Erzulie with her jewels and gossamer veils, Yemoja to whom the rivers and seas are sacred; Oya, first wife of the thunder god and herself in charge of winds and rains" (127). Marshall displays two loving adults expressing themselves sexually in a way that is tinged with neither neurosis nor pathology. This is a subversive portrayal of Black sexuality that disrupts the dissemblance Blacks often enact to combat the negative controlling images, such as those of the insatiable Black buck or the jezebel, at the heart of dominant American sexual ideology (Collins, *Black Sexual Politics* 56).

To be clear, my intent is not to valorize heterosexual sex as inherently subversive. Rather, I want to draw attention to the ways in which even supposedly normative desire is often circumscribed within the ideals of respectability politics and to argue that this refusal to conceal it is important and disrupts the politics of respectability.[15] Jay and Avey's sex life at the beginning of their marriage resists respectability politics by exemplifying an intimate connection that is reciprocal, affirming, and unashamed. The infusion of African-derived images from Haitian *vodou* (Erzulie) and Yoruba/*Santería* faiths (Yemoja and Oya) throughout the description of Jay and Avey's lovemaking also links sex-positive intimacy to a Diasporic consciousness. Thus Jay and Avey's intimate practices are connected to the transgressive syncretic religious practices of peoples of African descent who were brought to the Americas—practices, such as the ring shout, that preserved African cosmologies under the guise of Western religious symbols. The implication here is that just as their ancestors combated repression and hostility by outwardly displaying deference to dominant ideology while, nevertheless, continuing to worship in ways they saw fit, so may Jay and Avey navigate their hostile racist world of post–World War II America by holding on to the Diasporic rituals that sustain them while pursuing mainstream success, instead of succumbing to normative ideals that require submission to dominant ideas and, ultimately, cultural erasure.

Another significant Johnson family ritual connected to an ethic of community support and accountability involves reciting poetry, especially to their eldest daughter, Sis. On Sundays, Jay regales them with "memory fragments of poems he had learned as a boy" in segregated Kansas (125). Jay recites, not Western classics, but rather classics of the Harlem Renaissance, a choice that foregrounds his connection to and pride in African American art in a time when Black art forms were either ignored by or deemed inferior to their mainstream counterparts. And although these are only pieces of poems, the fragments are both poignant and sustaining: "'. . . *I bathed in the Euphrates when dawns were young . . . ,*' [Jay] loved to recite, standing in his pajamas in the middle of the living room" (125; emphasis in original). He is choosing to share Langston Hughes's "The Negro Speaks of Rivers," foregrounding the sections that reference Africa. This cultural choice, which emphasizes a Diasporic connection that is a major leitmotif in the novel and throughout Marshall's oeuvre more generally, underscores the centrality of positive Diasporic rituals to the maintenance of resilient Black families.[16]

This moment is also especially telling as an exemplification of an ethic of community support and accountability, considering that Jay's audience consists of Avey and a very young Sis, who is so enthralled "her eyes would all but take over her small face" (125). Jay and Avey are purposefully teaching their daughter positive images of Blackness and their heritage, combating Jay's complaint that the "Schools up north didn't teach colored children anything about the race, about themselves" (125). The schools do not teach Black students about "the race," but, Marshall insists, Jay and Avey can and do make the choice as parents to teach Sis about this aspect of her heritage. Therefore, when Jay recites Hughes' "I, Too, Sing America" ("*I am the darker brother / They send me to eat in the kitchen / When company comes . . .* "), they are openly critiquing the racist Jim Crowism that plagues Black life in the North and the South (49). Jay and Avey reject racist narratives and institutions and affirm their family as a safe, loving space that resists social erasure. In this way, the novel focuses our attention to their family practices as transgressive because these practices move beyond repressive ideology that would seek to simply reify dominant racial hierarchies that require the Johnsons' subordination. Jay and Avey's unabashed use of music and poetry as restorative healing practices within their family makes the case that rejecting respectability politics in family life is not a romantic ideal but a pragmatic way for Blacks to navigate the world despite their seemingly marginalized status.

Praisesong compels us to consider these acts as *rites* or sacred practices that are therapeutic and that reveal Avey and Jay's recognition of
the importance of taking care of themselves in a world intent on viewing
them as inferior. Avey muses that the rites she and Jay performed were
intentional acts of support, "*praisesongs* . . . [that] had both protected
them and put them in possession of a kind of power . . . " (137; emphasis
mine). In this recollection, praisesongs are small, but significant, affirmations: "They were things which would have counted for little in the
world's eye. To an outsider, some of them would even appear ridiculous,
childish, *cullud*. . . . They had nonetheless been of the utmost importance. . . . Something vivid and affirming and charged with feeling had
been present in the small rituals that had once shaped their lives" (136–
37; emphasis in original).[17] Although these activities might be called
"cullud," a word that gives Blackness a negative connotation and makes
it therefore of questionable repute to some, in fact the very connection
to African American culture is part of what makes their rituals special
and affirming and illuminates their family as a unit whose members
are joined to support and sustain one another in fundamentally healthy
ways. The juxtaposition of the affirming things the Johnsons previously
practiced with the reality of their travel on a Jim Crow bus is important to note as well, however. Although they must travel in a manner
that reinforces their second-class status, Jay and Avey's trips to Tatem
undermine the normativity and authority of forces, such as de jure segregation, that would be disruptive to their familial connections. That
they move through these hostile segregated spaces to acknowledge and
affirm a Diasporic ritual reinforces the notion that these activities, which
provide a type of spiritual sustenance that supports them individually
and as a collective, are fundamentally rooted in their status as people
of African descent living in the Americas. Ultimately, the Johnsons'
praisesongs not only affirm their family but help to create and sustain
it in ways that affirm the significance of Diasporic connections to the
well-being of Black people, emphasizing that Black families can flourish
by retaining aspects of their heritage even as they navigate mainstream
American society.

A Harsh and Joyless Ethic

The music, poetry, and intimate relations of the Johnsons' early family life reflect the potential and significance of an ethic of community
support and accountability, yet Jay and Avey's subsequent swift descent

into a family bound by respectability politics underscores the couple's tenuous and ambivalent attachment to these practices and to an ethic of community support and accountability more generally. For a time, the Johnson family is able to navigate the larger world seemingly without sacrificing the special rituals that connect to their heritage and that act as succor in a hostile society. Nada Elia contends that until the confrontation on Halsey Street, "Jay and Avey had thought very positively of themselves as Black people. . . . They knew their own worth, a worth that nevertheless remained on the margins of 'success' as defined by the dominant discourse" (90). I would complicate Elia's contention, however; for although Jay and Avey generally think of themselves positively during this time, their burgeoning class bias, as evidenced by Avey's desire not to be associated with her neighbor on Halsey Street well before the momentous argument, opens up the possibility for further entrenchment in a repressive politics of respectability. That is, although they listen to the blues and recite African American poetry, they also distance themselves from other Blacks that they perceive as lower class, despite (or perhaps because of) their own tenuous class status. By trying to avoid the pitfalls and instability of poverty without recognizing their own complicity with prejudice and classism, Jay and Avey become increasingly invested in an alienating respectability politics that fundamentally alters their family and produces an ambivalence that eventually erodes their positive cultural connections and destroys their intimacy. *Praisesong*, then, highlights the ways in which an ethic of community support and accountability at the heart of the family's traditions cannot fully coexist with the paradox of respectability politics, thus making a larger claim: family practices cannot resist repression by rejecting some norms while reifying other equally problematic beliefs, and when Black families attempt to resist repression by reinscribing problematic beliefs, significant complications arise.

Praisesong describes the worldview that Jay and Avey will adopt for most of their marriage as a type of American Dream informed by a "harsh and joyless ethic" (131). This "harsh and joyless ethic" is a manifestation of kyriarchy, what Elisabeth Schüssler Fiorenza calls a "complex pyramidal system of intersecting multiplicative social structures of superordination and subordination, of ruling and oppression" (211). When Jay and Avey succumb to the allure of respectability, they are not only ascribing to a group strategy that aims to improve their lives but also investing in kyriarchy, a system of domination that will allow them some measure of social power and control if they subscribe to its tenets.

I use the term *kyriarchy* as opposed to *patriarchy* because the former underscores the potential opportunities for even marginalized peoples to be complicit in the oppression of others. In other words, kyriarchy foregrounds the ways in which individuals with differing levels of power can exert (or attempt to exert) power over others in order to increase their own social or political standing. Although respectability politics began as a group strategy aimed at helping African Americans achieve full citizenship in American society, its reliance on repressive tactics has often made it a tool of kyriarchy. Thus the Johnsons' "harsh and joyless ethic," or their investment in the ideals of respectability politics, is part of a discourse that helps sustain the workings of kyriarchy. However, this ethic requires extreme sacrifice and constant vigilance because it is so difficult to maintain. Put another way, it creates the paradox of respectability, which in turn incites ambivalence toward family relations, often in the form of, simultaneously, a desire to uphold the family unit at all costs and an intense degree of unease or resentment toward this duty.

The particular manifestation of respectability politics in *Praisesong* emphasizes a steadfast devotion to family, places a strong emphasis on self-respect and honor, adheres to rigid gender roles and identities, advocates a strong sense of individual and collective vigilance against perceived impropriety, and rejects the notion that institutionalized racism, sexism, and class prejudice are deterrents to material success and the proverbial American Dream. Two things are also very clear under this "harsh and joyless ethic": unsuccessful Blacks are simply lazy or lack the wherewithal to succeed and thus produce dysfunctional families; and women's apparently unstable minds and overly fertile bodies need particular policing because, if unchecked, they have the potential to become uncontrollable forces that destroy families. Together, these notions serve to reinscribe a dominant discourse about the danger and inherent inferiority of those who are poor, Black, and female. The catalysts for these conservative narratives and the "harsh and joyless ethic" more generally are exemplars of failure to attain the American Dream: the Halsey Street neighborhood, the first place that the Johnsons make as their family home, and an unnamed neighbor who symbolizes the street's danger. Halsey Street and the Halsey Street woman are negative memories that support long-standing and dominant discourses of what constitutes appropriate behavior. As Belinda Edmondson argues, "The American Dream is linked in this way to a masculine quest for power and status and *modernity*" (164; emphasis in the original). However, these memories not only represent what not to do but also reflect how tenuous the

Johnsons' notions of success are, for the couple conjure them up repeatedly as justifications for deeper entrenchment within respectability politics, highlighting a deep-seated anxiety around class and social status.

Praisesong gives respectability politics a street address in the specter of Halsey Street, which becomes the antithesis of success and "civilization" in the novel.[18] Although the couple and their children experience many happy times over the twenty years that they live in their fifth-floor walkup on Halsey Street, Jay later remembers only the street's noisy confines and teeming tenements, reducing both the locale and their time there to an unfortunate episode of their lives, one that should be neither fully remembered nor repeated. The novel depicts both Jay and Avey opting to buy into a politics of respectability that seeks to dismiss places like Halsey Street as sites of decent, viable family life. Consequently, Halsey Street becomes the driving force behind Jay's relentless pursuit of material wealth. Indeed, like Silla in Marshall's first novel, *Brown Girl, Brownstones*, Jay becomes obsessed with material prosperity. The precautions guard against any slippage back to Halsey Street, the antithesis of success and mainstream acceptance. The memory of their humble beginnings galvanizes Jay into decisive action; he spends the rest of his life amassing a small fortune and fortifying his family against any potential loss. Now certainly, it is responsible to keep one's family fed and insured, and it is also admirable to work hard. However, Jay's bomb shelter–stocked kitchen pantry, his neurotic dependency on insurance policies, and the breakneck pace of his work all convey less a person who is thoughtful and prepared for emergencies than a patriarch invested in rigid notions of respectability and therefore preoccupied with control and insecure about his origins and precarious manhood (89). Jay collapses his role as husband and father with that of superhuman provider, effectively erasing any other aspect of himself, as if being a responsible family member necessarily meant self-effacement. Frances Smith Foster argues that "the myth of missing manhood rests on present-day expectations and assumptions, beginning with the definition of the two words most important to its interpretation: 'husband' and 'fatherhood.' This myth also confuses 'fatherhood' with 'patriarchy'" (133). In other words, although Jay claims to be acting only out of concern for his family's well-being, what is illuminated is that because he is invested in a kyriocentrism that fundamentally challenges his self-worth, he is engaged in a Sisyphean battle to prove himself as modern-day patriarch who has truly escaped the stigma of Halsey Street. Thus respectability politics is debunked as a viable social strategy and is instead illuminated as a destructive paradigm that can succeed in destroying one's sense of self while one pursues economic success and social acceptance.

The memories of Halsey Street not only prompt Jay's headlong pursuit of success but also function as a major point of friction in Jay and Avey's marriage. The threat of Halsey Street, and its concomitant dangers, becomes a refrain Jay can reference in order to coerce Avey's submission. Marshall writes, "Whenever there had been a discussion between them about money, whenever they had argued, in fact, he had never failed, no matter what the argument was about, to bring up the subject of Halsey Street, holding it like a Sword of Damocles over everything they had accomplished" (88). Just as the legendary Sword of Damocles underscored the precariousness of the emperor in the Greek legend, so does Halsey Street symbolize the precariousness of the Johnsons' hard-won status. Jay's use of this symbol persistently skews what is remembered and what is passed on to their family. Although this passage reveals Avey's incredulity at Jay's ability to reference Halsey Street in every dispute, the novel highlights Jay's unyielding fixation on their former home as evidence of the paradox of respectability's stranglehold upon their family. Jay's continued denunciation of Halsey Street (especially via the accusation, "You must want to wind up back where we started") becomes a refrain that is a rejection not just of the apartment but also of their family's beginnings and the family's possible devolution into poverty and all the narratives surrounding the poor. Halsey Street becomes not just a painful memory for Jay and Avey but also a symbol of the pathological Black family. Thus for Jay rejecting the street also involves rejecting any notion of functional life in Black urban or ghetto spaces. *Praisesong* illustrates the myopia of respectability politics, revealing that this ideology often refuses to validate ways of living that do not live up to the mythical ideal and that while this refusal may afford a family like the Johnsons some measure of social acceptance, it often does so at the cost of familial love and intimacy.

In *Praisesong*, the paradox of respectability also engenders family discourses that thrive on unequal power dynamics between men and women. Black people, and Black women in particular, have the potential to be contaminated by the ills of Halsey Street unless they are vigilant in policing themselves and allow themselves to be policed by others. The Johnsons' unnamed neighbor, whom I call the Halsey Street woman, fitfully embodies the specter of female contamination. The Halsey Street woman, who is just a few years Avey's senior, spends every Saturday morning the same way: scouring beer gardens for her ne'er-do-well lover, a man just a few years older than Jay, who has spent much of his weekly earnings cavorting with friends and other lovers. The woman's loud grievances are not singular but representative of many women in relationships marked by poverty, nihilism, and misogyny, on Halsey Street and in other environs: "Her rage those dark mornings spoke not only for herself but for the thousands like her for blocks around, lying sleepless . . . waiting, all of them, for some fool to come home with his sodden breath and half his pay envelope gone" (108).

Nevertheless, Avey, with her civil service job and responsible husband, does not empathize with or even pity these women. Instead, because of her pointed investment in kyriarchy, Avey subscribes to a rather narrow notion of respectability and initially distances herself from the Halsey Street woman: "She thought she was better. She didn't want anything to do with her kind. She couldn't wait till she could move on from around them" (108–09). The Halsey Street narrative thrives on what Candice Jenkins has termed the salvific wish, or the "earnest longing to rescue the Black community from . . . narratives of pathology," in which Black women in particular embrace traditional bourgeois standards of propriety in an effort to counteract accusations of immorality and sexual deviance (23). Because Avey adheres to the salvific wish and a discourse of exceptionalism rooted in kyriarchy, she claims no kinship with the Halsey Street woman, choosing instead to view her (and "her kind") as the scourge of the neighborhood. Thus *Praisesong* compels our attention to the ways in which respectability politics does not simply produce decency or accountability, as its proponents claim; rather, it is a fundamentally divisive and individualistic ethic that erects rigid borders between people who are perhaps not all that different from one another.

When Avey is pregnant with the couple's third child, the tenuous divide between her and the Halsey Street woman collapses and the paradox of respectability in the Johnsons' family life comes into full view. Out of work and confined to the fifth-floor walkup with two small children, Avey briefly loses her facade of respectability and sense of class distinction. She is extremely isolated; not only is she forced to quit her job and remain home all day while Jay works, but she is far from her family and friends (103).[19] These factors precipitate a sort of breakdown: she imagines Jay bedding a svelte white coworker and then considers her own imminent, and most likely horrifying, experience of childbirth (100–101).[20] Imagining Jay to be unfaithful, a heavily pregnant Avey confronts him and vows, *"Goddamn you, nigger, I'll take my babies and go!"* (110; emphasis in original). Her words eerily echo the weekly harangue of the

Halsey Street woman; for a moment "it seemed that they had changed places with the two down in the street; had even become them" (110). Jay's response, "Do you know who you sound like . . . who you even look like?" (106) becomes a refrain concurrent with "You must want to wind up back where we started"—another Sword of Damocles in Jay's arsenal to subdue Avey once she steps outside what he sees as appropriate behavior for women (88). The fact that these are Jay's dying words reflects his struggle with the paradox of respectability.[21] The Halsey Street woman (and her partner) have become symbols not only of how not to create respectable family but also of how precarious the Johnsons' family is. *Praisesong* problematizes the Johnsons' class pretensions by exposing that very little divides them from their peers on Halsey Street. In that way, the novel undermines the legitimacy of the politics of respectability, underscoring that it provides inadequate coping mechanisms for Black families dealing with poverty or other oppressive social constructs and exposing it as a failed political project.

The novel further challenges the paradox of respectability by showing the ways in which it prompts Jay and Avey to dismiss the sustaining African American cultural practices of their pasts even as they also suffer from their absence. Jay and Avey's notions of respectability not only advocate for an extreme work ethic but also encourage a type of cultural effacement. Before the confrontation on Halsey Street, Jay and Avey take family trips, read poetry together, and spend evenings lovemaking. After the confrontation, they become more financially prosperous but also more emotionally bereft as they leave the affirming rituals behind: "The yearly trip south became a thing of the past. . . . So did the trips they used to regularly make over to Harlem to see their old friends, and the occasional dance they would treat themselves to. All such was soon supplanted by the study manuals, the self-improvement books, and the heavy sample case containing the vacuum cleaner" (116). The activities they begin to eschew in favor of mainstream success are cultural activities tied to their identification as Black people.[22] Avey and Jay's understanding of success disparages African American heritage in favor of upholding a particular brand of respectability politics rooted in hostility toward Diasporic practices. Therefore, despite their increased economic stability, Jay and Avey's quality of life and their connection to their family are drastically decreased. The loss of sustaining rituals, which notably have no replacement in the narrative, marks the Johnsons' family life as sterile and alienated from larger systems of support, drawing attention to the ways in which respectability politics functions as an inadequate social model in that it often neglects fundamental aspects of Black identity and family life.

Praisesong underscores that while Avey seemingly accepts the changes in her family life without complaint, the paradox of respectability makes her view these circumstances with a profound sense of ambivalence: "The closing for the house in North White Plains had taken place, the actual move was only weeks away, when suddenly she found herself thinking not so much of the new life awaiting them but of the early years back on Halsey Street, of the small rituals and private pleasures" (122). Avey and her husband have put most of their effort into leaving Halsey Street behind; nevertheless, it is clear that leaving the rituals and pleasures of the Johnsons' life there is not only a mistake but an unnecessary one. Avey recognizes this mistake, albeit implicitly, and this nostalgia prompts ambivalence when she should ostensibly be delighted to move out of their old neighborhood. *Praisesong* underscores the destructiveness of the paradox of respectability, illustrating that it can produce alienation, ambivalence, and estrangement, even as respectability politics is presumably supposed to catalyze cohesiveness and stability for Black families.

When the Johnsons move to the aptly named suburb of North White Plains, not only does their world become increasingly insular and centered on material gain, but both Jay and Avey become mouthpieces for conservative kyriocentric rhetoric surrounding race and class that is gaining traction even as the civil rights movement is gaining momentum, effectively rejecting any notion of solidarity with working-class Blacks. Jay in particular comes to see his economic success as a consequence of leaving behind the rituals and cultures of his earlier life.[23] Although Avey questions her husband's stance, she too ignores the evidence of institutionalized disparities and rejects solidarity with other Blacks in her embrace of respectability politics. Avey ignores clear evidence of racism in an effort to pretend it does not exist and to affirm her status as a poised, respectable lady. Rather than railing against any instance of discrimination, Avey uses silence (and its requisite feigned ignorance) as her armor in combating anything distasteful.[24] When she encounters racist snubs while dining in the exclusive Versailles room on her luxury cruise, for example, she rationalizes the behavior away: "There were some things in this life, she once tried explaining to Marion, she simply refused to let bother her" (47). Avey's refusal to be angry is actually a desire not to feel anything, and her strategy of ignoring anything even remotely unpleasant obstructs not only her relationship with her daughter Marion but her perception of the world around her.[25] This circumstance underscores another way in which respectability politics fails its adherents: it may bring Avey and her friends to the Versailles room, but it cannot make them welcome there. In other words, adhering to the politics of respectability may allow a Black person to be tolerated in some venues, but it in no way guarantees acceptance into mainstream culture—a cautionary tale for Blacks who may view respectability politics as a one-way ticket to improved social standing. Thus Avey still exists on the margins of dominant society even as she desperately desires full admittance to its rights and privileges through her belief in respectability politics. In this scenario, *Praisesong* forces us to consider the detrimental ways in which the politics of respectability often succeeds in reifying the racist system from which it emerges and that it seemingly attempts to help its adherents escape.

Avey's respectability politics renders her particularly hostile toward the civil rights movement because it would force her to recognize her connection to others and to admit to the disparities and injustices she herself faces, despite her class status. For example, Avey becomes incensed when Marion phones her parents from the front lines of the Poor People's March: "She seemed to hear in the background the great hungry roar of the thousands encamped in the mud near the Lincoln Memorial, the sound reaching out to draw her into its angry vortex, to make her part of their petition. And not only that. She had also seen, in a sudden vivid flash, the poor half-crazed woman from Halsey Street" (140).[26] Avey retreats to the apparent safety of her notions of respectability and recoils at the very idea of joining in the civil rights struggle, viewing the marchers as part of a chaotic mass.[27] Rather than viewing them as peaceful protesters invested in an ethic of community support and accountability and voicing their disapproval of an inherently unequal economic system, or even as kindred spirits to the Ibo who walked across the water to freedom, Avey is appalled at the mere notion of so many gathered expressing antiestablishment opinions. Her visceral reaction to the perceived noise of the event (which is imagined because this reverie takes place in the brief seconds before she accepts Marion's collect call) underscores her own marked silence and the discomfort she feels when others call that silence into question.

Avey also resents Marion's call because any mention of class struggle conjures memories of the Halsey Street woman, a symbol of familial dysfunction and a constant reminder of who Avey might become if she fails to suppress any spontaneous emotion. Through this description, respectability politics does not strengthen family ties or bonds of affinity and accountability; rather, it fosters estrangement and alienation with others, for in this moment, Avey's relentless desire for upper-class status social acceptance not only rejects solidarity with other Blacks but creates a wedge between herself and her activist daughter. *Praisesong*, then, reveals that respectability politics brings to African Americans not so much the possible power that it promises as estrangement from the self and others and the potential devastation of Black families.

Finally Making It Across

By the time we see Avey on the cruise, she is completely entrenched in narrow notions of respectability, has virtually forgotten the pleasures of Halsey Street, is seemingly content with her bland, bourgeois pride, and has, in fact, worked hard to forget Aunt Cuney. When suddenly plagued by nausea, hallucinations, strange dreams, and vague feelings of misgiving, Avey packs her six suitcases (plus a shoe caddy and requisite hat box—pointed reminders of her excess baggage), puts on her best dress (with gloves and hat to match), and heads to the mainland of Grenada, hoping to quickly catch a flight back to the States (50). One of the most disconcerting moments for Avey during this aborted vacation is the dream about her Aunt Cuney, who becomes a symbolic reminder of the potency of repressed obligations to kin. During the dream, when Aunt Cuney beckons her to walk over to the Landing and join a ritual dance, not unlike the ring shout of her childhood, Avey firmly rejects her. Because Avey is so fixed in her desire to keep up bourgeois appearances (as noted by her emphasis on her wardrobe: summer suit, hat, gloves, stockings, patent-leather pumps, and fur stole), she at first refuses to risk even these trappings of wealth and respectability by walking through the brush, rocks, and rough grass to get to the Landing. Marshall writes elsewhere in the novel that Avey believes her clothes assure her that "she would never be sent to eat in the kitchen when company came!"—a perverse reference to Langston Hughes, so unlike the celebration of poetry the Johnsons enacted during those early years on Halsey Street (49).

Sensing Avey's attachment to these markers of class and wealth, Aunt Cuney begins to tear the clothes from her body, literally divesting her niece of her class privilege and the facade of respectability: "The fight raged on . . . with the fur stole like her hardwon life of the past thirty years being trampled into the dirt underfoot" (45). The physical fight in the dream is a thinly veiled metaphor for the ambivalence that marks

Avey's adult life as she struggles with her call to an ethic of community support and accountability and her desire for middle-class status via respectability politics, unable to reconcile the two. While the dream ends with Aunt Cuney and Avey locked in epic combat between North White Plains and the Landing, Avey's battle continues in her waking hours as the dream of Aunt Cuney triggers a whole chain of events. Through the depiction of Avey's confrontation with Aunt Cuney, *Praisesong* invites us to consider the ways in which one's past cannot be ignored or traded in for social status without serious consequences.

To that end, dis-ease, or an extreme estrangement from the self and an acute disconnection from others fostered by social constructs such as respectability politics, manifests itself in several ways in *Praisesong*.[28] Avey's dis-ease is depicted as the bodily manifestation of the toxicity of the paradox of respectability, a physical outpouring of the effects of ambivalence. However, dis-ease is not the marker of pathology but the rejection of, or attempt to reject, repression. Throughout Avey's cruise (and even before then), she has other strange hallucinations as well. While dining with her friends in the Versailles room, she does not recognize herself—seeing only a "woman in beige crepe de Chine and pearls" (48). Another time she notices that the woman she sees in the mirror is something of an enigma, "the composed face with its folded-in lip and carefully barred gaze. She was clearly someone who kept her thoughts and feelings to herself" (48).

While Avey's doctor trivializes her concern, Avey's sense of self-misrecognition symbolizes her ambivalent disconnection, the disconnection Aunt Cuney challenges in the infamous dream.[29] Catherine John notes, "This temporary inability to see is an inversion of the visionary third sight that blesses the Ibo and touches both her great-aunt Cuney and her ancestral namesake, Grandma Avatara" (191). In other words, the fact that Avey does not recognize herself and that this misrecognition increasingly occurs is a marked example of both the internalized rupture of consciousness and the urgent need for the return of an ethic of community support and accountability in her life. Avey experiences a psychic collapse manifested in the flesh—a fragmenting of the self, in which the mind and the body are imagined as separate, warring entities.

Nevertheless, the recognition of dis-ease reflects the possibility of reclaiming the ethic of community support and accountability that Avey has experienced in her past. Awaiting a flight to New York in a posh hotel in Grenada, Avey has both a breakdown and a breakthrough. In a section tellingly entitled "Sleeper's Wake," she remembers her marriage to Jay and their move from Halsey Street to the suburbs. Several times the typically demure and soft-spoken Avey cries out, "Too much!" in an effort to "make up for the silence of years" (138). These exhortations are one of the first verbal steps she takes toward claiming her voice, as opposed to Jay's final strangled cry of protest at his death. The refrain reflects the fact that Avey finally recognizes that the sacrifices they made were indeed too much, that "they had behaved, she and Jay, as if there had been nothing about themselves worth honoring!" (139). As the section's title suggests, she has begun to awaken from a sleep of complacency to a waking consciousness, where the ambivalence of her past is called into question. Avey's exhortations reject the politics of respectability that asked for self-effacement, in favor of grounding herself in more sustaining Diasporic rites.

Ultimately, she decides that she and Jay *could* have done things differently, could have "wrested, as they done over all those years, the means to rescue them from Halsey Street and to see the children through, while preserving, safeguarding, treasuring those things that had come down to them over the generations, which had defined them in a particular way" (139). Avey finally rejects the "harsh and joyless ethic," realizing that material success does not necessitate spiritual death or social isolation, that, indeed with awareness, vigilance, strength, distance of mind and heart, and celebration of the flesh, one could escape Halsey Street but still retain its positive ministrations (139). Avey's understanding of family shifts radically from her previous definitions: at this point, family is not just a reason to insulate oneself with wealth or to buffer oneself with social standing but a unit that helps one positively negotiate the world and even change one's surroundings.[30] Avey's revelation also reiterates that an ethic of community support and accountability is not necessarily hostile toward material success but insists that Blacks employ a hermeneutics of suspicion toward ways of negotiating the world that seek to estrange them from supportive communities while they pursue economic stability, illuminating such thinking as ultimately violent, destructive, and futile.

Therefore, once Avey is set onto a path of healing from the dis-ease of ambivalence and the paradox of respectability, she does so by connecting to kinship networks that foreground the significance of elders and ancestor figures. Like Aunt Cuney, out-islander Lebert Joseph introduces Avey to an aspect of an ethic of community support and accountability that pays homage to ancestors through rituals marked as African retentions.[31] The aged Lebert is a trickster figure (like his namesake Legba, the *vodou* god of the crossroads and a trickster figure) who spurs Avey toward healing after finding her bewildered at an existential (and literal) crossroads.[32] Lebert acknowledges that the ancestors, or the Old Parents, are rather vengeful if unacknowledged: "All of a sudden everything start gon' wrong and you don' know the reason. You can't figger it out all you try. Is the Old Parents, oui. They's vex with you over something" (165). Lebert (un)knowingly diagnoses Avey's case. She has indeed vexed an Old Parent—as evinced by her dream brawl with Aunt Cuney.

Likewise, Avey's life has been disrupted and turned around through her lack of accountability and her neglect and dishonor of her past. Lebert's admonition reflects the errors in eschewing the past; his declarations about the Old Parents also signify the confusion some Blacks across the Diaspora presumably feel when they abandon the sustaining rituals and modes of support that may have nurtured them in favor of the allure of respectability politics. Lebert's subsequent claim that "just because we live over this side don' mean we's from this place, you know. Even when we's born here [in Grenada] we remain Carriacou people" resonates with the same underlying epistemology as Avatara's ideology about the Ibo (163–64). For Lebert and other out-islanders, living and working in Grenada, which is described as the more westernized area of the sister islands, is not enough to make them forget Carriacou or to dishonor the Old Parents' memories. Every year it is their custom to take a two- or three-day excursion back to Carriacou to unite with their families and honor their ancestors. Like Avatara's words before him, Lebert's statement is a metaphor about the lived experience of those across the African Diaspora: one does not have to eschew one's heritage to live and thrive in the West. This point has particular significance for the post–civil rights era in which the novel is set and published. It suggests that conforming to dominant ideals of respectability is not a guarantee of social acceptance, a poignant claim during a time when culture wars sought (and seek) to erode the gains made by African Americans and to call into question their move into fuller social prominence.

To that end, *Praisesong* invites us to consider the out-islanders thriving not despite their excursion but *because* of the trip, revealing the efficacy of an ethic of community support and accountability with regard to personal success. The taxi driver, a native Grenadian who transports Avey from the pier to her hotel and who is an unabashed adherent of respectability politics, admires the Carriacouans' work ethic, apparent business acumen, and sense of unity, although he is baffled and angered by the Carriacouans' dogged insistence on making the yearly excursion.

According to him, the out-islanders are "serious people. Hardwork-ing. They come to live here and before you know it they're doing bet-ter than those like myself that's born in the place. . . . They's a people sticks together and helps out the one another. Which is why they gets ahead" (78). Indeed, "the Carriacou Excursion" epitomizes an ethic of community support and accountability and serves the same purpose as Jay and Avey's record playing and poetry reciting decades earlier did: it is an affirming and sustaining experience that bolsters the out-islanders to participate in their daily lives. Again, the depiction of the Carriacouans in Grenada insists that one can in fact thrive in the Americas by holding onto sustaining Diasporic practices and finding strength in a collective.

Ultimately, Avey's experiences with Lebert and later with his daughter Rosalie and with other Carriacouans prepare her to begin reenacting an ethic of community support and accountability with others.[33] Unlike the colossal *Bianca Pride* she sails in from New York to the Caribbean, Avey takes the short trip from Grenada to Carriacou on a rickety schoo-ner. While the *Bianca*, which literally means "white," is a symbol of the bloated excess and respectability politics that sicken Avey, the *Emmanuel C*, which means "God is with us," is a humble and unassuming vessel that leads to her liberation.[34] Avey departs from pride in symbolic white-ness, removes her excess baggage, and moves toward a sense of self-worth not rooted in the markers of bourgeois material success.[35] As a part of her purging of repressive respectability politics, Avey's experience of dis-ease is heightened; what begins as vague discomfort gives way to outright illness in which she vomits and soils herself. Although morti-fied, Avey has no choice but to submit to the care of the out-islanders and begin relinquishing control. The elders do not make a showy display of Avey's illness; their decorum is so profound that they literally shield and shroud her body from view.[36] "It is these women," notes Carole Boyce Davies, "who function as midwives directing her to a re-birth of con-sciousness, who represent the continuity with her Great Aunt Cuney and those other elders of her childhood" ("Black Woman's Journey" 30). Thus the women's formalized response reflects an ethic of community support and accountability, a manifestation of extended kinship and care, even though they are strangers to her. Avey's experience on the *Emmanuel C* suggests that kindness and care, rather than propriety and class stand-ing, are the true markers of kinship and that they challenge the suprem-acy of respectability politics as the most acceptable mode of behavior.

The celebration Avey attends on her last night in Carriacou is the culmination of her move toward an ethic of community support and accountability.[37] After Lebert and his kin lead the Beg Pardon, the other elders of the community begin the nation dances, performing slightly varied shuffling movements, not unlike the ring shouts of Avey's childhood, that represent snippets of remembered African heritage. Increasingly, Avey feels a kinship to the proceedings: "All that was left were a few names of what they called nations . . . *The bare bones. The burnt-out ends.* And they clung to them with a tenacity she suddenly loved in them and longed for in herself. Thoughts—new thoughts—vague and half-formed slowly beginning to fill the emptiness" (240; emphasis mine). Avey is not a passive observer of the proceedings. The nation dances galvanize her into action, if only mentally at this point. She admires the dancers who proudly celebrate, even if what they honor is depleted remnants. They honor the charred remains of their ancestral heritage, while still living in a markedly different present. Thus their celebration becomes a linking of the entire community as fictive kin rejecting the attempts to destroy their culture. In this way, the novel depicts an ethic of community support and accountability as a way for Blacks to pragmatically connect with one another despite what may or may not remain lost or unremembered. Rather than simply lamenting the destruction that slavery and colonialism have wrought, the nation dances, while certainly not dismissing the violent legacies of these institutions, reflect the resourceful and transgressive ways in which Blacks have formed kinship networks and communities throughout the Diaspora. The ethos invoked by these rituals calls for an understanding of Black family life in the Caribbean and the United States that rejects a narrative of scarcity and lack in favor of a nuanced perspective that emphasizes Black people's transgressive agency.

The novel also portrays a hybrid cultural identity, via the creole dances, that also reflects an ethic of community support and accountability. After viewing the nation dances, Avey joins the creole dances, adding the steps she saw in Tatem and experiencing the feeling of connection she felt as a child venturing to upstate New York with her family and other Blacks.[38] After years of fighting her familial obligations and denying her heritage, Avey has arrived: "She had finally after all these decades made it across. . . . Now, suddenly, as if she were that girl again, with her entire life yet to live, she felt the threads streaming out from the old people around her in Lebert Joseph's yard. And their brightness as they entered her spoke of *possibilities and becoming even in the face of the bare bones and the burnt-out ends*" (249; emphasis mine). Although not of Caribbean descent, Avey recognizes the connections between the communities across the Diaspora.[39] The individuals in the circle become part of an affinity group, just as the silken threads connected her to other Blacks from across the world when she was a child. In other words, as Pascha Stevenson insists, "It is those connections—those silken threads binding her to this Black community, pulling her back to her childhood in Tatem and stretching forward into a future defined by a discourse of fabric, interrelatedness, infinite ties—that support and maintain kinship" (153).

Because Avey cannot "call her nation" she can participate only in the creole dances; nonetheless, this is not a lamentable exclusion but rather an example of how postmodern Blacks who are not rooted in every specific detail of their heritage can still have a positive reconciliation with their history and with the notion of Diasporic kinship. Only a few of the eldest participants of the proceedings can call their nation. The other dancers, especially the young people, such as Rosalie's housekeeper Milda, happily join the creole dances in a moment of marked pan-African unity. The creole dances signify generative possibilities that exist in the face of loss, another exemplification of an ethic of community support and accountability. Thus, while not all the islanders can call their nation, all of them can participate in a dance that reflects a melding of traditions in a particularly "New World" context. In a sense, the elders form a protective guard around the young people. The older nation-callers at the edge and the younger creole dancers perform a visual display of circles of meaning that symbolize different examples of an ethic of community support and accountability across the Diaspora. In the end, the participants in the creole dances embody different but similarly significant engagements with ancestral heritage. Whether dancers proudly display the "burnt out ends" or unabashedly participate in a medley of improvised steps in the frenzied jump-up, both the nation dance and the creole dance are praisesongs to Diasporic experience. Neither ritual is privileged, highlighting the efficacy of both as forms of community support and accountability that affirm a variety of Black experiences.

Exhorting the Next Generation

The rites that Avey undergoes in Carriacou (re)initiate her into a new world of understanding; indeed, Avey vows to spread the word like Coleridge's Ancient Mariner. However, in her case, Avey vows to stop young, upwardly mobile Blacks, younger versions of Jay and herself who are heirs to the promises of the post–civil rights era, those in danger of forgetting themselves and their culture, "as they rushed blindly in and out of the glacier buildings, unaware, unprotected, lacking memory, and a necessary distance of mind. . . . She would stop them and before they could pull out of her grasp, tell them about the floor in Halsey Street and quote them the line from her namesake" (255). That is, as an exhorter, Avey will retell the story of the Landing and remind her listeners that, like her ancestor Avatara, their bodies can be in their offices pursuing success, but their minds can be connected to their heritages, that one world need not be relinquished for the other and that personal and communal politics are not necessarily mutually exclusive.

She is therefore poised to urge the next generation of African American strivers living in an era that asserts the seemingly impossible coexistence of affirmative action and Reaganomics that they can be like their Diasporic brethren, the out-islanders in Grenada, who have not relinquished cultural affirmations for material success. In that way, Avey seeks to reveal the tragic cost of the paradox of respectability—ambivalence, estrangement, pain, and regret—consequences that may not necessarily outweigh even a large measure of material success, especially in the tumultuous post–civil rights era of the 1970s and 1980s. Thus, despite its upbeat ending, *Praisesong* is a cautionary tale for 1983 and beyond. The novel warns that the price of social currency is high and that, rather than bankrupting themselves to gain access to the American Dream, Black people have the power to pursue other options.

Besides proselytizing the rising African American elite, Avey vows to teach her grandsons with the same unwavering dedication as her Aunt Cuney did her, reasserting the importance of an ethic of community support and accountability with her biological kin. When spending the holidays with her eldest daughter Sis and her two sons several years before, Avey saw her youngest grandson "crying amid the scores of presents he had received, all because he had not been given a toy xylophone he had fallen in love with when out shopping with her and his mother the day before" (138). Initially, Avey silently admonished Sis for spoiling the child. However, after her epiphany about the importance of small rites and rituals, Avey reconsiders. It is this grandson that Avey especially wants to reach; she identifies him as a kindred spirit, one who already eschews materialism for "something . . . simple, yet containing all the magic in the world" (138). Thus Avey's grandmothering is also profoundly marked by her experiences; rather than viewing her grandson as ungrateful, her shifting perspective understands the boy's behavior as a desire for simple pleasures rather than an inappropriate willfulness.

In addition to sharing her perspectives with upwardly mobile workers and with her grandchildren, Avey's story and experience of an ethic of community support and accountability is portrayed as relevant not only to the upwardly mobile workers and the grandchildren that she seeks to teach but to scores of others in the world of the novel. Her youngest daughter Marion's teaching and social work positively influence Avey because she vows to run a summer camp of sorts in Tatem with not only her grandchildren but also some of her daughter's struggling students, whom she calls her "sweet lepers."[40] By including this group in Avey's audience, the novel makes clear that the notions of self-care and the ethic of community support and accountability set forth in the novel are not limited to an age, a gender, or a socioeconomic class; rather, honoring oneself and one's heritage while striving is a lesson to be learned by all within (and undoubtedly without) the Diaspora. Ultimately, Avey's future pupils form a diverse group that both reflects the makeup of Black communities across the Diaspora and serves as a revolutionary model for social change through communal support systems. Through Avey's embrace of an ethic of community support and accountability, *Praisesong* reveals a possible trajectory even for those who are seemingly inextricably bound up with respectability politics. The novel draws attention to a practical model for recognizing and reconnecting to healing practices already rooted in Black communities through Avey's gradual return to more sustaining and sustainable family practices.

Therefore, while Avey's vow to accost young Black women and men might seem romantic or even fantastical, her plans to renovate the house she has inherited from Aunt Cuney and pass on the legacy of Ibo Landing ring with the same pragmatic determination that the novel shows Jay and Avey having in their pursuit of upward mobility, minus the self-effacement. Cheryl A. Wall contends that the "novel does not suggest that this privileged protagonist will give up the material possessions she has or promise to buy no more. It is not that idealistic. It is heuristic, however, in its plea to its African American readers that they perform rituals of remembrance that connect them to a history they too often ignore or dismiss" (208).[41] Thus *Praisesong*'s exhortation is about the possibility of practical self-renewal, community engagement, and transformation, not nostalgic rhetoric or romantic imaginings of cultural connection. Although the novel ends in triumph, it is clear that Avey's hard-won transformation is not guaranteed to persuade others—the Grenadian cabbie, for example, who takes Avey to her hotel, who is entrenched in respectability politics and thus is scornful of the Carriacou Excursion, failing to understand that honoring cultural connections need not preclude financial success. Avey imagines him laughing off her conversion: "Crazy. The American Black woman gone crazy he would think to himself, and blame it on the excursion" (255). Likewise, Lebert's "grands and great-grands" who have never seen the excursion and who are ensconced in life in New York, Toronto, and elsewhere may never be convinced of the value of honoring the Old Parents. These facts do not necessarily undercut Avey's triumph; rather, they put Avey's journey in perspective and temper the notion that the excursion and the discourses surrounding it might be a panacea for all the problems arising from deeply entrenched notions of respectability politics.

Praisesong effectively rebukes conventional wisdom about the effectiveness of respectability politics in Black family life, underscoring instead the dangers of the paradox of respectability. The novel not only depicts a community of praise singers recovering one of their own but also advocates for an ethic of community support and accountability and the reclamation of a Diasporic ethnic identity as a possible defense against the soul-numbing effects of racism, sexism, and classism in the post–civil rights era. Avey's experiences in Grenada and the neighboring Carriacou underscore the importance of sustaining African American and Caribbean communities with distinct and complex links to their Diasporic heritage. Avey successfully transitions from disconnected socialite to a woman vowing to use her power and privilege for good, rejecting repressive narratives of family success in favor of a more culturally affirming ethos of kinship. Overall, the novel is a praisesong not just to Avey but to the whole Diasporic experience. And while Avey may not be able to "call her nation" like the elders in Carriacou, she does have access to the sentiment behind this act, and that sentiment is significant. Avey's rejection of the paradox of respectability and her retelling of the Landing story become a sort of praisesong to memory, one that may very well not end with her.

2 / Sins of the Mother? Ambivalence, Agency, and the Family Romance in Jamaica Kincaid's *Annie John*

When asked why she crafts iconoclastic characters that often exhibit a sort of "negative freedom," Antiguan author Jamaica Kincaid explains, "Perversely, I will not give the happy ending. I think life is difficult and that's that. I am not at all—absolutely not at all—interested in the pursuit of happiness. I am not interested in the pursuit of positivity. I am interested in pursuing a truth, and the truth often seems to be not happiness but its opposite" ("Jamaica Kincaid" [Snell]). Kincaid's insistence on being "perverse" to readers and reviewers in search of trite happy endings reflects her ongoing interest in creating challenging, unsettling work. Throughout her oeuvre, her obsessive reworking of mother-daughter themes troubles normative notions of family in favor of pursuing what she sees as darker, but more relevant, truths. In texts such as *At the Bottom of the River, My Brother*, and *The Autobiography of My Mother*, for example, Kincaid depicts vexed family dynamics that exemplify "negative freedom" and that consequently reveal as much about conflict and alienation as they do about familial affection and loyalty. Thus Kincaid, like other contemporary Black women writers from the Caribbean such as Erna Brodber, Michelle Cliff, and Merle Hodge, invokes a hermeneutics of suspicion toward normative notions of respectability and Black family life and foregrounds the ambivalent connections at the center of many families as a result.

Kincaid's semiautobiographical first novel, *Annie John* (1985), part bildungsroman and part searing indictment of the dissolution of a mother-daughter relationship, is likewise a case study in "negative freedom."[1] The novel, set in colonial Antigua in the middle of the twentieth century, traces the young protagonist Annie's life as she experiences childhood and adolescence under the watchful eye of her domineering mother, Mrs. John, and her close-knit community.[2] Like other novels of education, *Annie John* reveals the various rites of passage Annie experiences in school, at home, and throughout her community. Much of the novel's most pointed action, however, involves Annie's growing discomfiture at her changing relationship with her mother and her (in)ability to reconcile her desire for autonomy with her desire to have an unchanging relationship with her mother. *Annie John* paints a largely vexed portrayal of family, and of motherhood in particular. Mrs. John is a protégé of Victorian sensibilities who is a bit of a domestic tyrant, colluding with colonialism and other forms of kyriarchy. Annie's ultimate disconnection from her mother, much as in a typical bildungsroman, reveals a heroine poised to maneuver the world on her own terms, away from the stifling confines of her natal home.

Yet inasmuch as *Annie John* is about Annie's ambivalence toward her mother, the novel also takes part in a larger discussion of women's roles in families within Black women's literature in the Caribbean and the United States. Like *Praisesong for the Widow*, and other Black women's literature in this tradition, *Annie John* compels us to consider ambivalence born of the chafing restrictions of respectability politics as a defining feature of many Black women's social conditions, particularly in the wake of colonialism. *Annie John* draws attention to respectability politics through the notion of "young lady business," or the training Annie receives in art, domestic duties, etiquette, music, and general education that will make her "fit" to be a bourgeois wife and mother someday. The novel also invites us to consider respectability politics through the portrayal of Annie's mother, who, though not the architect of the "young lady business," which is an institutionalized social construct, is a most ardent convert who zealously seeks to indoctrinate her daughter into its ideology. This chapter's analysis of *Annie John* contends that Kincaid's novel illuminates the role of the paradox of respectability, in which some Blacks aspire to be respectable according to the ideals of respectability politics but also find it difficult, if not impossible, to live up to their professed ideals—a tension that often provokes ambivalence in familial relationships.

This ambivalence is a complicated confluence of desire to be close with one's family and dread of such closeness. More specifically, ambivalence—in the form of Annie's desire to be close to Mrs. John alongside intense feelings of repulsion toward her mother—calls into question the efficacy of Mrs. John's adherence to respectability politics and her collusion with hegemonic ways of knowing, such as the "young lady business." Thus, while Mrs. John does succeed in raising Annie (to at least appear) as a "young lady," her increasing estrangement from Annie, her inability to diagnose Annie's adolescent dis-ease, and Annie's ultimate departure from Antigua mark Mrs. John's efforts as troubling and problematic. Respectability politics in the world of *Annie John*, as elsewhere in African American and Black Caribbean women's writing, may succeed in improving the lives of Blacks to a degree, but it is also a politics of surveillance and repression that seeks to control Black women's bodies and render them pliant, obedient colonial subjects—and ultimately estranges Black women from one another.

This chapter argues that *Annie John* not only portrays family systems built on respectability politics as flawed and problematic, like the other texts I discuss in this book, but also invites us to consider truly viable family units as built on an ethic of community support and accountability that features flexible and expansive notions of family, including networks of both biological and fictive kin and interrelating communal and personal politics. Such notions of family are seen in Annie's relationship with her maternal grandmother, Ma Chess and in Annie's homoerotic friendships with other young women. The novel also exemplifies an ethic of community support and accountability through its portrayal of enriching Diasporic rituals and traditions, such as the spiritual system of obeah. As in *Praisesong for the Widow* and other texts discussed in this book, Diasporic rituals are particularly significant because they represent a subversive form of resistance to hegemonic systems of power and act as examples of social sustenance that are rooted in traditions at the core of Black communities. Moreover, *Annie John* shows that an ethic of community support and accountability necessitates a rejection of a narrow respectability politics based on kyriocentric colonial mores and a reimagining of intimacy and family beyond dominant hegemonic social structures. Indeed, *Annie John*, like the other Black women's novels studied in this book, forces us to consider that Black women possess the agency to circumvent respectability politics and that means to do so are often already present in their communities.

Moreover, *Annie John* does not dismiss Mrs. John out of hand but illustrates the presence of an ethic of community support and accountability in the depiction of Mrs. John's community of obeah healers and her negotiations around empowering Annie. Much as Paule Marshall's

Praisesong depicts syncretic religious practices, *Annie John* underscores the potential for intimacy and communal support within transgressive African Diasporic spiritual practices, support that is available even to those entrenched in respectability politics. Furthermore, the novel incites us to trouble any easy demonization of Mrs. John by illuminating the complex negotiations she undertakes in raising Annie while under the burden of the paradox of respectability, negotiations that reveal the tensions between her pragmatic desires for upward mobility and her transgressive desires to empower her child. *Annie John*, then, is really the story of two Annies, mother and daughter, and the ways they engage their world through their social positions in their family. Thus this chapter critiques Mrs. John's respectability politics while also acknowledging the novel's depiction of Mrs. John's tenuous position as a Black woman raising a genteel yet empowered daughter in a world where (Black) women's choices have always been fairly circumscribed.

A Closer Look at Mrs. John

Part of the reason Mrs. John is largely dismissed or even castigated in studies of *Annie John* is that the novel itself is markedly ambivalent about family and about motherhood in particular. The novel privileges a daughterly perspective that rarely promotes easy recognition of Mrs. John's full humanity, even as the novel depicts a daughter lamenting a mother not honoring a daughter's desire for that particular type of connection. Critics of *Annie John* or of Kincaid's works more generally rely on this daughterly perspective to make meaning of the novel regardless of their theoretical perspective. That is, although critics who understand the novel in psychoanalytic terms, as a bildungsroman, as evidence of Kincaid's autobiographical concerns, or as a postcolonial allegory (with the mother symbolizing the mother country) employ theoretical methods that seem to have little in common, their conclusions largely converge: almost all privilege a daughterly perspective that identifies Mrs. John as the novel's main obstacle and antagonist.

Psychoanalytic readings of the novel, for example, have mostly focused on the trope of the family romance and the female Oedipus complex, contending that the novel is a book-length lamentation on the rupture of the pre-Oedipal bonding of mother and child.[3] Critics who use autobiography as a point of departure in Kincaid studies come to similar conclusions about the role of the mother in *Annie John*.[4] Kincaid herself certainly invites such a reading, sardonically claiming in an interview,

"I've never written about anyone except myself and my mother. I'm just one of those pathetic people for whom writing is therapy" (Kincaid, "Jamaica Kincaid" [Cudjoe] 402).[5] The autobiographical line of critical inquiry, like the psychoanalytical method, favors the perspective of a daughter who is perceived to be at odds with an all-powerful mother figure. Similarly, postcolonial readings of *Annie John* look at Mrs. John primarily as the source of Annie's alienation in the novel, arguing that much of Annie's ambivalence toward Mrs. John is symbolic of the colonial subject's ambivalence toward the mother country.[6]

Together these critical perspectives promote an understanding of ambivalence in *Annie John*, but they can also help reify a problematic discourse in their emphasis on the proverbial sins of the mother. Consistently aligning a complex mother figure with all that is wrong with hegemonic systems of power can succeed in not so much challenging these systems as reinscribing the supremacy of antifeminist ideologies that first narrowly define and then demonize motherhood. Analyzing Mrs. John and Annie as complicated and flawed figures that engage respectability politics in a variety of ways while also struggling with its ideals offers a richer, more nuanced view of the novel. My focus on the novel's elucidation of the paradox of respectability draws attention to hegemonic systems of power and the characters' investments in them without simply vilifying Mrs. John. Thus my reading illuminates the complicated contours of Black women's connections to one another and to systems of power in ways that are attuned both to the issue of agency in reifying repression and to the ambivalence born of the burden of respectability.

Greg Thomas's work is a notable exception to the prevailing critical perspective on Mrs. John, as he argues more for scrutinizing both Annie's unresolved sexual desire for her classmates and her desire for her mother, along with Kincaid's increasingly conservative ethos throughout her oeuvre—claims that I take as a point of departure in my own analysis of *Annie John*.[7] Thomas contends that there is a recurrent problematic theme in Kincaid's work, namely that of the mother who has "fallen" from the pedestal on which her daughter placed her, and asserts that it does little to shed new light on family dynamics in the Caribbean.[8] And while it is outside the scope of this chapter to theorize on Kincaid's entire body of work, I am mindful of Thomas's assertions in my own analysis of Mrs. John. More specifically, my analysis pays particular attention to both Annie's and Mrs. John's reification of respectability politics that ultimately damages their connection to one another, rather than simply focusing on Mrs. John as a singular culprit.[9] Looking beyond a daughterly perspective to include a nuanced view of the portrayal of Mrs. John yields vital information about *Annie John*, information that adds a critical dimension to the study of Caribbean women's literature.

Moving beyond a daughterly perspective means that Annie's narration of the idyllic parts of her childhood can be problematized in interesting ways that further illuminate the roles of respectability, ambivalence, and an ethic of community and support in the novel. By Annie's account, she blossoms under the careful attention of her devoted, older parents,[10] and she describes her life until age twelve as nothing short of utopian: "I was given my tea—a cup of cocoa and a buttered bun. My father by then would return home from work, and he was given his tea. As my mother went around preparing our supper, picking up clothes from the stone heap, or taking clothes off the clothesline, I would sit in a corner of our yard and watch her. She never stood still. . . . She might stoop down and kiss me on my lips and then on my neck. It was in such a paradise that I lived" (25). Annie's childhood seemingly takes place in a domestic paradise where she takes voyeuristic pleasure in observing her mother. Mundane household tasks become eroticized under Annie's daughterly gaze (cooking, washing, and ironing share the same space as kissing), linking sensual pleasure with the domestic space.

Nonetheless, despite Annie's seductive description, the true nature of Mrs. John's work is less romantic: she is a housewife performing her daily duties and not a hedonist reveling in sensual pleasures as she readies the evening meal. Put another way, Annie's completely domestic paradise is invested in the dynamics of a nuclear family master narrative central to a politics of respectability. Interestingly, Annie's father seems almost peripheral, while Mrs. John and Annie exist in blissful symbiosis of an almost prenatal variety. Nonetheless, although Annie's father is mostly absent from the scene, his presence lingers: Mrs. John is tending the home (that Mr. John has built with his own hands) and serving him an afternoon snack, just as she does for Annie. Thus, while Annie emphasizes her mother's majestic beauty and power, this description does not belie the actual power dynamics at the heart of this family. In actuality, this moment exposes respectability politics at work rather than being a pleasant snapshot of Annie's life "before the fall." Recognizing the contrast between Annie's misrecognition of this moment's true import and the reality of the moment's larger meaning underscores not only the pervasiveness of respectability politics but also its power to engender a nostalgia for a past that never was.

While Annie is upset when her childhood is replaced by the multiply-ing demands of womanhood (or perhaps more accurately "ladyhood"), the novel underscores that Annie's "paradise" is false, not only because her memory is faulty, but also because this "Eden" is largely dependent upon a respectability politics centered on Mrs. John's servitude to both Annie and her father. Mrs. John dutifully performs the role of a petit-bourgeois wife: she is the primary caregiver for Annie, tends the house, cooks the family meals, and waits on her husband.[11] While Kincaid does not portray Mr. John as a tyrant, she does describe a man catered to by his wife. Kincaid writes, "*As my mother made my father his breakfast, my father would shave. . . . Then he would . . . quickly bathe in water that he had instructed my mother to leave outside overnight in the dew*" (13; emphasis mine). In addition to preparing breakfast especially for Mr. John, Mrs. John has been "instructed" by her husband as to the proper care of his toilette. While Kincaid depicts several instances of Mr. John lounging in his bath, there are no moments where Mrs. John lingers in a bath (the only moments of Mrs. John slowly bathing are the medicinal obeah baths she takes to ward off the evil intentions of her husband's former lovers). Besides catering to her husband, Mrs. John is consumed with taking care of Annie: cooking, cleaning, washing, ironing, and oth-erwise attending to her headstrong daughter. Lounging and play are not options for Mrs. John in her family; she is too busy serving.

Upon closer examination of the novel, Annie's childhood takes place, not in a prelapsarian paradise but in a site of unpaid and under-rec-ognized labor at the heart of traditional Western marriage. Therefore, Annie's nostalgia for a paradise lost should invite a critique of respect-ability politics at work in the world of the novel and not simply a critique of Mrs. John. Mrs. John's seemingly ceaseless obligations and Annie's growing resentment of her mother reflect the paradox of respectability. That is, according to the ethos of respectability in the novel, Mrs. John is a good person only when her life is absolutely devoted to her husband and daughter. That Mrs. John's behavior as a petit-bourgeois housewife is in service not only to her family but to the colonial state should not be forgotten. The dominant systems of power that seek to naturalize family systems with strong patriarchs served by submissive women are reified through the workings of the John family.

Rather than sympathizing with her mother's plight, however, Annie has learned far too well from the dominant narratives that devalue domestic labor while also making it mandatory for most women, respectable or otherwise. As she grows up, Annie recoils at the drudgery of Mrs. John's married life, admitting, "Looking at how sickly [Mr. John] has become and looking at the way my mother now has to run up and down for him, gathering the herbs and barks that he boils in water, which he drinks instead of the medicine the doctor has ordered for him, I plan not only never to marry an old man but certainly never to marry at all" (132). On the one hand, Annie is perceptive enough to recognize the less-than-romantic aspects of vowing to love someone for better or for worse, which suggests that she implicitly understands the roles of duty and power within the larger cultural narrative of marriage. On the other hand, Annie sees her mother's toil as both pitiful and inexcusable. Evelyn O'Callaghan suggests that Annie "blames her mother for the consequences of the fall, the sentence handed down for the female sin of sexuality: that is, the wifely duty of submission. . . . Worse, mother/ Eve insists on the same fate for her daughter!" (*Woman Version* 57–58). O'Callaghan argues that Annie perceives Mrs. John as duplicitous and particularly dangerous because the latter seeks to project her seeming lack of autonomy onto her unwilling child; in other words, her primary goal is to reify the sexist cultural practices that confine her. However, I think there is also space for challenging Annie's interpretation of her mother's behavior. Indeed, part of Annie's disgust at her mother's decision is that an older Annie recognizes that Mrs. John must split her attention between her husband and her child, for, as Laura Niesen de Abruña argues, Annie "sees perhaps why her mother could no longer be her first love after she had married a man so much older than herself" (286). Both Annie and Mr. John are extremely demanding; the novel's depiction of their inflexibility underscores the power of their incessant claims for attention and illuminates the demands of respectability politics and its requisite desire for maternal submission.

Throughout the novel, other situations not only portray Annie's behavior toward her mother as intensely ambivalent and flawed but also reveal her daughterly investment in the misogyny of respectability politics. When Annie and Mrs. John engage in an intense argument and Annie declares herself the victor, her first reaction is: "I looked at my mother. She seemed tired and old and broken. Seeing that, I felt happy and sad at the same time. I soon decided that happy was better" (102). But when Mrs. John gives an arch reply, Annie reassesses the situation: "It was I who was tired and old and broken, and as I looked at my mother, full of vigor, young and whole, I wanted to go over and put my arms around her and beg forgiveness" (103). On the one hand, this exchange may seem little more than a minor power play between mother and daughter, a routine occurrence in a novel of education perhaps. Nonetheless, this moment is quite revealing because it underscores the routine nature of Annie's ambivalence toward her mother. She feels pleased to have bested her in a shouting match and, in the same moment, wants to reconcile with her. Moreover, her notions of who emerges and remains "young and whole" or "old and broken" are in a constant state of flux, calling her other assessments into question. Her selective memory and her particular (mis)perceptions of events color the narration and prevent any transparent reading of Annie's voice, except to acknowledge its deep-seated ambivalence. Any consideration of the novel must grapple with Annie as an unreliable narrator who rails against the injustice of respectability politics while also adhering to the misogyny that is sometimes a consequence of subscribing to this ideology.

An Anglophile and an Agent

At first glance, Mrs. John, like the powerful matrons Aunt Becca in *Crick Crack Monkey* and Helene Wright in *Sula*, is most obviously invested in a rather Victorian ethos of respectability. She is steadfastly devoted to her family and consumed with very particular notions of dignity and honor. To that end, she is a passionate supporter of training her only child in a myriad of bourgeois social graces—a process Annie derisively identifies as "young lady business." Annie muses: "Because of this young-lady business, instead of days spent in perfect harmony with my mother, I trailing in her footsteps, she showering down on me her kisses and affection and attention, I was now sent off to learn one thing and another" (27).[12] Mrs. John's insistence that Annie become a "young lady" reflects an investment in colonial notions of decorum and respectability. Evelyn O'Callaghan notes, "The 'young lady business' is a class-based construct ('lady' rather than 'woman') which . . . was engrained in the colonial education girls received in the West Indies" (*Woman Version* 55). The portrayal of the respectability politics of the "young lady business" indicts the binary of "lady" versus "woman" as both destructive and divisive. As expressed in the novel, a "lady" is articulate, well educated (in the British system), accomplished in Western arts, and well versed in etiquette, not to mention chaste, modest, industrious, and, perhaps most importantly, obedient to her elders. "Ladies" become teachers and nurses and then marry respectable gentlemen. A "woman," on the other hand, is the marked opposite of a lady; she is an adult female who lacks the education, social graces, and social standing of a "lady." She works, but certainly not in a "respectable" career. She has children outside marriage and perhaps never marries at all.[13] Mrs. John wants Annie to grow up to become a respectable "lady," so that she will benefit from the social standing and privilege such a label affords, rather than a "woman," who presumably will have few to no benefits within her society.

Thus in *Annie John* "young lady business" is a discourse of respectability based on a colonial Caribbean model of acceptable behavior in which Blacks can access social power and privilege by adhering to a strict set of ideals regarding propriety that is rooted in kyriarchy, a system of social hierarchies connected to intersecting sets of oppression. The ideals of respectability politics as evidenced through "young lady business" are not simply part of a social strategy aimed at ameliorating Annie's life. Because of respectability politics' dependence on repressive practices, it is fundamentally connected to kyriarchy, a system of domination in which individuals with varying degrees of power dominate or try to dominate others as they navigate various social hierarchies. The tensions between the professed goal of respectability politics and the reality of its investment in kyriarchy—the very system that prompts the necessity of respectability politics—creates a paradox of respectability in which the characters wish to uphold the tenets of respectability politics even as they are not fully able or even willing to do so.

Because of this paradox of respectability, Mrs. John's desires are fraught with ambivalence. Her notions of success as a parent are notably limited and informed by colonialism; thus, for Mrs. John, success is raising a genteel young woman who will sail to England, study nursing, and marry a respectable man. But we must also acknowledge that Mrs. John's vision for Annie, though clearly questionable, is well intentioned in its goal to give Annie as much power as she can wield in a hostile world. Alison Donnell articulates a compelling model for Mrs. John's social location. She argues for the replacement of the concept of "double colonization"—which rightfully underscores the multiple oppressions women of color face in the Caribbean—with the notion of Black women as "double agents," which properly connotes how Caribbean women mobilize gender, ethnicity, and cultural identity as a "site of resistance, affirmation and oppositional agency" (8). I replace "colonization" with "agency" here not to efface imperialism but rather to recenter Caribbean women's negotiations of power. Mrs. John acts as an agent, albeit one of limited and problematic powers because of her investment in rigid respectability politics: she seeks to lay a foundation for Annie to reap the few privileges she can attain as a young Black woman coming of age in a British colony. It is imperative that she give Annie the tools to survive in a hostile society, for as Patricia Hill Collins has argued, Black mothers throughout the Diaspora must invariably "[balance] the need for physical survival of their daughters with the vision of encouraging them to transcend the boundaries of the sexual politics of Black womanhood" (*Black Feminist Thought* 185). Thus, while Mrs. John's investment in respectability is seemingly sensible, that investment often interferes with her goals to empower. This tension, or paradox of respectability, arises because Mrs. John's strategy for social mobility is built upon kyriocentric foundations.

Therefore, when Mrs. John refuses to create a dress identical to hers for Annie, she is not simply denying her daughter's wishes. Instead, Mrs. John understands that "as a result of female demonization, [she] has to train Annie in accordance with societal, patriarchal conventions, lest she be seen in an unfavorable light" (S. Alexander 63–64). The novel allows us to consider Mrs. John as someone seeking to control her daughter but also as a woman caught in the unrelenting demands of colonial discourse and respectability who is seeking, however problematically, to harness respectability politics the best way she believes she can. Thus what is problematic is not so much Mrs. John's intentions as her lack of alternative resources and an expansive vision that does not center on normative notions of respectability; in attempting to empower Annie, Mrs. John relies on a discourse designed to promote women's submission. This tension produces a cautionary tale that reveals what is at stake for Black women in the Caribbean who must navigate respectability politics.

Mrs. John's deference to respectability politics profoundly complicates her relationship with Annie, particularly because it incites Mrs. John to police her daughter's burgeoning sexuality. For example, when Mrs. John observes Annie in what is really an innocent exchange with a group of young men, one of whom is a childhood friend, and calls her a "slut," the moment is painful for both Annie and her mother. Annie feels shame because of Mrs. John's misinterpretation of the events and her unduly harsh criticism, yet Mrs. John also voices her shame at the mere possibility of having raised a "womanish" daughter who would blatantly engage in sexual impropriety, as a "lady" would never do. It seems that after all the cajoling and special attention, Mrs. John has failed in raising a daughter who can properly "conduct [herself] when speaking to young men" (102). Dianne Simmons argues that Annie's reaction to her mother's demands is the bewildered response of a beleaguered child forced to cope with "an impossibly contradictory map of the world" given to her by her mother (30). Simmons's claim is only partially true, however. Annie is indeed given an impossibly contradictory map, but her mother is not the sole cartographer. The novel's depiction of Annie's confusion invites a larger critique of a Western family economy rather than a singular indictment of Mrs. John's duplicity. Certainly, Annie's narration compels this demonization of Mrs. John; however, the novel also invites a critique of how the unrelenting demands of hegemonic structures of oppression influence Mrs. John's conflicting behavior.[14] This moment can be understood not just as an indictment of Mrs. John's misinterpretation of the events but also as a condemnation of the prevailing narratives of respectability that mark young lower-middle-class Black women such as Annie (and perhaps a young Mrs. John) as uncontrollable, hypersexualized creatures and that prompt mothers such as Mrs. John to buy into this racist and sexist rhetoric.

Annie's brief realization after their heated exchange expresses as much: "When I looked down it was as if the ground had opened up between us, making a deep and wide split. On one side of this stood my mother, bent over my dinner cooking in a pot; on the other side stood I, in my arms carrying my schoolbooks and inside carrying the thimble that weighed worlds" (103). The novel not only contrasts Mrs. John's domestic world, symbolized by her pot, with Annie's reality as a schoolgirl with her books but also invites us to consider how these images represent discourses of respectability that seemingly divide the women from each other but in many ways serve the same purpose in their kyriocentric society. The image of the widening chasm between two women, one bound by "ladyhood" and domestic duties (and their associated narratives) and the other bound by the dictates of impending "ladyhood," reveals a vexed situation for all. Despite whatever good intentions Mrs. John may have, her actions reveal that adhering to a repressive politics of respectability necessarily creates schisms between women because it both upholds and replicates reigning hegemonic systems of power aimed at disenfranchising women and estranging them from one another.

Yet rather than recognizing her mother as a victim of kyriarchy and imperialism who is also invested in the politics of respectability invoked by these systems, Annie mostly views her mother as a duplicitous serpent aiming to beguile her out of an Edenic childhood, just as the biblical serpent tricked Eve. This misrecognition is, in many ways, as destructive as Mrs. John's desires for ladyhood. The moment where Annie imagines a widening chasm between herself and her mother is a brief moment of lucidity; otherwise, she is unwilling or unable to see Mrs. John as a similarly colonized body, a body that experiences erasure and abuse in the face of the Anglo-Victorian bourgeois mores of colonial Antigua (Tiffin 912). Mrs. John's behavior in fact troubles notions of maternal dominance (e.g., the emasculating Black matriarch) by revealing that in this case the seemingly all-powerful "matriarch" is struggling under the same oppressive demands as Annie. Mrs. John, then, engages in the precarious balancing act of following colonial dictates only inasmuch as they are useful to her. Though certainly an accomplice, she is an uneasy one who lives in a colonial world with few choices. Not dismissing Mrs. John but instead paying close attention to her complicated subject positions, along with the ambiguity of Annie's perception of her, garners a richer understanding of the scope of respectability and family dynamics in *Annie John*.

* * *

In addition to portraying the troubling effects of respectability politics in the novel's primary mother-daughter relationship, *Annie John* invites us to consider Mrs. John as an agent who is invested in healing family practices that can be understood as acts rooted in an ethic of community support and accountability. Not unlike Avey in *Praisesong*, Mrs. John taps into affirming communal practices, Diasporic rituals, and subversive practices that help shape her notion of family, perhaps as much as her investment in respectability does. For example, Mrs. John's notion of education is informed by an ethic of community support and accountability. It is important to note that Mrs. John does not privilege the domestic over the academic but encourages Annie to excel at both. Simone A. James Alexander notes that, although they are competing discourses, both literary training and domestic training are symbols of freedom: "The juxtaposition of the literary (written) and the domestic (oral) speaks to the need for negotiation. Mrs. John epitomizes this negotiation, for although her domain is the kitchen, she instills in her daughter the importance of literary training" (60). Mrs. John encourages Annie to excel in school and is disappointed when Annie returns with less than excellent grades or displays inappropriate behavior at school. Mrs. John's emphasis on education is an expression of an ethic of community support and accountability that affirms her daughter's marked intelligence and encourages her intellectual development, a transgressive act that emphasizes how Black women can skillfully navigate a hostile (post)colonial world bent on their subordination and have done so in the past. Thus Mrs. John's attitude toward education illuminates how Black women can act as complicated double agents who have investments in kyriarchy but also challenge and resist kyriocentric ways of knowing and moving about in the world.

Mrs. John's sense of education moves beyond the yard and school-house to include training her daughter to be an independent woman in the world, thereby undermining colonial dictates that would make Annie a social subordinate. The novel portrays Mrs. John imbuing Annie with a sense of purpose and responsibility from a young age. For example, when Annie is only five, Mrs. John trains her to run errands by herself: "My mother had placed three pennies in my little basket, which was a duplicate of her bigger basket, and sent me to the chemist's shop" (139). When Annie successfully returns from the errand, Mrs. John is ecstatic: "Her eyes filled with tears and she swooped me up and held me high in the air and said I was wonderful and good and that there would never be anybody better" (139–40).[15] Throughout the novel, Mrs. John constantly pushes her daughter toward independence and self-sufficiency. Thus Mrs. John continually strategizes for her daughter's success in a hostile colonial space, even though she does so with decidedly mixed results, reflecting how difficult it is for Black women in colonial Antigua to pursue upward mobility without relying on normative ideals of respectability.

Mrs. John's penchant for storytelling also reflects an ethic of community support and accountability. In the trunk kept beneath Annie's bed—incidentally, the same trunk that a headstrong sixteen-year-old Annie Senior used to depart from her parent's home—Mrs. John keeps mementos of Annie's childhood, and, when airing out this trunk she regales Annie with stories of her childhood: Annie's "biting phase" or the time Annie burned her elbows on a coal pot. Each time Mrs. John eagerly and graciously submits to Annie's extended requests for stories about her life: "On and on my mother would go. No small part of my life was so unimportant that she hadn't made a note of it" (22). These tales do not simply buy into the lady/woman binary, or recount child-hood play or illustrate simple nostalgia; rather, they are used to build Annie's self-esteem. The narratives Mrs. John spins from objects in the trunk symbolize characteristics—such as strength, intellectual achieve-ments, and independence—that often deviate from normative standards of ladyhood. In the larger context of colonial Antigua, this self-esteem building is both significant and crucial. Mrs. John's stories emphasize skills that social-climbing Black girls like Annie will need not only to survive but to thrive in a society in which they are actively marginalized.

Yet the space in which the storytelling takes place is also a site of kyriocentric servitude. These stories not only recount moments of Annie's life that foreground the special bond she shares with her mother but also emphasize the tensions of the paradox of respectability that Mrs. John both enacts and passes on to Annie.[16] Thus it is with pointed irony that Mrs. John tells these stories of fierce female independence while circumscribed in a family system that often finds such traits untenable. The juxtaposition of these elements should remind readers of the ways both Annie and Mrs. John are caught up in the paradox of respectability and of Black women's complicated negotiations within families throughout the Caribbean. The tensions between respectability politics and a more transgressive ethic depicted in *Annie John* in many ways mirror the tensions and negotiations Black women experience in the face of colonialism and suggest that a more nuanced understanding of their choices is needed to understand how Black women can and do participate in family life.

The significance of Mrs. John's trunk as a symbol of both the potential of an ethic of community support and accountability and the pervasiveness of respectability politics cannot be overstated, however. When Mrs. John was sixteen, she "packed all her things and left not only her parents' house in Dominica but Dominica itself for Antigua. Her father and she had had a big quarrel over whether she would live alone, as she wished, or would continue to live in her parents' house, as her father wished" (105). Mrs. John was openly resentful of her father's dictates and the respectability politics of her natal home and paved her own way, leaving Dominica for Antigua alone. Defiance and self-determination defined a young Annie Senior. Therefore, the trunk and the stories attached to it are not simply pieces of nostalgia; they are also symbols of both intergenerational female power and resistance to kyriarchy. On the one hand, Mrs. John and the repurposed trunk of her youth represent the potential to challenge one's family structure and to rebuke hegemonic authority. Annie Senior left home to live as she wished, and despite the perilous journey she endured from her childhood home to her adult home, she survived and went on to create a new family. Her desire for independence transgressed the respectability politics her father adhered to, revealing Annie Senior to be a woman with the marked determination to defiantly choose the parameters of her own life. Yet Annie Senior grew up to become Mrs. John and ended up reifying many, though not all, of the same aspects of respectability politics she had defied with her own parents, provoking the same paradox she had sought to escape. Mrs. John, especially considered alongside the symbolism of her trunk, reflects the ambivalence born of the struggle between an ethic of community support and accountability and respectability politics and the uneasy and often problematic ways these epistemologies are negotiated.

Although she casts her mother in the same role as that in which Mrs. John cast her own father, Annie realizes, if only implicitly and ambivalently, that Mrs. John provides a transgressive example of speaking truth to power, an example she can draw upon as she navigates the world. Take, for instance, Annie's critique of colonialism, which is directly connected to her mother's critique of her own father. When Mrs. John discovers that her father, Pa Chess, is increasingly infirm, she recognizes the irony: the very person who sought to control her movements is now unable to move. Annie reflects, "After she read the part about Pa Chess's stiff limbs, she turned to my father and laughed as she said, 'So the great man can no longer just get up and go. How I would love to see his face now!'" (78). Mrs. John's pithy phrase about her father so resonates with Annie that she rightfully links it with the fall of another oppressive figure. Annie writes, "The Great Man Can No Longer Just Get Up and Go" beneath a picture of a shackled Christopher Columbus in her school textbook during class. While the defacement of the book embarrasses Mrs. John, she has clearly served as a model for this subversive behavior, despite her desire to have Annie be a docile and well-behaved pupil and, therefore, a model "young lady." In other words, Mrs. John's assessment of her own tyrannical father directly catalyzes Annie's transgressive thinking about another repressive patriarch, for Annie writes the provocative phrase in her schoolbook right after hearing her mother say it: "When I *next* saw the picture of Columbus sitting there all locked up in his chains, I wrote under it" (78; emphasis mine). Mrs. John's own rejection of the paternal law of her natal home initiates a questioning spirit in her daughter, who treats her textbook as a palimpsest in which she literally writes over history. Mrs. John appears again as an influential agent who instills Annie with the skills to be a critical thinker and to be wary of respectability politics and tyrannical (male) power, even as Annie identifies her mother as a similarly despotic force.[17] Nevertheless, it is clear that Mrs. John is unable to recognize and reconcile her domestic resistance with larger institutional resistance and that this tension results in ambivalent relationships within her family. In this way, *Annie John* invites us to consider that ambivalence is born of the frustrations of seemingly irreconcilable ideological differences not only for Annie, but for Mrs. John as well.

A Sacred Circle of Women

Annie John also explores the potential for an ethic of community support and accountability through obeah, an African Caribbean spiritual practice that legitimizes female power through both magical and curative rituals.[18] In the novel, *obeah* also refers to a belief system in which the supernatural exists alongside the natural in daily life and the dead walk among the living.[19] The depiction of obeah in *Annie John* exemplifies an ethic of community support and accountability in several ways. For one, it is a rejection of the primacy of Western spiritual practices, as it is a syncretism of African and Judeo-Christian cosmologies. Syncretic practices such as obeah often serve as a way to resist colonizing forces that seek to delegitimize or erase any remnant of Diasporic spiritual practice; thus they are potential models of resistance to other aspects of colonization. Furthermore, obeah troubles notions of the mind and the body as fundamentally separate units, providing the potential for resistance against hegemonic powers by emphasizing the potential for Black people's agency through spiritual practice rooted in Diasporic rituals. However, what is perhaps most striking about obeah is that women can be its most powerful practitioners, administering folk medicines, cures, and poisons for a variety of physical and mental ailments. As Donna Perry notes, "The obeah woman's charms have the power to transform reality: they can undo curses, heal wounds, even destroy enemies" (251). Women in the world of *Annie John* who practice obeah use it for healing and as a magical and curative defense, particularly against malice and jealousy, and come together to form a type of family. When Annie is to depart for England, for example, Mrs. John sends all of Annie's jewelry and underclothes to her obeah woman "to protect [Annie] from evil spirits and every kind of misfortune" that might befall her to thwart her trip (134).

Women in *Annie John* are under constant threat from malevolent spiritual forces, often metaphysical manifestations of kyriarchy, and they use obeah and their obeah community to combat this. For example, Annie and Mrs. John in particular are always aware that they are never quite safe from the spite of Mr. John's former (and perhaps current) lovers. Routine events—a minor illness, the strange behavior of domestic animals, broken pottery, and misunderstandings between friends—have sinister undertones (14–15). Mr. John's current/former lovers, who apparently continue to vie for his attention or who desire recompense for his betrayal, seek to dethrone Mrs. John from the seat of her marital and maternal authority with "bad spirits." At other moments, Mrs. John must envelop a young Annie in her own skirts and run away from women with "angry voice[s] saying angry things" that they encounter on their way home from the market (17). The novel reveals Mrs. John's vulnerability and the tenuous position of women more generally within kyriarchy—other women can seemingly wrest her family away from her with serious threats to her person at any moment.

That vulnerability gives even greater meaning to Mrs. John's desire for Annie to be educated and have more choices than she has had and further suggests that even Annie's seemingly blissful childhood home was not secure. Mr. John is also revealed as a philanderer who is apparently immune from these attacks and whose reputation remains unimpeachable, another privilege of the kyriocentric structure of Caribbean family systems based on notions of women's respectability and men's reputation. For while the women in *Annie John* are enmeshed in a matrix of respectability politics, Mr. John might be best understood under the rubric of reputation. Regarding the gender politics of the colonial Caribbean, Peter J. Wilson notes, "Reputation stipulates the minimum requirements for adult manhood and respect . . . that a man should father children. . . . Beyond the minimum of fulfillment, there is a great scope for differences in reputation. A man who fathers many children by many women is 'stronger' than one who only has a few" (150–51). Thus there is a clear double standard concerning sexual activity for men and for women, especially for women who aim to ameliorate their class standing. Mr. John is no less respectable for having fathered several children with several women; indeed, he is very highly regarded.

While Mrs. John counters threats to her family with her own use of obeah, she uses obeah to intercept and repel her rivals' malicious advances, not to hurt them. Obeah, then, exists as an aspect of an ethic of community support and accountability that helps Mrs. John counteract the inequity of kyriarchy within a supportive kinship network, suggesting that Black women's spiritual practices rooted in transgressive Diasporic rituals reflect an agency necessary to help challenge or repel hegemonic notions of power.[20] That is, Mrs. John's use of obeah illustrates the practice as part of an ethic of community support and accountability that reveals possible ways for women to combat circumstances that seek to pit women against one another. In her obeah practice Mrs. John contacts a variety of female sources: a professional obeah woman, her own mother, and a trusted woman friend. After gathering their advice, she is able to prepare the proper medicinal bath "in which the barks and flowers of many different trees, together with all sorts of oils, were boiled in the same large caldron" (14).

With regard to obeah, Mrs. John acts not on her own but as part of a supportive community, where other women seeking to protect themselves and their offspring share charms and cures they can use against hostile forces in their lives. Thus, although Mrs. John has vocal enemies, she can call upon an equally strong network of kin to support her. Mrs. John is involved in a community of transformative women, what Kathleen Renk has described as a "mother-centered world associated with magic," one that will keenly protect its interests (48). These agents create an intimate women's space. In it, Mrs. John ceremoniously bathes first Annie and then herself, deliberately washing their bodies with protection. This is a moment of particular closeness for mother and daughter that, while suggesting a re-creation of prenatal bonding, is unlike Annie's memories of domestic paradise because it is not simply in service to the "respectable" family. Thus obeah, like the family generally, has the potential to be anything from divisive to emancipatory, depending on its adherence to repressive prevailing discourses of power. For Mrs. John in particular obeah exemplifies the potential for an ethic of community support and accountability to challenge respectability politics and the hegemony of kyriocentric family systems. In that way, *Annie John* invites us to consider obeah, a common practice throughout the Anglophone Caribbean and one that is connected to similar spiritual practices such as *vodou* and *Santería*, as having the potential to be a transgressive form of power for Black women in the Caribbean.

Intergenerational Agency

Mrs. John does not limit her use of obeah to repelling her husband's lovers; she also attempts to use it when Western medical practices no longer suffice, revealing it to be a powerful alternative epistemology. Like Avey Johnson aboard the *Bianca Pride*, Annie experiences a dis-ease that is a manifestation of intense emotional suffering brought on by toxic respectability politics: at age fifteen, she contracts a mysterious depression-type illness that forces her to stay in bed for months.[21] Mrs. John first listens to her husband and takes Annie to a British physician, Dr. Stephens. However, when his vague prognosis proves less than fruitful, Mrs. John contacts Ma Jolie, a renowned practitioner of obeah recommended by her mother, to cure her daughter. In this scenario, however,

Mrs. John must weigh her investment in two distinct and competing systems, for her husband disapproves of obeah. Mrs. John appeases her husband's notions of respectability rooted in Western ideas of reason by arranging Annie's medicine cabinet so that the "offensive" obeah cures are hidden behind the prescriptions from Dr. Stephens, paying homage to her husband's belief in traditional Western medicine in order to navigate the potentially choppy waters of her marriage (117–18).

Obeah, like other social and spiritual practices that fall outside acceptably mainstream behavior, is not immune to the restrictions of hegemonic family discourse, as is seen in the handling of Annie's illness. Even as obeah can be a source of power for women, and can provide a type of feminist kinship, it can also be circumscribed by hegemonic discourses of family when respectability politics are dominant. However, the potential for an ethic of community support and accountability remains: repressive norms never fully subsume practices such as obeah. Despite her husband's disapprobation, Mrs. John does incorporate her own notions of health care in her treatment of Annie.[22] While accommodating her husband's wishes, Mrs. John does not retreat from her belief in the validity of obeah cures. Instead, she counters Mr. John's adherence to Western medicine, foregrounding her own oppositional agency by recognizing the false power in a methodology that dictates that healing power is restricted to men with diplomas and machines (Karen Brown 123). The incident underscores the uneasy relationship between these competing discourses in Black women's lives and the complicated and delicate ways they negotiate these discourses.

It is the arrival of Ma Chess, Mrs. John's mother, that most illuminates the potential for an ethic of community support and accountability in the world of *Annie John*. When Ma Jolie's formidable knowledge of herbs and natural cures fails to cure Annie, Ma Chess unexpectedly appears from Dominica "on a day when the steamer was not due," underscoring the importance of elders' knowledge in obeah practice (123). Ma Chess is an obeah woman of unparalleled power and part of Mrs. John's spiritual support network. Annie admits, "Whatever Ma Jolie knew, my grandmother knew at least ten times more" (123).[23] Kincaid describes Ma Chess as a woman who has a preternatural ability to heal and is especially attuned to Annie's mysterious illness.

Interestingly, upon her arrival, Ma Chess does not prescribe routine obeah cures, for she suspects Annie was not harmed by an obeah curse.[24] Instead she nurses Annie back to health by reenacting some of the things that Mrs. John did for Annie before their estrangement: "Sometimes at night, when I would feel that I was all locked up in the warm falling soot and could not find my way out, Ma Chess would come into my bed with me and stay until I was myself. . . . I would lie on my side, curled up like a little comma, and Ma Chess would lie next to me, curled up like a bigger comma, into which I fit" (126). Here, although Annie is silent, her body performs a sort of speech act, literally signifying a pause and the respite she is taking from life because of her illness. According to Moira Ferguson, Annie, in taking the position of a "comma," "has transformed herself into a sign of language with voice" (68). That her grandmother signifies an even larger pause that Annie herself fits into reflects the nature of Annie's convalescence and the pivotal type of care she receives from Ma Chess. Indeed, this period is one of metaphoric rebirth: Annie lies fetuslike inside her grandmother's curved embrace until she is able to find her way out. In these instances, Ma Chess performs curative speech acts, transgressing beyond the bounds of Western medicine and respectability politics to heal Annie in a holistic way.

It is important to note that it is Annie's grandmother, and not her mother, who ultimately cures Annie. Neither Ma Chess nor Mrs. John offers any commentary on Annie's recovery; Ma Chess simply leaves when Annie gets better. It is perhaps Mrs. John's conflicted consultation with both Western medicine and obeah, not to mention her adherence to a politics of respectability, that prevents her from rightly diagnosing Annie's illness as a mental/physical breakdown or dis-ease, a circumstance that Ma Chess quickly discerns. Put another way, Mrs. John's preoccupation with Western epistemologies obstructs the full utility of obeah's spiritual practices for her.[25] Thus Ma Chess's transformative (grand)mothering supersedes Mrs. John's momentary ineffectiveness. "For some of the older generation of Caribbean women," Helen Pyne-Timothy suggests, "the penetration of European cultural values into the African cosmology was not so intense or so desirable. Most of these systems of belief, syncretism, are beginning to appear in Annie's mother's universe" (242). Nevertheless, Ma Chess does not single-handedly save Annie. In the end, Annie does recover, and it is because of the combined and concerted effort of women in her community—Mrs. John, Ma Jolie, and her grandmother Ma Chess—highlighting that healing often occurs through the concerted efforts of a circle of women engaged in an ethic of community support and accountability.

Mrs. John and Annie have Ma Chess as a role model of oppositional agency, for in the novel she is singular in her resistance to the tyranny of respectability politics. A practitioner of obeah and a natural healer, Ma

Chess stands in direct opposition to the repressive politics of respectability represented by both her husband and her son-in-law. Like her daughter, Mrs. John, Ma Chess initially tries to adhere to respectability politics and negotiate her own beliefs with those of her husband, Pa Chess, a Methodist minister—a negotiation that results in a profoundly ambivalent relationship between the two. Because of her investment in respectability politics, when their beloved son, Johnnie, becomes ill, she allows her husband to dictate the terms of his medical treatment. When Johnnie dies, seemingly from an obeah curse (a telltale worm emerges from his body upon his death), Ma Chess refuses to adhere any longer to her former notions of family and respectability. She disregards social convention, leaves the Methodist Church, and all but divorces her husband: "From that day on, Ma Chess never spoke to Pa Chess again, even though they lived in the same house. She never said a word for him or against him, and if his name came up she would absent herself in spirit— and in body, too, if his name continued to come up" (125). The fact that she is married to Pa Chess in name only, despite their cohabitation, and does not speak to him suggests that Ma Chess has found a striking way to navigate a relationship with someone who has dictated the rules of engagement for most of their marriage. In other words, when Ma Chess decides to "absent herself" from Pa Chess, she shifts and decenters the power dynamic in the family.

However, rather than seeking to dominate or even punish the man who controlled much of her life, she simply erases him and proceeds to act independently, as if she were a widow. Thereafter, Ma Chess wears only black, in mourning for her son, and openly practices obeah. The trajectory of Ma Chess's life reveals a vexed relationship with a range of repressive and transgressive family ideologies. Until Johnnie's death, Ma Chess negotiates between the two ideologies until it is clear that, for her at least, these philosophies are fundamentally incompatible. The novel draws attention to Ma Chess's ethic of community support and accountability as fully emerging from the destructiveness of respectability politics. Her experience of marriage and motherhood becomes the ultimate cautionary tale of the high cost of respectability but also offers up a possible avenue of resistance and agency. In a sense, the novel's portrayal of Ma Chess therefore invites us to consider a possible direction for Mrs. John and women like her, who ambivalently engage both sets of discourses.

Ma Chess's rejection of respectability politics can also be understood in opposition to another dominant male figure, her son-in-law, Mr. John.

The two share a general wariness of each other: "Ma Chess and my father kept out of each other's way—not so much because they didn't like each other but because they didn't see the world in the same way. Ma Chess once asked my father to tell her exactly what it was he really did, and when he said that he was off to build a house she said, 'A house? Why live in a house? All you need is a nice hole in the ground, so you can come and go as you please'" (126). While Kincaid forestalls Mr. John's response, considering his pride in his vocation as a carpenter and house builder, Mr. John would undoubtedly be aghast at his mother-in-law's suggestion. Much as in her estrangement from Pa Chess, Ma Chess counters conventional notions of propriety and respectability in her relationship with her son-in-law. Although she is clearly skeptical, she is never openly disrespectful of Mr. John, and once Annie recovers she leaves for Dominica without a goodbye. Yet her disdain for Mr. John's affectation of Western ways is palpable, especially in their exchange about housing choices, and the efficacy of her traditional medicines trumps what Karen McCarthy Brown calls Mr. John's "naïve empiricism" with regard to his unyielding faith in Western medicine (123).[26] Not surprisingly, her pointed distrust of hegemonic social mechanisms of respectability (like the Church or even Western styles of living) matches her emphasis on her own personal freedom to move, eschewing mores that would compel her own subordination and women's subordination in general.

Both Ma Chess's rejection of respectability politics and the supremacy of male authority and the emergence of her own independent worldview evolve from her status as a mother and grandmother. Ma Chess returns to her Diasporic healing practices when Western medicines fail to treat her son, and she continually advises her daughter and granddaughter in traditional healing ways. She is a striking example of the possibility of motherhood as a site of politicized resistance, even in the face of repression. While she does not supplant Annie's father (indeed, his medicines remain at the front of the medicine cabinet), she does challenge the supremacy of his knowledge, revealing that epistemologies can be powerful and transgressive even when they are not dominant. Ma Chess's subversive role and the position of the obeah cures become a fitting metaphor for the interaction between dominant discourses and oppositional narratives, or, put another way, a model for an ethic of community support and accountability in the face of pervasive respectability politics. Ma Chess both indicts respectability politics and foregrounds the transgressive ways Black women have enacted and can enact resistance and agency.

Unlike her mother, Mrs. John does not completely abandon respectability politics and its compulsory heterosexuality for her own independence. Instead, Mrs. John has traded in her father's absolute power for a seemingly egalitarian relationship with a much older man. Such unions are often one of the few viable compromises that might allow women a measure of security and social status in a highly stratified society. However, while it may offer Mrs. John some degree of power to be a respectable married woman on her own terms, such a union does little to challenge the status quo. Donna Perry notes of the marriage of Mr. and Mrs. John that "this is no romance plot, at least not in the conventional sense, but one based on mutual respect and admiration" (251). While clearly operating within the parameters of a traditional heterosexual union, Mrs. John secures herself a degree of power (that is, social and financial security) in her society, creating a matrifocal world, albeit a co-opted one. Her shrewdness has enabled her to make an advantageous match, for although she does not escape her husband's control, she does skillfully negotiate the terms of engagement. The compromise that is her marriage becomes another site that illustrates the complications and ambivalence that attend negotiations between prevailing cultural norms regarding respectability and more radical notions of female independence, another tension that forces us to consider the struggles between these epistemologies as defining Caribbean family life. Ultimately, I would argue that the choices made by Ma Chess and Mrs. John suggest there are multiple coping strategies for navigating kyriocentric family structures, strategies that yield various (that is, unequal) forms of agency for Black women across the Caribbean.

Girl/friends

These coping strategies begin early in life in the world of *Annie John*, with Annie enacting an ethic of community support and accountability with others besides her mother in an effort to compensate for the shifting dynamics in her natal home. For example, Annie's clandestine friendship with the Red Girl is a relationship that affirms Annie's distaste for the "young lady business." While Annie is forced to bathe and brush her teeth daily, wear clean clothes, and attend Sunday school every week, the Red Girl's mother does not force her to do any of those things.[27] However, besides Annie's envy of the Red Girl's freedom from cleanliness habits and social obligations, what is most intriguing about the Red Girl is her general shirking of conventional gendered expectations.

Not only does her physical appearance reject the respectability politics of colonial girlhood, but her activities—climbing trees "better than any boy," playing marbles, and visiting the forbidden lighthouse—transgress all notions of general propriety (58). The Red Girl becomes a kindred spirit for Annie, evidence that her disdain for respectability politics is not singular or unique. Eventually, Annie and the Red Girl begin having homoerotic encounters, in which the Red Girl alternately pinches and kisses Annie, a sensation Annie describes as "delicious" (63). Thus the friendship between Annie and the Red Girl underscores the ways children can potentially resist the ubiquity of respectability politics by instituting their own standards of conduct and their own understandings of intimacy.

Also, when Annie begins a new school, right at the advent of the "young lady business," she almost immediately discovers a strong community of support and accountability with her classmates. Annie notes, "My life in school became just the opposite of my first morning. I went from being ignored, with hardly a glance from anyone, to having girls vie for my friendship, or at least for more than just a passing acquaintanceship" (48–49). While during this period Annie's home life is one of perceived disapprobation and tension, Annie's life at school is one of affirmation and validation. Her friendship with her classmate Gwen is also a particularly important source of support. In fact, this relationship, much like Annie's relationship with the Red Girl, is described in mostly romantic language. For example, in depicting the two girls, described by their friends as the "Little Lovebirds" (60), meeting to walk to school, Kincaid writes, "We'd set off for school side by side, our feet in step, not touching but feeling as if we were joined at the shoulder, hip, and ankle, not to mention heart" (48). In another instance, Annie kisses Gwen on the neck, sending the latter "into a fit of shivers, as if someone had exposed her to a cold draft when she had a fever" (50–51). Although Kincaid has dismissed any sort of queer sexuality for her characters in the text, the repeated scenes of homoerotic yearning and passion seem to be something other than platonic sentiments.[28] Indeed, the novel's attention to homoeroticism challenges the compulsory heterosexuality endemic to the politics of respectability and suggests the variety of ways that Black women can viably create intimacy and community.

What is perhaps most significant about Annie's experiences with Gwen, her classmates, and the Red Girl is that they provide Annie with a support system outside her family. For example, while Annie must dissemble with her mother, she can be almost completely open with Gwen:

"We told each other things we had judged most private and secret: things we had heard our parents say, dreams we had had the night before, the things we were really afraid of; but especially we told of our love for each other" (48).[29] Annie's intense friendships with Gwen, the Red Girl, and her other classmates illuminate the significance of Black women's connections to one another, connections that often begin in childhood. Furthermore, they provide a space where she and her peers can, in relative safety, explore their sexuality in a world where simply being seen speaking with a boy can bring you censure, thereby challenging the regulations of respectability politics. This tension implicates the paradox of respectability because queerness is deviant, yet any interest in boys is likewise considered deviant. Kincaid writes, "On our minds every day were our breasts and their refusal to budge out of our chests. On hearing somewhere that if a boy rubbed your breasts they would quickly swell up, I passed along this news. Since in the world we occupied and hoped to forever occupy boys were banished, we had to make do with ourselves. What perfection we found in each other" (50). This passage describes a homoerotic environment where young women try to discover both the pleasures and mysteries of puberty. Indeed, in some respects Annie's schoolgirl community is not unlike Mrs. John's community of obeah healers. Both communities transgress the bounds of respectability politics while also providing support and affirmation of Black women's agency. Again, it is important to note that Annie creates this support system just as her relationship with Mrs. John begins to sour. Ultimately, the depiction of Annie's school community foregrounds the necessity of fictive kin and an ethic of community support and accountability for both children and adults.

However, Annie, the heir to the struggles of both Ma Chess and Mrs. John with respectability politics and an ethic of community support and accountability, ultimately reifies much of what she rails against within her own circle of friends. For example, when Gwen goes from being a cherished confidante to an "annoying acquaintance," this is more than a routine evolution of a childhood friendship (129). Annie believes that Gwen's desire for her to marry her brother Rowan so they "could be together always" is the ultimate betrayal, final proof that Gwen has succumbed to the allure of respectability politics (93). Nevertheless, while Annie dismisses Gwen's matchmaking desires, she does so in a way that echoes her dismissal of Mrs. John. Annie is unable to recognize Gwen's complex negotiation of balancing her desire to keep their friendship intact with her understanding that the rules of heteronormative coupling make female friendships visibly less important than heterosexual marital relations. Thus, when Annie sanctimoniously rejects Gwen, what she has ultimately done is reject her girlhood community that has sustained her thus far. Indeed, I would argue that while the novel invites us to consider that Annie's illness is partially the result of her estrangement with her mother, it is also partly instigated by her own internalization of respectability politics, which affects not only her relationship with her mother but also her relationships with other young women and her perception of herself. The dissolution of Annie's own girlhood friendships, then, provides another cautionary tale about the consequences of respectability politics and their corrosive effect on identity and intimacy in both children and adults.

The End of "Young Lady Business"

At the end of the novel, it seems that Mrs. John is indeed successful, albeit in a limited way. She has seen her daughter through school. Annie can cook, clean, and sew. She has not disgraced herself with any boys, and she is going to study nursing in England. Annie will certainly have more choices than Mrs. John will or Ma Chess ever did. And when Annie comes into her own voice at the end of the novel (signaled by the declaration of her name), this is a reflection not only of her own personal choice but of her participation in a legacy of agency previously instantiated by her grandmother and her mother. As Ann R. Morris and Margaret Dunn argue, "Jamaica Kincaid's *Annie John* is a very positive work. Though it ends with a young woman's departure for an alien world, the implication is not just that she will be able to return to the land of her mother but in addition that she herself knows this, that she has in effect been empowered in her search for self-identity" (225).[30] It would seem *Annie John* succeeds in profiling a matrilineal legacy of transformative womanhood and an ethic of community support and accountability.

Mrs. John's victory is hard-won, however; her efforts are only partially successful because of Annie's ambivalence toward her family and community, underscored by the fundamental misunderstandings between herself and Annie. For while Annie comes to voice because of the efforts of her mother and grandmother, soon after her realization of her own growing up, she muses: "I had made up my mind that, come what may, the road for me now went only in one direction: away from my home, away from my mother, away from my father . . . away from people who said to me, 'This happened during the time your mother was carrying you'" (133–34). The community that was to protect and empower Annie becomes the very thing that drives her away. The things Annie cites are explicitly related to her mother. In other words, Annie seeks refuge away from her mother and from those who would insist upon her honoring that ethic of community support and accountability.

Indeed, Annie's prolonged period of depression and illness is marked by erratic, though nonetheless symbolic and meaningful, behavior and reminiscences—such as imagining herself as a doll-sized Brownie traveling alone on a road and washing her parents' photographs "clean" of her picture. These thoughts and imaginings and her subsequent estrangement from her previous life as a carefree schoolgirl all denote Annie's position as an alienated young woman. It is perhaps no surprise that she decides to eschew all that she knows in favor of a future where she, and not her past relations, will apparently determine her life chances.[31] The overwhelming persistence of narratives about propriety and respectability rooted in the hierarchy of colonialism ultimately alienates Annie from herself and others, despite the presence of an ethic of community support and accountability with her friends and her mother's and grandmother's oppositional agency.

As Kincaid's avowed desire for the perverse contends, the novel provides neither a neat resolution nor a happy ending. It ends, rather, with an ambivalent Annie sadly sailing to England. Kincaid herself suggests that Annie's dismissive and antagonistic behavior toward her mother is partly evidence of adolescent stubbornness. When asked in an interview why Annie was "hardhearted," Kincaid replies:

> Well, it's a mask—she's not really hardhearted. She really wants
> to break down and be taken back in, but there's a parting place.
> She says she remembers that she's been told, "Once you start to do
> something, you have to see it through," and so she's got to see this
> thing through. But it's a hardness that has no substance, really, and
> if I were to continue to write this character—which I won't—you
> would see how the hardness is easily broken. She becomes enough
> of a woman to start imposing hardnesses on other people, but it's
> not a real hardness, and I think that the very last line shows that. It
> goes "It's as if a vessel of liquid had been placed on its side and now
> was finally emptying out." ("Jamaica Kincaid" [Cudjoe] 407)

Kincaid suggests that Annie's anxieties and ambivalences, the consequences of the paradox of respectability, will ebb away as she matures, just as the vessel of liquid slowly empties out. Nonetheless, this extranarrative explanation does little to ameliorate the fundamental anxieties at the heart of the novel. Competing narratives of family and respectability have created a brilliant but frustrated young woman who has been emboldened by maternal and communal care and who simultaneously wishes to be free of it. Kincaid contends that "perhaps twenty years later" there would be a reconciliation between Annie and her mother, although Annie has initially hardened herself in order to leave her home without regret ("Jamaica Kincaid" [Cudjoe] 407–08).

Thus, while Mrs. John is a complex figure who skillfully negotiates between cultural expectations and her own desire to give power to her daughter, at the end of the novel the reader is left with the impression that Annie is unlikely to recognize this or to see her mother's behaviors as anything but undermining. Put another way, the possibility for Annie to strike a balance in reconciling her mother's teachings with her own seems dismal indeed. The proverbial sins of the mother (and of women similar to her mother) trump any solidarity Annie might seek to claim with her community, underscoring that for some Black women alienation and estrangement are preferable to the complications of a familial love that is enmeshed within respectability politics.

3 / Daughters of This Land: Genealogies of Resistance in Edwidge Danticat's *Breath, Eyes, Memory*

Haitian American author Edwidge Danticat published her debut novel, *Breath, Eyes, Memory*, in 1994, a pivotal moment in Haitian history. That same year the nation's first democratically elected president in decades, Jean-Bertrand Aristide, returned to office with great fanfare after having been ousted in 1991 by a military coup. For some, Aristide, a former Catholic priest whose political philosophy invoked liberation theology, seemed to offer a radical shift in Haitian politics.[1] After years of dictatorships and weak interim governments, Haiti seemed poised to reject its previous authoritarian political history for a new, more egalitarian government with Aristide at the helm. This shift would presumably affect all aspects of Haitian society, including family life, as the family is a social construct that often reflects the workings of the state. Thus it is perhaps not entirely coincidental that *Breath*, a novel so concerned with challenging cultural narratives of family in the Haitian Diaspora, with rewriting a history that far too often has relegated women to the sidelines, if not made them invisible, appears in this moment of great political change. Indeed, in a sense, *Breath* arises out of the burgeoning liberatory sentiment also reflected in the major, albeit brief, political shift in Haiti.[2] Nonetheless, the novel is not a buoyant take on the possibilities of a new Haiti, but rather a staid and thoughtful meditation on the collision and collusion of the prevailing repressive discourses of respectability on women's lives and in their families in Haiti and its Diaspora.

Danticat's novel *Breath*, like texts from fellow contemporary Black women writers in the Caribbean and United States, advances contemporary discourse about the legitimacy of particular types of Black families; in this case, the novel invites critiques regarding the legitimacy of normative notions of female-headed households in an era pointedly concerned with respectability politics. In an interview, Danticat admits: "I wanted the book to have a matriarchal family. In my experience, I had seen many matriarchal families. . . . A lot of men were away—in the city, in the neighboring Dominican Republic working in the cane fields, or working in other countries. I wanted to explore how a family of rural women passes things down through generations" ("Interview" 186).[3] *Breath* depicts a family of single, working-class women living across the Haitian Diaspora in New York and the Caribbean who seek to ameliorate their social status by strictly adhering to respectability politics; namely, they employ a rigid understanding of propriety and family relations in an effort to compensate for the perceived shame of their lack of respectability due to their class and marital statuses and their sexual histories. Martine and Grandmè Ifé, in particular, are entrenched in an especially egregious manifestation of respectability politics: they actively reify dominant power structures within their family by routinely centering their perceptions of men's desires, using folklore and mother wit to suppress dissent among women, and perpetrating sexual violence on one another in both Haiti and the United States in the name of family honor. To be clear, I am not suggesting that the specific practices the Caco women engage in, such as virginity testing, are particularly Haitian rituals. Rather, the novel's depiction of virginity testing as a consequence of respectability politics draws attention to how structures of dominance can manifest within a family, even when that family consists primarily of women, and even as they migrate across the Haitian Diaspora.[4]

Recognizing the role of the paradox of respectability and the possibility for an ethic of community support and accountability is critical to a gaining a fuller understanding of Danticat's debut novel. Thus *Breath* does not indict the absence of men or the women's failure to live up to the rules of the "virginity cult"; instead, it compels a critique of the paradox of respectability, for the Cacos hold a stern allegiance to the ideals of respectability politics while finding it difficult or impossible to actually conform to these ideals. That paradox of respectability makes the Cacos' connections to one another ambivalent—for example, fostering both a sense of duty to one's family and extreme resentment about performing that duty—and ultimately threatens to destroy these connections altogether.

However, the novel's characterization of Atie and Sophie also draws attention to the possibilities for family systems that transgress normative paradigms to become sites of support, respect, and love. In *Breath*, an ethic of community support and accountability reflects expansive notions of kinship that trouble the boundaries of accepted social convention, emphasizing loving queer relationships, supportive fictive kin, and egalitarian heterosexual partnerships. Furthermore, unlike the normative notions of family that the novel presents, examples of an ethic of community support and accountability in the text reject the perpetuation of abuse in favor of women controlling (or seeking to control) their bodies. The novel's portrayal of an ethic of community support and accountability foregrounds the possibility of healing through storytelling, poetry, and holistic therapy, suggesting that communal Diasporic practices such as folklore and traditional healing can challenge the hegemony of respectability politics and center a range of women's experiences. Thus *Breath* reveals the possibility that the family can be more than a reiteration of repressive rules and a domestic expression of the state's surveillance and control and can instead feature a type of kinship that offers opportunities for, though certainly not guarantees of, support, healing, and change. Yet although *Breath* illustrates that Black women can rework Diasporic tradition and rituals to unleash transgressive potential, it also compels us to consider that without wide-reaching institutional change only some Black women will be able to truly move beyond the bounds of respectability politics, which for many others stymies the potential for healthy expressions of family.

The Cult of Virginity

Respectability politics in *Breath* takes the form of a staunch upholding of repressive tradition and duty, steadfast devotion to family and family honor, extreme deference, sacrifice, hard work, and strict notions of propriety. And much of the respectability politics in *Breath* revolves around extreme notions of sexual propriety, described in the novel as a "virginity cult." This virginity cult is not simply an exaltation of chastity but a cultural fixation on women's bodies and sexualities parading as a glorification of purity. Sophie muses: "I have heard it compared to a virginity cult, our mothers' obsession with keeping us pure and chaste. . . . I learned very early in life that virgins always took small steps when they walked. They never did acrobatic splits, never rode horses or bicycles. They always covered themselves well and, even if their lives depended on it, never parted with their panties" (154). The virginity cult is an aspect of respectability politics built upon a set of body fictions, narratives of women's sexuality that emphasize a self-effacing blend of chastity, modesty, and obedience that polices women (King vii).[5] The body fictions of the virginity cult are an organizing principle in the Caco family, a paradigm that governs many of the family's actions. Thus it is no wonder Grandmè Ifé, the eldest Caco woman, fervently believes: "If a child dies, you do not die. But if your child is disgraced, you are disgraced. And people, they think daughters will be raised trash with no men in the house. . . . If I give a soiled daughter to her husband, he can shame my family, speak evil of me, even bring her back to me" (156). According to this logic, heterosexual marriage is the only appropriate institution where a woman can be sexual: that is, she can be sexual only in service to her husband, unless she is willing to shame herself and her family. In this paradigm, a daughter's sexuality is an object of exchange in the marriage market and therefore can be devalued. Death of a loved one is a circumstance that does not fundamentally alter a person's social status, Ifé reveals, but a woman's sexual dishonor can absolutely destroy the social standing of one's family and even cause their social death. Thus, in such a schema, as portrayed in Nellie's family in Erna Brodber's *Jane and Louisa Will Soon Come Home* and in the community of Ruby in Toni Morrison's *Paradise*, family dynamics built on respectability politics are often dedicated to controlling women's sexuality, and such kinship is circumscribed by silence and repression.

Martine is a direct heir to the respectability politics of the virginity cult, and this circumstance profoundly influences and complicates how she mothers and how she understands the role of family. Her internalization of respectability politics is particularly ironic because she is a survivor of rape and sexual abuse. Her response to sexual violence is neither anger at the perpetrators nor critique of the social apparatus that sanctions such acts; rather, she turns to policing her daughter's body in an effort to (re)claim respectability. Thus Martine's notions of sexual propriety are much like those of the narrator of Jamaica Kincaid's short story "Girl," who admonishes her daughter "not to act like the slut she is so bent on becoming" (*At the Bottom of the River* 3), in that Martine places on her daughter the burden of maintaining a social reputation that hinges on the perception of her sexuality. Not only does Martine insist that Sophie not date until she is eighteen, vowing that Sophie will not be "wild like those American girls," but she shares two extremely painful cautionary tales about sex with her young daughter on the latter's first night in the United States, tales that reflect her adherence to repressive notions of respectability (56). She tells Sophie the truth about her conception, revealing, "A man grabbed me from the side of the road, pulled me into a cane field, and put you in my body. I was still a young girl then, just barely older than you" (61). The implication here is that a Tonton Macoute, a member of the state-sanctioned militia, raped Martine; thus the state-sponsored terrorism of the Duvalier regime is connected to Martine's very personal trauma.

Not unlike the fascist Trujillo regime in the neighboring Dominican Republic, the Duvalier regime relied on a strict system of surveillance and martial law to dominate all elements of Haitian society for almost thirty years. One of their most repressive creations was a militia called the Tonton Macoutes, a phrase that invoked a bogeyman legend from Haitian folklore. Danticat writes: "In the fairy tales, the *Tonton Macoute* was a bogeyman, a scarecrow with human flesh. *If you don't respect your elders, then the Tonton Macoute will take you away*" (Danticat, *Breath* 138; emphasis in original). Leaders in the Duvalier regime created a national narrative, knowingly taking an existing myth of the bogeyman and invoking it as the flesh-and-blood terror of the Tonton Macoutes. Thus, the Tonton Macoute became the manifestation of the state's willful lust for power and disregard for human life. I am not suggesting, however, a simple teleological link between language and action. Rather, while the discursive violence of the Macoute folktale does precede Duvalier's nefarious reimagining of the tale, both fictional and historical Macoutes are symptomatic of larger overarching systems of oppression present in Haitian society and in kyriarchy overall. That is to say, the various manifestations of the Macoutes underscore the ways in which this tyrannical discourse is not just a function of the discursive but the linguistic equivalent of the manifestation of kyriarchy.

In relaying the story of her rape at the hands of a Tonton Macoute, what is most important for Martine is propriety and respectability; one must stifle any outward appearance of weakness or immodesty. Rather than foregrounding her attacker's action as an assault, Martine emphasizes her impregnation with the phrase "put you in my body." Sophie describes Martine's tone as not sounding "hurt or angry, just like someone who was stating a fact. Like naming a color or calling a name," although later Sophie learns that Martine is plagued by nightmares in which she repeatedly relives both the virginity testing and the rape (61). Martine never blames her attacker; indeed, she mentions him briefly. Her internalization of the scripts of respectability—via the body fictions of the virginity cult—lays the onus of the attack on herself, rather than on her attacker or the systematic acceptance of violence that sanctioned her assault. So rather than reacting with anger to her attacker, Martine turns the anger inward to police herself and eventually turns it onto Sophie, thereby ultimately creating an ambivalent relationship between the two women.

While Martine envisions this self-policing as a way to emancipate herself from the memory of the rape, her actions are not liberating but imprisoning. In other words, Martine upholds the silencing she initially experienced as a victim of rape, further participating in her own erasure as part of a society that bases a woman's worth on her sexual "purity." The silencing and dissemblance at the center of this conversation illustrates a central paradigm in Martine's own mothering and in respectability politics. Self-policing is essential for proper, respectable womanhood, and Martine has so internalized the virginity cult that she not only represents this aspect of respectability politics herself but also raises Sophie with an acute awareness of it, as she truly believes that Sophie is an extension of herself. This emphasis on silencing underscores the inadequacy of respectability politics in truly helping Black female victims of violence across the Diaspora to gain a measure of agency or healing.

Martine also reveals another aspect of the politics of respectability's virginity cult in the second story she tells, describing the act of "testing" to her daughter: "When I was a girl, my mother used to test us to see if we were virgins. She would put her finger in our very private parts and see if it would go inside. . . . The way my mother was raised, a mother is supposed to do that to her daughter until her daughter is married. It is her responsibility to keep her pure" (60–61). There are two seemingly contradictory sentiments in this statement. On the one hand, Martine describes testing as an archaic social practice. The phrase "the way my mother was raised" places the act of testing in an outdated episteme, as if it were a discarded ritual. Yet Martine's tone, and the fact that she reveals this story immediately after telling Sophie it is her right to ask her anything as her mother, cements Martine's right—indeed, the familial right—to invade and investigate Sophie's body; and the larger discourse on children as property of their parents, who are their "custodians" and "guardians," seems to contribute to this phenomenon. Martine describes the enactment of the virginity cult as a duty—in her words, a mother's "responsibility." Rather than question the ethos that would so strictly police women's bodies, she, like Ifé, agrees that raising a "soiled" daughter is a disgrace.

Martine has the potential to talk back to or even decenter master narratives about women's worth by rejecting the virginity cult. Yet because she has so completely internalized repressive notions of respectability she does not see a way to circumvent this logic and instead zealously reinforces it. In other words, Martine buys into a respectability politics in which notions of women's proper behavior always reference prevailing paradigms that reduce women's worth to their value as units of sexual currency. Ultimately, Martine insists that her daughter not only should follow the routine dictates of the virginity cult and respectability politics more generally but also should expect to relinquish control over her body in other, even more invasive ways. Thus respectability politics is further revealed to have the potential to exact violence in ways that counter any claims for its greater good as a strategy for Black people's successful upward mobility.

Moreover, while Martine shares these stories in a misguided attempt to bond with Sophie, this scene draws attention to the paradox of respectability at work in Martine's life, namely in her ambivalence toward her past and in her inability to fully recover from either form of abuse—both of which ultimately foreshadow the vexed relationship she will have with her daughter and her own deteriorating mental state. Thus it is no surprise that when Martine learns of Sophie's relationship with Joseph she returns to the family legacy of testing in order to be sure that Sophie remains "whole." Martine resorts to a practice that is central to respectability politics: the policing of others. She polices her daughter's body the way her own body was painfully policed before her rape, although she herself was almost as traumatized by the testing as the rape that followed it, for she confesses: "I realize standing here that the two greatest pains of my life are very much related. The one good thing about my being raped was that it made the *testing* stop. The testing and the rape. I live both every day" (170; emphasis in original). The culturally sanctioned abuse Martine received from her mother is unequivocally aligned with the government-sanctioned rape Martine endured, underscoring that the actions constitute a set of symbiotic cultural practices, with the testing reinforcing the repressive notions of sexuality and dominance that sanctioned her rape and vice versa. *Breath* compels us to consider that normative discourses of respectability may succeed in producing some level of social acceptance but that more generally such politics do not create stable family units and instead undermine familial connections among women.

The occurrence of Martine's revelations about her rape and her testing in the same conversation explicitly links the two forms of violation as coeval and perversely symbiotic. The novel forces us to consider that the rape and testing are forms of violence that reinforce each other and the larger systems of kyriarchy. As I have indicated throughout this book, I use the term *kyriarchy* to refer to a system of power and domination that consists of multiple intersecting structures of oppression. *Kyriarchy*, as opposed to *patriarchy*, emphasizes how even those who are marginalized and have little social power or individual agency can broker power in ways that ultimately reify the larger constructs of domination in society. Testing is symptomatic of the rhetoric of the virginity cult and other aspects of respectability politics and, like the systematic sexual assaults that the Duvalier regime uses, is a tool of kyriocentric oppression. Although it is an assault, indeed a form of incest, carried out by family members, like the abuse perpetuated by the Macoutes, it is predicated on a body fiction of women's value as sexual currency. Thus, like other aspects of respectability politics, it functions as part of the state's apparatus to uphold kyriarchy.

Breath, Eyes, Memory also invites us to consider how respectability politics becomes naturalized when it is linked to long-held cultural traditions. Before he became president for life, a young François Duvalier and other Black intellectuals influenced by *noirisme* philosophy began calling themselves *griots* and hoped to reshape national and cultural narratives about Blackness and power in Haiti during and in the wake of U.S. occupation.[6] In 1938, Duvalier and other *griots* founded a journal called *Les Griots* that sought to create distinct narratives that emphasized Africa, not Europe or the United States, as the source of Haitian cultural pride and heritage. Duvalier and his fellow *griots* claimed to want to revolutionize Haitian society, but in reality they simply sought to change the color of the despots from the mulatto elite to the rising Black middle class, while keeping the masses of poor Blacks, especially Black women, subordinate.

In *Breath*, Martine draws on Haitian folktales to justify her abuse, much as Duvalier employed narrative mythmaking to uphold his regime. In particular, Martine attempts to distract Sophie during her testing with the story of the *Marassas*: "The *Marassas* were two inseparable lovers. They were the same person, duplicated in two. . . . The love between a mother and daughter is deeper than the sea. You would leave me for an old man who you didn't know the year before. You and I we could be like *Marassas*. You are giving up a lifetime with me" (84–85).[7]

In this passage, the *Marassas* that Martine describes are more than two people who look alike; more importantly, they are metaphysical twins. Myriam Chancy notes, "Martine . . . persists in describing her acts of sexual abuse in terms of a spiritual 'twinning' of souls," rather than as acts of violence and incest (122). Familial love, then, for Martine is about relishing sameness, not respecting difference. Informing Sophie that they could be *Marassas* in this moment obfuscates the issue of abuse with a narrative of "pure" maternal love and respectability that is superior to romantic love or sexual intimacy, yet one that nonetheless insists on and reinforces the notion that a woman's worth is based upon the denial of desire and the enforcement of silence. In this way, Martine's reasoning parallels the dictates that guided the Macoutes' and Duvalier's other attacks on women. Sophie's body must be an open book, yet one accessible only to her family and the state. Thus the sexual politics of the virginity cult reveals the imposition of potentially strict limitations of respectability politics in Black women's lives, especially when respectability politics often sanctions violence and promotes silencing.

The reframing of the *Marassa* tale in an abusive ritual foregrounds the paradox of respectability at work in Martine's actions, underscoring that the whole business of testing is ultimately less about Sophie's sexual awakening than about Martine's desire to control her daughter's body in a way that she could not control her own. Martine's actions represent a more widespread ambivalence toward and extension of the institutionalized abuse of Black women. As Donette A. Francis argues, by "focusing on rape as a crime against women which violates women's rights to protection and due process as citizens, Danticat highlights the ideological sexism operative in Haitian political culture, which systematically silences—through concealment, deferral, or dismissal—women's testimonies of sexual violations" ("Silences" 79). The testing, therefore, reifies the misogynistic narrative of the Macoutes' terror campaign within the parameters of the family, despite Martine's acknowledgment of the pain it has caused in her own life. It not only ensures that Martine will gain control over her daughter but further suggests that she and Sophie will be *Marassas*, for the same pain connects them.[8]

Although Martine insists that the virginity testing is about honesty, it is the epitome of violation, betrayal, and dishonesty, for Sophie must deny her burgeoning sexual feelings in favor of her mother's (and society's) ideas of women's appropriate desire and purity. Martine's actions reinscribe violence onto another prostrate female body. The vivid example of testing highlights that mothers like Martine can forcefully collude with the hegemonic state in exacting this silencing and violation, even as they claim to be concerned only with decency and propriety and even when they themselves are suffering as a result of similar violence. In the end, Martine's (re)telling of the tale of the *Marassas* acts as a defining and silencing story that echoes prevailing cultural scripts about women's respectability and submission.

Ironically, testing fails in every way for the Caco family. "Because testing may occur after the fact [of sexual intercourse], it only indicates whether or not the daughter has already had sexual intercourse. Therefore, it can neither prevent consensual sex, nor protect the daughter from rape"—nor ensure marriage, this last being particularly important (Rossi). Indeed, despite Ifé's efforts, neither Martine nor Atie gets married, and both women are haunted by their experiences of incest and other violence. Thus adherence to normative notions of respectability is far from a guarantee of upward social mobility. Furthermore, these circumstances suggest that sexual politics based on repressive paradigms of respectability politics rarely produces positive familial relationships among Black women. On the contrary, *Breath*'s depiction of the history of sexual abuse in the Caco family suggests that truly functional Black families cannot have repression and violence at their core.

Poetry Is Not a Luxury

In addition to Martine's vexed and problematic experience of family, the novel draws attention to troubling kinship practices through the example of Grandmè Ifé. Ifé is the matriarch of the Caco family and, like elder figures such as Aunt Cuney, Mama Day, and Ma Chess in late twentieth-century Black women's literature, is the guiding force for many of her family's traditions. Her name is an allusion to the revered city of Ifé (also known as Ilé-Ifé) in southwestern Nigeria, a central site of Yoruba culture that is considered to be the birthplace not only of the Yoruba but of life in general. Just as Ilé-Ifé is where modern Yoruba can trace their ancestral history, Ifé Caco is where Martine, Atie, and Sophie can trace their familial legacy. This pointed naming, connecting the Caco family elder with the honored African locale, emphasizes the centrality of African retentions in Haitian culture, especially among the older generation.

Furthermore, the importance of Oshun, goddess of rivers, sensuality, and fertility, in the establishment of Ilé-Ifé underscores a powerful portrayal of motherhood that, though mythical, reflects the possibilities in the novel for an ethic of community support and accountability.[9]

In Yoruban cosmology, "The figure of the Goddess Osun reminds us that women were critical to the founding of the world. Moreover, contrary to the biblical story of Genesis, the Osun narrative challenges the hegemony of male deities and their neglect and discrimination against female agency" (Olupona viii). Oshun's victory over the duplicitous male gods takes place at Ilé-Ifé, offering a striking counternarrative to the ways women figure in Judeo-Christian creation stories. In the Yoruba creation story a female goddess rights wrongs instead of leading an innocent male (and subsequently all of humanity) into ruin. Thus Ifé's connection to Ilé-Ifé and to Oshun illuminates the potential for the Cacos to create a family system that is not wholly rooted in Western paradigms of womanhood and respectability.[10] Indeed, this naming suggests that family can be reframed to emphasize women's power in positively shaping discourse and that Diasporic traditions in religion and storytelling can be one way to recognize and (re)claim Black women's agency.

Traditional storytelling, such as what Grandmè Ifé and others perform throughout the novel, is not simply entertainment but a significant epistemology that shapes cultural discourse over the generations. Indeed, storytelling in the novel more generally reflects the importance of Black women's roles in shaping social discourse and passing on cultural scripts in family and communal life. Because of Ifé's status as the community's "talemaster," her stories become both framing narratives in the novel and the master narratives that reflect family and cultural myths (123). One story is a long narrative centered on a beautiful young girl and a handsome lark, where Ifé reinscribes normative notions of family and respectability politics. The little girl meets the bird on her way to school and he offers her a large, sweet pomegranate "for the honor of just looking at [her] face" (124). This pattern (the looking and the receiving of the fruit) goes on for days until the lark eventually asks her to travel with him across the sea to a faraway land. She must relinquish her heart to a "king who will die if he does not have a little girl's heart" (125). However, the girl tricks the lark and cleverly replies, "I didn't tell you this because it was a small thing, but little girls, they leave their hearts at home when they walk outside. Hearts are so precious. They don't want to lose them" (125). The lark allows the girl to return home for her heart and the little girl runs back to her family, never returning to the forest. Grandmè Ifé ends the tale with the warning that "if you see a handsome lark in a tree, you had better know that he is waiting for a very very pretty little girl who will never come back to him" (125).

This story is rife with layers of allegorical meaning. According to Meredith Gadsey, "It could be argued that this tale was created in response to the experience of the Middle Passage as a cautionary tale to warn the descendants of enslaved Africans against the dangers of beguiling strangers" (165). Gadsey's claim has merit, especially considering the African connection in Ifé's name, not to mention Ifé's marked reverence toward Guinea, cited in the novel as the location of the afterlife. The story could also be an allegory of the ambivalence of migration, referencing the lure and desire to be drawn away from home (Haiti) across the sea (the United States or Europe) and the cleverness of leaving one's heart at home.

However, there is another layer to this cautionary tale, one that foregrounds the significance of respectability in the Caco family. The courtship (with the admiration that borders on lust, given the kissing and the ripe fruit) and the palpable sensuality at the center of the tale imply that this story is not simply about a little girl and a bird. The specter of the erotic hovers in the background of this story—especially through the symbol of the pomegranate, which invokes the myth of Demeter, Persephone, and Hades. Just as Hades lured Persephone into the underworld (and away from *her* mother for half the year) with a pomegranate, so does the lark intend to seduce the little girl in Ifé's story away from her family with the enticing fruit. The Greek myth revolves around separation from one's mother and childhood and initiation into the adult world of sex and heterosexual loyalties, anxieties similarly at the heart of *Breath*. Just as the Persephone/Demeter myth is, on one level, about the changing seasons (of both the harvest and human life cycles), the lark story is a larger cultural narrative about the stages of life: girlhood and school, the allure of wanton pleasures and sexual desire in youth, and the duty to family that ideally marks heteronormative adulthood.

The little girl and the handsome lark can also be seen as symbolizing women and men respectively, reflecting, in particular, the choices, albeit the limited ones, that the little girl (and by extension, women) face in this society: she can leave her home for a faraway king who wants her heart (marriage), or she can stay safely ensconced in her family (spinsterhood). Though Ifé presents these as distinct choices, they are not all that different; indeed, they are slight variations on similar fate. Whether choosing the husband or the natal family, the little girl is not choosing independence, for there are no options that leave the girl free to do as she wishes. This folktale operates as both a seeming justification of kyriarchy and an indictment of the ways in which kyriarchy circumscribes Black women's options, revealing the potential complexity of Diasporic folktales and their representation of Black women's lives.

Grandmè Ifé delivers the story of the lark and the girl as a cautionary tale, though not one about the dangers of oppressive family life. Instead, she advises her listeners to be clever, like the little girl, and leave their hearts at home. Ifé does not admit that this story is as much about suffocating in the narrow "safety" of the familial home as it is about the potential dangers of sex or even the marriage bed, for, as Nancy Gerber suggests, "Ifé believes it is better to remain within the safety of home and family than to succumb to the dangers of the erotic" (40). However, as I have argued, the home Ifé mythologizes is safe only if you ignore the ritual of testing and other forms of violence in the domestic sphere. In this instance Ifé tells a story that is committed to preserving kyriocentric standards of sexuality and respectability, upholding an ideology that "inscribes the conflicts between female autonomy and filial duty" (Gerber 80). However, while Ifé is in collusion with forces that seek to disempower women, her goal is actually to keep her female listeners safe, although she is certainly willing to leave them with few choices in the process. The conflict at the heart of this tale foregrounds ambivalence and reflects the thwarted possibilities signified by Ifé's name. Although her name represents the potential power of transgressive discourse, Ifé's allegiance to respectability politics undermines this possibility in how she enacts or even discusses kinship. By extension, the novel invites us to consider how conceivably empowering cultural practices, such as storytelling, employed by Black women lose their efficacy if they are ultimately used in the service of bolstering respectability politics and subsequently reifying the hegemony of kyriarchy.

In the other main story that Grandmè Ifé tells, she again signals a conflict between independence and obligation, depicting family as a potentially constraining site for women. She tells Sophie: "There is a story that is told all the time in the valley. An old woman has three children. One dies in her body when she is pregnant. One goes to a faraway land to make her fortune and never does that one get to come back alive. The last one, she stays in the valley and looks after her mother" (119). Sophie interprets her own family history within this story, with the last child being her Tante Atie, who initially raises her and then takes care of Ifé in her old age.[11] This story about the old woman with three children is, in a way, the sequel to the story of the little girl and the lark; it narrates what happens to the little girl when she returns home and is engulfed by respectability politics. In other words, Atie is the grown-up version of the little girl who "left her heart at home" and who embraces respectability politics for much of her life.

While early on, Atie, as Sophie's guardian and mother figure, ambivalent about her liminal social position, "reinscribes scripts of biological motherhood" by urging Sophie to think only of Martine as her mother figure, later on Atie significantly reconfigures her understanding of family, becoming a vocal proponent of an ethic of community support and accountability (Hewett 130).[12] Thus the tale of the woman with three children does not entirely sum up Atie's life. However, the burdensome conflict between independence and duty, in addition to the nearly impossible standards of respectability, fuels much of the conflict in Atie's life and spurs the ways in which she thinks about family. Atie advocates for transgressive and affirming experiences of family that emphasize mutual support and not dominance or repression.

Unlike Grandmè Ifé, Atie is not a revered master storyteller in her community; nonetheless, she is a mother figure who passes down important tales to her kin. And unlike Martine, whose storytelling is perverse, Atie, as Sophie's surrogate mother, frequently uses her storytelling to soothe and empower her charge. She teaches Sophie about her family genealogy and eventually fosters in her a keen interest in the history of her family.[13] When an inquisitive Sophie asks about her parentage, Atie supplants a gentle folktale for the more painful truth: "One time I asked [Tante Atie] how it was that I was born with a mother and no father. She told me the story of a little girl who was born out of the petals of roses, water from the stream, and a chunk of the sky. That little girl, she said, was me" (47). While Atie often uses storytelling as a way to impart family histories, in this moment she makes a choice to shield Sophie from knowledge of her violent conception. However, I would argue that Atie's choice in storytelling is not a willful occlusion or even an act of shame. Rather, it reveals a transgressive desire to rework narratives of shame and violence into an enchanted world for Sophie. Atie reworks their family narrative to be one of triumph rather than one of pain and submission. However, Atie's stories are not well-meaning delusions: instead, they constitute a challenge to the notions that Martine and Ifé reify from the prevailing scripts of respectability. Atie's ethic of community support and accountability thus reflects an alternative form of agency, even (or perhaps especially for) Black women who are marginalized by respectability politics.

In contrast to her own mother, Atie is committed to disrupting normative discourses, and to that end she enacts an ethic of community support and accountability by imparting stories that not only teach but also inspire. For example, Atie tells a young Sophie a parable about living with difficulties not to immobilize her but to empower her: "[Atie] told me about a group of people in Guinea who carry the sky on their heads. They are the people of Creation. Strong, tall, and mighty people who can bear anything. Their Maker, she said, gives them the sky to carry because they are strong. These people do not know who they are, but if you see a lot of trouble in your life, it is because you were chosen to carry part of the sky on your head" (25). For one, this parable is meant to teach Sophie that difficult situations are, in fact, routine. Moreover, this story, coupled with Atie's earlier story of Sophie as a girl made from rose petals, water, and "a chunk of the sky," signals Sophie as one of the Guinea people of Creation, foreshadowing Sophie's eventual role not only as a transgressive storyteller but as a survivor. To be clear, Atie does not glorify suffering or martyrdom; rather, she enacts an ethic of community support and accountability by encouraging Sophie to view herself as a survivor rather than as a victim. Connecting the two tales emphasizes empowerment and agency, and a rejection of the narrow notions of family and respectability that Ifé and Martine's stories provide. Atie's stories also explicitly link the Caco women to Diasporic folk tradition and are another instance of Atie's commitment to retooling family narratives with a transgressive consciousness.

Ultimately, Atie's stories, unlike Martine and Grandmè Ifé's tales, do not reveal ambivalent or wholly negative images about womanhood, sexuality, duty, and autonomy. Atie's own actions underscore that she is not simply reinscribing repressive aspects of Haitian oral tradition but crafting concepts of identity and kinship that foreground transgressive ways of knowing and that suggest similar possibilities for Black women across the Diaspora. Atie not only (re)tells stories but eventually also rewrites stories in her own words, emphasizing that orality and oral traditions allow for continued revisions and additions. This perception is clear from Martine's (re)interpretation of the *Marassas* narrative. However, while Martine's perverse behavior undermines Sophie's sexual agency, impedes her own healing, and reinscribes respectability politics, Atie's storytelling illustrates that empowerment via oral traditions can stem from both the possibility and the presence of subversive revisions to storytelling and family histories that happen over time. Black women need not abandon cultural traditions and rituals, for these are not necessarily inherently repressive. *Breath* foregrounds the necessity of recalibrating our understanding of Black women's agency in enacting and transforming traditions.

Atie's behavior and thinking become increasingly more radical over time, highlighting the possibilities for an ethic of community support and accountability. Part of this paradigm shift occurs when Atie becomes literate and begins not only to tell stories orally but also to write them down. In an interview, Danticat declares, "I would never be one of those people who romanticizes illiteracy. And just because you write things down doesn't mean you don't remember them or lose the oral traditions. On the contrary, you now have two different ways of telling your story" ("Interview" 190).[14] Atie exemplifies this perspective: when Sophie returns to Haiti as an adult, Atie has renounced her earlier idea that her time for school has long past. She fervently pursues literacy, becoming a voracious reader and writer, taking reading lessons from Louise and writing poems in a tattered notebook she takes everywhere. Despite Grandmè Ifé's disapproval of Atie's relationship with Louise—their bond is just shy of being described as a lesbian relationship—Atie is committed to becoming literate.[15] When Ifé questions her nightly reading lessons with Louise, Atie retorts, "Reading, it is not like the gifts you have. I was not born with it" (107). Thus Atie pointedly takes time to hone her skills, despite her mother's disapprobation. Atie's burgeoning literacy and the concurrent confidence she displays in pursuing it mark her as a woman committed to a hermeneutics of suspicion that challenges respectability politics concerning women's behaviors. She subsequently becomes Sophie's primary model for a type of resistance to repressive family discourse that is couched, nonetheless, in Haitian sensibilities. Atie's behavior illuminates the strategies that Black women employ to challenge social constraints without divorcing themselves completely from their communities.

While Atie's literacy spurs her toward a type of transgressive consciousness, even before she learns to read and write, Atie's notions of family have long challenged respectability politics. Before Atie fully rejected burdensome notions of women's roles in families, she had an openly ambivalent, questioning spirit regarding the paradox of respectability: "According to Tante Atie, each finger had a purpose. It was the way she had been taught to prepare herself to become a woman. Mothering. Boiling. Loving. Baking. Nursing. Frying. Healing. Washing. Ironing. Scrubbing. It wasn't her fault, she said. Her ten fingers had been named for her even before she was born. Sometimes, she even wished she had six fingers on each hand so she could have two left for herself" (151). Atie details the specific dictates that guide women's behavior in families: according to this rubric, a woman's hands are machines that are to be used only in service of her family. Thus Atie insists on gaining literacy and writing poems as a way to reject these burdens of respectability and to reclaim her two hands in an activity that she deems important.

As Valérie Loichot contends, through Atie's behavior, "women's previously written bodies graduate to writing bodies," thus illuminating the ways in which the female body has been understood as a sort of palimpsest (94). Martine aligns literacy with marriageability and the virginity cult, telling Sophie, "You are going to work hard here . . . and no one is going to break your heart because you cannot read or write. You have a chance to become the kind of woman Atie and I have always wanted to be. If you make something of yourself in life, we will all succeed. You can *raise our heads*" (44; emphasis in original). Atie rejects this framework outright: she does not use her new skill to win back Donald Augustin, the man who spurned her because of her lack of education, or to become connected to another man.

Atie does not learn to read or write poems to impress or gain the favor of others, although her literacy does help foster a closer bond with Louise. For her, literacy is not simply a vehicle of social mobility with the purpose of "raising our heads"; it functions as a method of loosening constraints of repressive narratives to make way for affirming modes of thought and action. Atie's defiance and her shifting positions of scorned lover, surrogate mother, and rebellious poet are poignant examples of transformative womanhood and an ethic of community support and accountability in the novel and, specifically, for Sophie, provide examples of how women can resist repressive respectability politics and can talk back to culturally sanctioned systems of familial oppression.

Atie's defiant poetic voice is in stark contrast to her previously muted self mired in respectability politics. She is quite different from a younger Atie, who earlier, according to Martine, "lost her nerve" and did not follow through on taking night classes when Sophie was a child.[16] The older, more embittered Atie rebels against those community mores that disapprove of a middle-aged peasant woman devoting her time to reading and writing, challenging the prevailing notions of what is acceptable for an unmarried woman in her family: "They train you to find a husband. . . . They poke at your panties in the middle of the night, to see if you are still whole. . . . They make you burn your fingers learning to cook. Then you still have nothing" (136–37). Thus Atie's nightly reading lessons and her intense relationship with Louise reflect a type of ethic of community support and accountability that openly defies the constraints she has previously conformed to and gives her a way for her to fight against the "nothingness" she feels characterizes her life. Atie rejects the virginity cult and other aspects of respectability politics that demand a woman's "purity" and submission, openly critiquing a system that forces women into subservience, supposedly in exchange for security and protection, but then leaves them disempowered and without options. In this way, both Atie's poetry and her overall subversive behavior counter Ifé's tale of the lark and the girl and her stance on a woman's "proper" duties. Atie recognizes that her body has been used in the production of both family and cultural narratives that deny her basic autonomy, and she rails against this violation. Atie stands as one of the strongest examples of an ethic of community support and accountability, consistently challenging, reworking, and denouncing repressive notions of family. Her stance on art and storytelling contradicts her society's expectations of poor Black women's actions because she partners her desire for creativity with her vocal desire for agency.

Atie's interest in literacy becomes, in many ways, a narrative of both transgression and independence; she asserts not only her desire to learn and practice her poetry but also her desire to do what she pleases rather than suppressing her desires for the sake of her family. The products of her study are pointedly subversive works. One night, after a family dinner, Atie reveals one of her poems:

She speaks in silent voices, my love.
Like the cardinal bird, kissing its own image.
Li palé vwa mwin,
Flapping wings, fallen change
Broken bottles, whistling snakes
And boom bang drums.
She speaks in silent voices, my love.
I drink her blood with milk
And when the pleasure peaks, my love leaves.   (134–35)[17]

This poem's meaning is multivalent. The piece is paraphrased "from a book of French poetry that Louise had read when she was still in school" (135). In a sense, the poem is something of a new creation because Atie refashions it from Louise's paraphrase. However, Atie's poem stands out for several other reasons that all challenge respectability politics. For one, it is a decided achievement for a woman who, until recently, was unable to write her poems down. Moreover, it is a subversive act to translate a French poem into Creole, so often considered a bastardized language. The opening lines "She speaks in silent voices, my love. / Like the cardinal bird, kissing its own image" also invoke the women in Atie's family. The image of the "cardinal bird" reflects their last name of Caco, and the concept of a scarlet bird kissing its own image is a more positive invocation of the myth of the *Marassas* that runs through the novel.

Atie's poem is also a radical reimagining of a folktale told earlier in the novel, a reimagining that directly challenges the respectability politics of the virginity cult. The original story recounts how a wealthy man turns down many girls to marry a poor black girl that he feels certain is a virgin. He plans to drink a few drops of her blood with milk on his wedding night. But the bride doesn't bleed, and the man, to save his honor, which requires that he hang the bloody sheet out in the courtyard the next day, cuts her between the legs to get blood that he can show. Instead, the bride bleeds to death, and the man displays the sheets and drinks the blood-spotted milk at her funeral. In this cautionary tale about a man's hubris and desire to prove his manhood through his wife's virginity, the women in the original story—the murdered bride, the countless other girls who are passed over—are silent and their bodies speak their worth, as is generally the case in the politics of the virginity cult. That is, their bodies are sites where discourses of masculinity trump whatever notions of selfhood and agency the women might possess, for a woman's worth in her family and society is based on her value as sexual currency. And, as Semia Harbawi suggests, "The irony [of the folktale] is that society wants to prevent women from bleeding (losing their virginity), and then wants them to bleed to prove their wholeness" (41). However, in the retelling, Atie "has taken the place of the male hero," thus troubling the notion of a silent female lover in the poem's very first line and the silenced women throughout the original folktale (Chancy 131). The women's voices in Atie's poem reject the repression of the respectability politics that characterized the earlier story. Like the female speaker, the lines about the cardinal bird kissing its own image also signify the covert romance between Atie and Louise: the speaker's lover leaves at the end of their trysts, as Atie must leave Louise at the end of their nightly rendezvous. Thus the poem also subversively queers the poem by reframing desire in the realm of same-gender loving, calling into question respectability politics by problematizing heteronormativity and conformity to normative gender and sexual roles. Moreover, while the original folktale involves sex, it is not celebratory in any way: the bride experiences a postcoital death and the story's tone emphasizes tragedy and remorse. Atie's poem, on the other hand, emanates passion, sensuality, and enthusiastic mutual desire. Overall, the multilayered interpretations of Atie's poem indicate the complexity of the poem and of Atie's newfound poetic voice. Thus Atie's very act of writing supplants the male-identified folktale with the voice of a female author, creating an alternative narrative that emphasizes feminist orality and same-gender desire.

Like the Diasporic group of travelers in *Praisesong for the Widow* and the community of obeah healers and Annie's girlhood friendships in *Annie John*, Atie's relationship with Louise offers another perspective on family, one that emphasizes an ethic of community support and accountability. Although Atie and Louise do not formally cohabit, they spend a significant amount of time together and have an intimate emotional bond. As two poor, unmarried women openly enjoying each other's company, they challenge the notion that their lives are insignificant because they have neither men nor biological children. They embrace their sexual desire for one another (the novel implies that more than reading goes on during their nightly reading lessons) and Atie in particular reclaims her status as a parent to Sophie.[18] This romantic pairing, though disapproved of by the elder Grandmè Ifé and presumably marginalized by the community at large, is one way to reimagine what partnership and family might look like if one decentered respectability politics and its attendant virginity cult and instead emphasized the egalitarian loving and partnership at the center of an ethic of community support and accountability. Whereas Atie's relationship with Donald Augustin was characterized by unfulfilled longing and major disappointment, she finds encouragement, support, and intimacy with Louise. Indeed, it is Louise who teaches Atie how to read. Atie and Louise's relationship, which is built on friendship and trust, counters the oppressive relationships throughout the novel that revolve around issues of power and dominance.

Yet for all of the virtues of the ethic of community support and accountability that Atie and Louise create, *Breath* does not necessarily invite us to consider that their family is particularly viable in their community. As the speaker of Atie's poem declares, "Just as my love peaks, my lover leaves," so do Atie and Louise ultimately separate. Desperate to escape the violence and unrest (she witnesses Macoutes killing a fellow vendor outside her beverage stand), Louise eventually sails to the United States without Atie, who is devastated by her departure. Though Atie and Louise loved and supported each other, the combination of Ifé's marked disapproval (which culminates in her buying Louise's pig, thereby giving Louise enough money to buy passage on a boat to the States) and the sheer force of the repressive social systems (symbolized by the Macoutes terrorizing the townsfolk) undermines the viability of their relationship. So while Atie and Louise's relationship presents a possible alternative to prevailing heteronormative notions of family and respectability, such a pairing may falter in isolation. I am not suggesting that Atie and Louise have the only queer relationship in La Nouvelle Dame Marie. However, it is clear that they are two women on the margins of their society for a host of reasons (including age, class, gender, marital status, and sexual orientation) and that these various factors influence the viability of their family. The dissolution of Atie and Louise's partnership underscores the tenuousness of an ethic of community support and accountability in the face of seemingly unrelenting politics of respectability and kyriarchy more generally.

Thus, despite Atie's turn toward poetry and her erotic life with Louise, she does not triumph completely over respectability politics. Atie's dis-ease, or chagrin, to use Ifé's term, and her pointed distaste of systems that have left her "as empty as a dry calabash" are the flipside of the regenerative power she exhibits as a poet and with her commitment to literacy. Atie's experience of chagrin is not unlike Avey's feeling of dis-ease in *Praisesong*; however, unlike Avey, Atie does not seem to be moving toward healing. Although Atie attains literacy and some degree of sexual freedom, she is estranged largely from both Martine and Ifé and never breaks free from her second-class status as an unmarried, queer woman in her community. When Louise leaves for the United States, she is left without a companion, noting that she "will miss [Louise] like [her] own skin" (145). Despite all of her resistance, Atie is marginalized and lacks access to power. The combination of her age, gender, and class, in addition to her sexual orientation, and her isolation from a larger network of supportive kin or community undermine much of her efforts. Thus for Atie the acts of coming to voice and successfully reshaping family narratives are not a sort of panacea. Atie challenges respectability politics but is still overwhelmed by the pervasiveness of its burdensome social practices in her family and community. The complicated portrayal of Atie in *Breath* underscores that for Black women changing language (or addressing discursive violence) without significantly changing (or escaping) the systems of oppression that uphold practices such as respectability politics results in only partial success in changing notions of family dynamics. Repressive modes of family remain powerful when women are isolated from networks committed to rejecting violent and pervasive paradigms.

A Little Closer to Being Free

The legacy of respectability politics is almost as damaging to Sophie as it is to Ifé, Martine, and Atie. Danticat illustrates that the body fictions that engender the virginity cult and testing do not simply condemn premarital sex; they render any sort of positive sexuality as taboo. Because of this, Sophie becomes her mother's *Marassa*, as she is unable to distinguish her mother's experience from her own.[19] Sophie admits: "*Her nightmares had somehow become my own*, so much so that I would wake up some mornings wondering if we hadn't both spent the night dreaming about the same thing: a man with no face, pounding a life into a helpless young girl" (193; emphasis mine). Martine's notions of sexuality become the script that dictates Sophie's life. And because she has taken on Martine's nightmares, Sophie identifies sex—even within the socially approved marriage bed—as vulgar and disgusting. She confides to her grandmother: "I have no desire, I feel like [sex] is an evil thing to do" (123). Sophie experiences the paradox of respectability, as she internalizes the repressive dictates of the virginity cult that conflate sexual assault with consensual intercourse and identifies all desire as immoral and all pleasure as sinful. In a sense, respectability politics works perhaps too well, for Sophie can barely submit to what she identifies as her wifely duties—regularly acquiescing to her husband's desires without complaint or coercion. The novel compels us to consider that because of Sophie's indoctrination in the virginity cult these "duties" are abhorrent even in contexts where such expression is permissible. Thus, while Sophie and Joseph have a generally loving and egalitarian relationship, the ingrained body fictions about sexuality dominate their relationship and adversely affect their partnership intimacy, making the case that, unless challenged, rigid notions of respectability not only can breed ambivalence within and toward family but also can undermine what could otherwise be healthy forms of kinship.[20]

Nevertheless, despite Sophie's negative experiences, the novel foregrounds the possibility of contesting repressive family politics through Sophie's coming to voice. First, unlike Martine and Ifé, yet like her Tante Atie, Sophie, after an initial acceptance, openly critiques the systems that oppress her family. However, unlike Atie, Sophie is eventually able to flourish in spaces that encourage her coming to voice, most notably in her community in Providence, Rhode Island, and with her husband Joseph. It is Sophie and Joseph's relationship that most fully highlights the possibility of a viable ethic of community support and accountability. Joseph is Sophie's partner, a spouse who respects women and is the "kind of man who could buy a girl a meal without asking for her bra in return" (68). Indeed, their courtship and later relationship is characterized by a high degree of emotional intimacy. Joseph becomes Sophie's confidant and they share their pasts and their hopes for the future with each other. Furthermore, Joseph is an attentive father and supportive spouse, especially regarding Sophie's therapy. Joseph is also a musician who "had been to Jamaica, Cuba, and Brazil several times, trying to find links between the Negro spirituals and Latin and island music" (73). Joseph, even in his limitations, represents a progressive masculinity that largely rejects kyriarchy and has an awareness of Diasporic connections. For example, when he first meets Sophie he tells her, "We have something in common. *Mwin aussi.* I speak a form of Creole, too. I am from Louisiana. My parents considered themselves what we call Creoles" (70). Rather than viewing Sophie as an exotic Other he can possess, Joseph claims cultural solidarity and Diasporic kinship, declaring that because he is African American rather than American (read: white), he and Sophie are "already part of each other" (72).[21] The ethic of community support and accountability in Sophie and Joseph's relationship is not unlike Marshall's Diasporic project in *Praisesong*, whereby Blacks from various parts of the Diaspora are not simply similar but linked together in a shared history that matters.[22] Overall, *Breath* compels us to consider that family systems rooted in an ethic of community support and accountability—based on shared understanding, respect, and support—are not only possible but also necessary to transform previously repressive paradigms, such as respectability politics, for Blacks across the Diaspora.

Sophie's marriage gives her the space to rework her notions of family positively by giving her the resources and space to work out her issues. Indeed, from the relatively safe space of her new family and community, Sophie also carries on the Caco family tradition of storytelling—pointedly retelling the tales of her Grandmè Ifé and her Tante Atie. Sophie, in her role as storyteller, rejects the notion that women must remain silenced and simply subject to the will of bogeymen, real or imagined, and connects the grotesque fairy tale to her own family history: "My father might have been a *Macoute*. He was a stranger who, when my mother was sixteen years old, grabbed her on her way back from school. . . . When he was done, he made her keep her face in the dirt, threatening to shoot her if she looked up" (139). Here Sophie rewrites both the fairy tale and Duvalier's urban legend and, as Donette A. Francis suggests, "undresses the seemingly benign innocence of a cultural system that enables 'the bogeyman' who haunts numerous Haitian women to 'roam the streets' unchallenged"; she "tells the story of her mother's rape as an intimate witness and her version relays more graphic details than her mother's, linking the violation of the body to the inability to speak" ("Silences" 81). Sophie's retelling begins as a myth, then includes a critique of state-run terrorism, and finally ends up as an intimate account of her own background. She recounts not only a portion of Haitian history but also how the war waged on women's bodies intimately connects to her family. Put another way, she rewrites a family narrative, clarifying that her mother is a victim and a survivor and that state-sponsored terrorism, in the form of the masked Macoute, is the perpetrator. Although Martine would not and could not voice this part of her personal and cultural history, Sophie acts as a genealogist who gives voice to the history of Martine and the countless other women who have been terrorized by these government-sponsored bogeymen. She rejects the notion that one can heal by helping to perpetuate one's own silence. Thus *Breath* illustrates the ways in which cultural traditions such as storytelling can be tools to indict oppression, while also affirming familial love and loyalty.

While Martine rejects medical help for her ongoing trauma, Sophie participates in both individual and group counseling, and these counseling sessions become another set of spaces for Sophie to experience affirming types of community and healing. The illustration of healing work in *Breath* is part of a tradition of twentieth-century Black women's writing that invokes what Farah Jasmine Griffin identifies as "textual healing."[23] It is important to note that, like the treatment of Velma in Toni Cade Bambara's *The Salt Eaters*, the medical attention Sophie receives is a blend of Western medicines and familiar cultural practices, and the significance of this combination cannot be overstated. For example, Sophie's therapist, Rena, is an African American who is both a medical practitioner and a *Santería* priestess and who literally embodies the coexistence of two seemingly oppositional epistemologies. These two epistemologies, which coexist, not in a vexed fashion, but rather in a type of symbiotic harmony, foreshadow the potential for Sophie to gain a more holistic appreciation of ways of knowing. In her sexual phobia group sessions, Sophie confides to other women of color who have experienced sexual trauma by the hands of their own relatives.[24] In their sessions, this group of fictive kin recite affirmations to counteract the ambivalent and negative feelings they have about their bodies, literally rejecting the damaging politics of respectability: "We are beautiful women with strong bodies. . . . Because of my distress, I am able to understand when others are in deep pain. . . . Since I have survived this, I can survive anything" (202). They also write their abuser's name on a piece of paper and ritually burn the paper in every session, signifying their attempts to release their connection to the abuse. The fact that this *Santería* ritual involves the burning of writing is a clear signification on the burning away of oppressive family narratives and practices and foregrounds the healing practices of an ethic of community support and accountability as pragmatic strategies for combating the violence of respectability politics.[25]

While Sophie's problems are not alleviated in one session, she recognizes she is on the path to healing insofar as she disrupts these links to oppression. Therefore, Sophie comes to recognize that her actions as a mother hold great import and could potentially hurt Brigitte, her baby daughter, as much as her mother hurt her. In this moment when she decides to sever her ties to the abusive behavior of her past, Sophie imagines her actions affecting her yet unborn grandchild, the child who would be the recipient of Brigitte's abuse and thus another traumatized woman in the Caco family. Sophie acts to break this cyclical pain of testing and the virginity cult and to disrupt this unwanted, yet persistent, legacy. Sophie's daughter Brigitte symbolizes the positive potential for the Caco women. Thus not only does Sophie actively rework the narratives of respectability and family she has lived by to protect her daughter (and heal herself), but she does so without completely abandoning her family history, naming her daughter Brigitte Ifé after her own grandmother and thereby signifying the potential for a healthy continuation of her motherline. The healing practices of an ethic of community support and accountability that challenges respectability politics are ultimately generative, not only reconnecting family members but also helping to forge new connections.

Sophie is also able to confront her feelings of shame, anger, and fear in her private meetings with her therapist, Rena, and doing so helps her resist the constraints of the virginity cult and respectability politics. When she expresses to Rena her distaste in calling Marc her mother's "lover," her therapist astutely assesses, "I think you have a Madonna image of your mother," pointing to the respectability politics Sophie has associated with Martine (220). Rena's questioning reveals how much Sophie has internalized the ethos of the virginity cult not only for herself but for Martine as well. Thereafter, Sophie begins to break down her mental image of her mother as "pure," an image that she has also used to judge her own sexual behavior. Because Rena is an initiate of Caribbean modes of cultural and spiritual thought and practice, she is not dismissive of Sophie's opinions, yet Rena still challenges her to reassess the ways in which she has held on to debilitating notions. Rena and Sophie's relationship illuminates how transgressive healing practices often already exist in Black women's communities and support networks, challenging the notion that Blacks must reject such practices in order to improve their lives.

Not only has Sophie thought of her mother in terms of the rigid sexuality of respectability politics, she has also revered her as goddesslike, a notion that has helped foster her problematic ideals of motherhood. In particular, while Tante Atie raised her, Sophie imagined Martine as a particular manifestation of the *vodou* goddess Erzulie: "As a child, the mother I had imagined for myself was like Erzulie, the lavish Virgin Mother. She was the healer of all women and the desire of all men" (59). It is interesting to note that Sophie associates her mother with the sensual manifestation of the goddess, Erzulie Freda, especially considering the rigid notions of sexuality under which she grew up. While initially a water goddess, Erzulie, in her many forms, is associated with the Virgin Mary in the syncretic melding of *vodou* and Catholic cosmologies in Haiti.[26] Although Erzulie Freda doubles as the Virgin Mary, she acts more as a sensual mother goddess than as a symbol for chastity, as she is a decidedly erotic figure. Michel Laguerre contends: "Ezili is the most charming and sensuous lady in the Voodoo pantheon. She is lovely, beautiful, and wealthy. She not only has affairs with spirits . . . but she also has a number of mortal men on her list. It is supposed that she wears her hair long and, being a mulatto woman, is attractive" (71).[27] Erzulie Freda's powerful sexuality is in marked contrast to the discourse of the virginity cult and other sexist dictates of respectability politics that seek to suppress women. Sophie's desire to have a mother with unabashed sexuality underscores the paradox of respectability she is caught up in, underscoring both ambivalence and the potential for tapping into discourses that have more empowering notions of women's roles. However, the casting of Erzulie Freda as a wealthy mulatto (or sometimes white) deity diminishes some of her efficacy as a tool of empowerment, because as Myriam Chancy suggests, her "power—defined as both erotic and sexual—is derived from these combined class and race distinctions" (123). Thus, while it seems as if the Caco women could challenge respectability politics through identification with the powerful Erzulie Freda, the fact that they are dark-skinned, working-class women means they cannot fully identify with the goddess, and this limits the icon's potential for inspiring resistance.

Nonetheless, Sophie eventually comes to identify her mother with another manifestation of Erzulie, Erzulie Dantò. Erzulie Dantò has some of the seductive qualities of Erzulie Freda, but as Karen McCarthy Brown notes, she is "an independent childbearing woman with an unconventional sexuality that, on several counts, flouts the authority of the patriarchal family" (228–29).[28] Sophie rejects the respectability politics of her past by beginning to reconcile these seemingly contradictory aspects of the goddess in her mother as linked to her healing. And although Martine never fully eschews misogynistic paradigms, she implicitly aligns herself with Erzulie Dantò, decorating her house in the goddess's signature color of red and growing hibiscuses in her backyard, underscoring the latent potential for her transformation and inclusion of an ethic of community support and accountability in her life. When Sophie prepares her mother for her burial, she dresses her all in red, illuminating the connection between her mother and the powerful *loa*. Sophie recognizes that her choice is controversial: "It was too loud a color for a burial. I knew it. She would look like a Jezebel, hot-blooded Erzulie who feared no men, but rather made them her slaves, raped *them*, and killed *them*" (227; emphasis in original). When Marc, Martine's boyfriend, objects, "Saint Peter won't allow your mother into Heaven in that," Sophie rejects his Judeo-Christian perspective, countering, "She is going to Guinea . . . or she is going to be a star. She is going to be a butterfly or a lark in a tree. She's going to be free" (228). Not only does Sophie claim Erzulie Dantò and take a step toward embracing her own power through sexuality, she does so by invoking the symbols redolent in her kinswomen's folktales. Here Sophie is a storyteller who, even in the face of Martine's death, builds upon the feminist narratives of family from her homeland, rejecting repressive conventions and respectability politics without abandoning folk wisdom. Claiming this already present (yet neglected for much of the novel) characterization of female sexuality opens up the possibility for rethinking family while also invoking Haitian *vodou* cosmology.[29]

Although *Breath* foregrounds therapy as a possible space for psychic healing and a reworking of the family, Sophie's reconnection to her biological kin is placed alongside her experience of holistic therapy as another potential method of rejecting respectability politics and enacting an ethic of community support and accountability. Indeed, all the women who help to nurture Sophie—Atie and Ifé, along with Sophie's therapist, and the members of her phobia group—eventually promote Sophie's active self-care. Relinquishing of burdensome ties to the past while remembering also to honor one's family is a tenuous balancing act that gestures toward a rejection of the self-effacement required by respectability politics. Grandmè Ifé, for one, is forced to recognize her collusion in Sophie's pain. She tells Sophie, "My heart, it weeps like a river . . . for the pain we have caused you" (157). Yet although Ifé apologizes, she also admits to the specific pressures mothers face in a kyriarchy that strictly polices women's bodies, pressures that can help engender family histories of abuse. She advises Sophie, "Now you have a child of your own. You must know that everything a mother does, she does for her child's own good" (157). This advice asks Sophie not only to lay blame on her family members who have hurt her but to recognize the systems of oppression that have influenced their behavior.

Moreover, Ifé's call for Sophie to liberate herself underscores women's power to shape family discourse positively through an ethic of community support and accountability. It is no surprise, then, that when Sophie leaves Martine's burial to confront her pain in the cane field, Ifé and Atie chant, "*Ou libéré?*"—or "Are you free of your burden?"—acknowledging the validity of Sophie's return to the site of her own violent conception. It is a turning point for the family to begin rejecting the painful past that has defined them for so long. The last line of the novel, where Ifé preempts Sophie's answer to "*Ou libéré?*" by saying, "Now . . . you will know how to answer," is especially telling (234). Although Ifé puts a finger to Sophie's mouth, this is not an act of silencing: Sophie can now consider how to respond on her own terms, rather than simply repeating what her foremothers have done. This conversation reflects a fundamental shift in emphasis in the Caco family—an emphasis on freedom and unity through the family, rather than subordination and silencing by one's kin. Ultimately, the novel's ending suggests that one can cast off the burdens of respectability politics without wholly rejecting one's family, community, and culture.

"Ou libéré?"

Breath, Eyes, Memory illustrates the pervasiveness of repressive types of family but emphasizes the empowering potential of decentering respectability politics. Sophie is not only an example of the viability of an ethic of community support and accountability but also the novel's most viable example of resistance, whose healing through feminist testimony reconnects her to her ancestral motherline. Unlike Martine, who simply reinscribes the violence she experiences, Sophie takes her cues from her Tante Atie and reimagines Grandmè Ifé's tales. Sophie does not abandon her family tradition of storytelling, for she is able to critique the stories and include them in her life and her understanding of the world when they are constructive and empowering. If, as Myriam Chancy suggests, "it is through the thematization of secrecy that the damage resulting from generational disruption is unveiled," then Sophie's breaking of secrets and silences through her folktales and family narratives is an attempt to illustrate how to connect the older generation to the younger in more positive ways (121).

Yet, as in many novels written by Black women in the Caribbean and the United States since the 1970s, it is the daughter who is ultimately able to experience the fruit of resistance.[30] In some ways, it is not surprising that Sophie is able to recover from her past and move forward: she is a married, middle-class, heterosexual woman with a relatively supportive partner and access to holistic health care. Despite her troubled past, her present is in many ways idealized. Her family members do not fare as well: Ifé is only partially converted, Atie is defiant yet marginalized, and Martine commits suicide before she can renegotiate her views on respectability. Sophie has come to voice and has spoken truth to power, yet many others remain silenced and shrouded. Sophie's transgressive narrative renders an incomplete victory, underscoring the strength and enduring legacy of respectability politics, especially for those isolated and marginalized by their non-normative subject positions. Sophie's partial triumph is an indictment of the enduring legacy of the paradox of respectability, the virginity cult, and the systems they engender and bolster, systems that more often than not alienate and isolate individuals rather than cohering them in families. This partial triumph is a cautionary tale that is particularly poignant considering the jubilant era for Haiti in which the novel is published. Like *Praisesong for the Widow*, *Annie John*, and other texts, *Breath, Eyes, Memory* persuasively argues that just as strength and knowledge can be inherited, so can ambivalence, pain, and repression, through the invocation of tradition, and that this inheritance is both persistent and pervasive, even in a post-Duvalier Haiti and its Diaspora.

4 / The Language of Family: Talking Back to Narratives of Black Pathology in Sapphire's *Push*

On August 22, 1996, President Bill Clinton signed the Personal Responsibility and Work Opportunity Reconciliation Act of 1996, more commonly known as welfare reform. The Clinton administration described the legislation as a "comprehensive bipartisan welfare reform plan that will dramatically change the nation's welfare system into one that requires work in exchange for time-limited assistance. The law contains strong work requirements, a performance bonus to reward states for moving welfare recipients into jobs, state maintenance of effort requirements, comprehensive child support enforcement, and supports for families moving from welfare to work—including increased funding for child care and guaranteed medical coverage" (Administration for Children and Families). Strict work requirements are the foundation of this legislation: heads of households must find employment within two years of receiving assistance and within months of receiving initial benefits they must work in community service programs (that is, volunteer) until they find employment. Additionally, families who get benefits have a maximum five-year cumulative limit on receiving welfare funds. While the reform has been relatively successful in getting people off welfare, it has been less successful in helping former recipients become self-sufficient because it largely removed a safety net for millions of the poorest Americans and moved other struggling families into a service economy that does not come close to providing a living wage.

One of the most striking aspects of welfare reform is its impetus, however. Certainly, reforming welfare is an agenda item for almost every presidential administration. Nonetheless, this 1996 legislation emerged during the height of the so-called culture wars, when the struggle between the political Right and Left over the direction of the country was part of a sensationalized national drama.[1] Frequently, poor and working-class Americans, especially people of color, were pawns in this national game, representing some of the most loathed aspects of American society: the abject, unassimilated masses who rather than pulling themselves up by their proverbial bootstraps became "welfare queens" and sucked the lifeblood from the nation, reproducing incessantly without adding anything to society except for increasing financial burdens. Thus the welfare reform that emerged from this period was based less on solid data than on the notion that welfare recipients had little incentive to work—that is, they had a skewed sense of personal responsibility— and that they therefore needed governmental intervention to help make them responsible, respectable citizens. The very title of the bill, the *Personal Responsibility* and Work Opportunity Reconciliation Act, reveals this ideology. Thus, while the legislation was ostensibly billed as a hand up rather than a handout, it was guided as much by deeply engrained notions about misplaced entitlements as by a desire to better the lives of the nation's poor.[2]

In 1996, the same year Clinton's welfare reform passed, New York–based poet-turned-novelist Sapphire published her controversial and provocative novel *Push*, an indictment of the ideology around the black poor that emerges out the culture wars era. *Push* may at first seem like an outlier in the company of other contemporary texts that foreground respectability politics in their consideration of family that I have discussed in this book so far. The novel's graphic depiction of the devastating effects of poverty, violence, and abuse may not immediately call to mind the dissemblance and strict emphasis on propriety, among other aspects, that typically exemplify respectability politics. However, like *Praisesong for the Widow, Annie John, Breath, Eyes, Memory*, and other texts that this book analyzes, *Push* troubles respectability politics, albeit in an unconventional literary form, by advocating for more transgressive expressions of family. An epistolary novel that employs journal writing, poems, and other first-person narrative devices, *Push*, like *Annie John* and *Breath, Eyes, Memory*, emphasizes the growing importance of educational communities in black women's empowerment. It is critical to recognize the significance of the interplay of ambivalence and respectability in the novel, in addition to the novel's subsequent delineation of an ethic of community support and accountability as a means both to resist repression and to foster intimacy and community.

Push might also seem like an exception to other texts featured in this book because of its particular depiction of Diasporic cultural connections. While the connections to African Diasporic culture are markedly apparent in novels such as *Praisesong for the Widow*, *Annie John*, and *Breath, Eyes, Memory*, the role of the Diaspora in *Push* is uniquely manifested. Precious is largely isolated from the outside world and thus from most Black cultural connections. Her main points of contact until she enrolls in the Diasporic community of the Each One Teach One school are her abusive parents and neglectful mainstream institutions, such as schools and hospitals. She is almost entirely estranged from other Blacks, save for her viewing of VHS tapes of Nation of Islam leader Louis Farrakhan and her casual encounters with Blacks in the streets of Harlem. Therefore, my discussion of Diasporic communities and practices in this chapter pays close attention to Precious's alienation, her desire for both respectability and community, her eventual experience in a Diasporic Black community, and her immersion in Black art, from music, novels, children's books, and poetry, that connects to Diasporic practices—an immersion that has some parallels to the experience of the protagonists in *Praisesong* and *Breath*. The particular depiction of African Diasporic culture and practices in *Push* serves to emphasize the significance and efficacy of culturally rooted practices and support systems for Black women and the dire consequences when Black women are left without them.

Push indicts the effects of the culture wars of the 1980s and 1990s by exposing the paradox of respectability, in which some Blacks wish to conform to the ideals of respectability politics but at the same time find it difficult, if not impossible, to live up to these ideals, and it chronicles the often debilitating consequences of not employing a hermeneutics of suspicion toward dominant notions of family. The paradox of respectability is particularly insidious because it incites individual and interpersonal tensions that often provoke ambivalent familial relationships. In *Push*, this ambivalence is a complex mixture of unquestioning loyalty and wary distrust toward one's family and/or community. More specifically, ambivalence, in the form of Precious's ardent belief in the healing properties of conservative Black nationalism and her increasing skepticism of its tenets, challenges the usefulness of her investment in respectability politics and her collusion with kyriarchy. *Push* compels us to consider respectability politics as the flawed strategy Precious and others employ that insists that they can overcome their misfortunes or bad experiences by behaving in ways that affirm repressive ideals of propriety emphasizing heteronormativity, Western ideals of physical beauty, jingoism, and other hegemonic constructs. *Push* consistently rejects easy solutions to Precious's challenges with family, especially casting doubts on the usefulness of the strident Black nationalism she initially identifies with in order to underscore that for Precious, and indeed others like her, viable forms of family and community cannot arise out of repressive paradigms; solutions romanticizing African ancestry and idealizing men's restoration as patriarchs fail to acknowledge and address the abuse, isolation, and poverty that has characterized her life.

Rather than having Precious be "saved" by the restoration of her biological family or by another, more functional heteronormative nuclear family, *Push* invites us to consider that healing is possible for Precious when she acts a poet and memoirist within an African Diasporic community that exemplifies an ethic of community support and accountability. This ethic is a type of intimate praxis based on mutual respect, love, and care that uses affirming Diasporic rituals, as opposed to romanticized revisions of African history, to support kin and that resists hegemonic power structures. For Precious, these Diasporic rituals include sharing personal writing and poetry rooted in both Black literature and a hip-hop aesthetic within her Each One Teach One community. Through these experiences of an ethic of community support and accountability Precious begins to truly resist and challenge the oppressive forces that have defined and excluded her. The women in Precious's reading class are a Diasporic community of abuse survivors who act as fictive kin, helping Precious reject her toxic biological family and begin to reject her reliance on a repressive politics of respectability through poetry and life writing. My analysis insists that the Life Stories class project in which the women participate is also the act of an ethic of community support and accountability that helps them work out, understand, and relate their tales of sorrow and triumph, openly combating violence, sexism, homophobia, and heterosexism, especially as these ideologies intersect with the issues of family. Ultimately, *Push* illustrates possibilities for disrupting the hegemony of normative notions of family, community, and support, for although the members of Precious's school family are not related by blood or connected by traditional notions of geography, they nevertheless constitute a viable community and a transgressive reworking of family and community.

Welfare Queen Remixed

Respectability politics in *Push* is a social strategy that protagonist Precious and some of those around her use to distance themselves from the stigma of being poor and Black and to align themselves with the values—and the social power—of mainstream American society. More specifically, respectability politics in *Push* includes a strict emphasis on normative notions of propriety, staunch heterosexism, idealization of conservative gender roles, and nationalism. Because Precious's biological kin are both destructive and dysfunctional in the extreme, much of her familial loyalty is toward the larger community she is connected to by her fascination with Black nationalist groups such as the Nation of Islam. Thus Precious's investment in Black nationalism as a method to combat her own social marginalization catalyzes much of her attempt to adhere to the ideals of respectability politics. To fully clarify the role of respectability politics in the novel, I foreground here the structures that engender Precious's vexed social status and her ensuing desire for normative respectability.

Controversy has surrounded *Push* since its publication in 1996 because of its depiction of working-class Black life. Set in the dystopic Harlem of the 1980s, the novel begins with Precious, a protagonist who, in Sapphire's own words, "has been raped by her father since she was seven years old. She's also been abused and battered by her mother, horribly. In addition, she's slipped through all the cracks in the educational system. So at sixteen, when the novel begins, she's still in junior high, unable to read and write, and pregnant with her father's second child" ("Sapphire's Big Push"). Not surprisingly, while some critics have cited the novel as an "affecting and impassioned work that sails on the strength of pure, stirring feeling" (Mahoney BR9), others have castigated it as a type of poverty pornography that glories in the supposed pathology of the so-called Black underclass, chronicling with explicit detail its supposedly characteristic abnormalities, idiosyncrasies, and vagaries. *Wall Street Journal* reviewer Vaughn A. Carney, for example, condemned the novel, asking, "Why does the publishing industry have this morbid fascination with the most depraved, violent, misogynist, vulgar, low-life element in the African American experience? Why is it that the industry is obsessed with and cannot get over the same old 'Color Purple' sausage stuffed into new casings?" (A14).[3] While such criticism may raise valid points about stereotypical depictions of Blacks in literature and popular culture, it clearly also betrays an investment in respectability politics that the novel itself resists. For reviewers such as Carney, *Push* should be held in contempt or dismissed because it illustrates the depraved, violent, and vulgar aspects of Black life. Carney's vehement critique of the novel in a conservative news outlet exemplifies what is at stake in *Push*'s characterization of the insidious effects of respectability politics on the ways in which the lives of poor and working-class Blacks are discussed.

Despite this marked criticism, Sapphire contends that her project in *Push* is much different: that, in fact, *Push* is a response to, and not a reification of, the prevailing narratives bandied about in the last decades of the twentieth century that link pathology to Black families. Sapphire asserts, "There's a blues song 'What's Been Done in the Dark Has to Come to the Light,' and I think that's something that stays on my mind. I always want to bring out what's been hidden or marginalized. Precious is more misunderstood than invisible, we hear about her every day. Every time Newt Gingrich opens his mouth it's about a welfare mother. I wanted to shed additional light. I wanted to show something behind the statistic" ("Artist with a Mission"). Sapphire identifies her own work as drawing attention to prevailing mythologies about Blackness that mobilize tropes such as the "welfare queen" to delegitimize the experiences of working-class Black women and their families. Sapphire insists that women like Precious have "existed on TV . . . but as a statistic—as an 18-year-old HIV+ woman who can't read with two children. I wanted to show her as a human being, to enter into her life and show that she is a very complex person deserving of everything this culture has to offer" ("Artist with a Mission"). Thus it is not that Precious's story is never told; it is that the story is usually told to blame poor Blacks, to justify social inequities, and to promote respectability politics, a project that Sapphire avows she is interested in disrupting. *Push* invites us to consider Precious not as an object of disdain but as an increasingly empowered woman who grapples with complex social issues, at times reworking traditional notions of family with transgressive sensibilities and at other times falling prey to repressive mores.

However, while *Push* does talk back to the tropes of the Black matriarch, the welfare queen, and the baby mama, it does not do so by championing invocations of respectability politics and offering up a functional Black nuclear family with a strong Black patriarch at the head or a bourgeois Black "lady" as appropriate role models. Instead, the novel features starkly incompetent social institutions that repeatedly fail their constituents, alongside what is perhaps the most depraved Black family in literature, and shows how the protagonist's life history propels her toward the allure of respectability politics. *Push* draws attention to how institutionalized inequities, along with internalized racism and sexism, create and foster ambivalence, nihilism, and the breakdown of Black families, rather than invoking the common refrain of poor choices, intrinsically malformed social practices, or the absence of strong paternal figures as the root of problems faced by Black families. Thus an analysis of the novel's depiction of family in the text must coincide with a detailed investigation of the institutions, such as school and medical systems, serving the family because these institutions profoundly affect Precious and Black women like her.

Prevailing American cultural narratives depict people like Precious as without value, as burdens in and on a social system primarily concerned with capitalistic consumption. Nikol G. Alexander-Floyd suggests that contemporary public discourse about Blacks is often reduced to the ubiquitous Black Cultural Pathology Paradigm (BCPP), a "popular set of assumptions about Black family breakdown and cultural deviance . . . [that] has had a devastating impact on Black communities, has served as the basis for White backlash to the Civil Rights and Black Power movements of the mid-twentieth century, and has been legitimized by various, competing constituencies, most notably that of nationalists" (3). Alexander-Floyd contends that the BCPP is not only dangerous because of its gross generalizations about Black people. It is also troubling because it places the full onus of Black poverty squarely on poor Black folk rather than addressing the myriad social institutions that contribute to poverty and marginalization (24). Similarly, Robin D. G. Kelley insists that in contemporary discussions of urban Blacks "there is a general agreement that a common, debased culture is what defines the 'underclass,' what makes it a threat to the future of America. Most interpreters of the 'underclass' treat behavior as not only a synonym for culture but also as the determinant for class. In simple terms, what makes the 'underclass' a class is members' common *behavior*—not their income, their poverty level, or the kind of work they do. It is a definition of class driven more by moral panic than by systematic analysis" (18; emphasis mine). Such notions of "the underclass" operate from a set of overdetermining paradigms that speak little to the nuances of poor urban Blacks' actual experience and serve to reinforce investments in respectability politics and kyriarchy more generally.[4]

Push compels us to consider that these notions of the underclass feed public discourse regarding poor Black families in ways that not only negatively affect Blacks in public policy, as evidenced by Clinton's welfare reform, but also influence how some Blacks, especially those who have internalized normative notions of respectability, see themselves, their families, and their communities. The novel illuminates how embracing respectability politics reflects a desire for some Blacks to attain and leverage social power and privilege, even if gaining this power means adhering to a strict set of ideals regarding propriety that is rooted in kyriarchy. By *kyriarchy*, as opposed to *patriarchy*, I refer to a system of social hierarchies connected to intersecting sets of oppression, whereby individuals with differing amounts of power and privilege—even those from traditionally marginalized groups—can dominate or attempt to dominate others as they navigate social institutions and interpersonal relationships. Respectability politics' reliance on repressive practices underscores its roots in kyriarchy, despite its history as a social strategy aimed at improving black people's lives. The tension between the presumptive goal of respectability politics and the reality of its investment in kyriarchy—the very system that prompts the need for respectability politics—brings about the paradox of respectability, or the ardent desire to uphold the ideals of respectability politics while being unable or even unwilling to fully adhere to them.

In the beginning of the narrative, even before she becomes literate and more fully comes into her voice, Precious is profoundly aware of her status as one of the "undeserving poor." This knowledge largely stems from her treatment not only at home but in school as well, for most officials have regarded her as the embodiment of pathology. She is dismissed as unreachable and disregarded as a potentially important member of society. In other words, officials, such as Precious's principal, believe that nice, respectable girls have the good sense to get up and use the bathroom instead of relieving themselves at their desks, rather than recognizing the telltale signs of abuse or another problem that might preclude Precious from doing so. Laurie Stapleton notes, "The education system itself is portrayed as governed and facilitated by teachers and administrators who have (inadvertently) indoctrinated themselves into supporting, and working within, a system that often silences or devalues students' holistic experiences" (215). However, I would argue that this indoctrination that Stapleton acknowledges is not entirely unintentional because Precious's painful treatment within the school system underscores the damaging effects of hegemonic kyriocentric oppression, acknowledging the ways in which even marginalized individuals might buy into the power of oppressing others. Thus *Push* illuminates the ways in which investments in kyriarchy have the potential to negatively affect the life chances for

Black women when such ideology is employed within the workings of social institutions, such as the educational system, meant to serve large sectors of the public.

School administrators are not the only officials who are mouthpieces for kyriarchy, for although help can be found in *Push* through social services such as alternative adult education, women's shelters, and twelve-step programs, often medical personnel and social workers fall short of consistent and compassionate care because they view Precious as disreputable and therefore undeserving. With the exception of the unnamed paramedic and "Nurse Butter," who help Precious during her first birthing experience, medical personnel treat Precious with indifference and disdain at best and outright hostility at worst. When Precious leaves home and takes baby Abdul to the hospital, she is barely tolerated by the nurses: "It's like they tired. I'm a problem got to be got out they face. . . . Nurse say lots of people get out of hospital wif no place to go, calm down, you not so special" (76–77). The notion that the nurses are tired—tired of being inundated with "charity cases" in particular—is reflected in the declaration that Precious is, in fact, "not so special." This nurse assumes that Precious is a problem, a welfare queen and jezebel whose voracious sexual appetite and conspicuous irresponsibility have left her homeless. Put another way, *Push* compels us to consider how normative notions of respectability inform the ways care is rendered, underscoring how Precious's life chances are diminished in the face of this discrimination. The health care system, then, is another site where poor Black women can face the disapprobation born of respectability politics.

Similarly, Ms. Weiss, Precious's caseworker at the Advancement halfway house, does not deviate from the prevailing script regarding Black pathology and respectability in order to offer Precious a level of care that could help improve her life. Ms. Weiss routinely presses Precious for her earliest memories of her mother and becomes frustrated when she refuses full disclosure because, for Weiss, Precious is not "someone deserving of help, she is seen as a drain on the system, a problem to be solved, a case to be 'managed'" (Bhuvaneswar and Shafer 113). Weiss's account of Precious in her case file reveals a skewed perspective and indebtedness to conservative notions of respectability. She writes, "The client seems to view the social service system and its proponents as her enemies, and yet while she mentions independent living, seems to envision social services, AFDC, as taking care of her forever" (120). Not unlike the bipartisan legislators who supported welfare reform in 1996, she believes that Precious's issue is a lack of personal responsibility and views support and independence as oppositional constructs, when in reality they may not be that antagonistic. To Ms. Weiss, "Precious' dreams of becoming well-educated and living independent are simply dreams, and in clinical terms, could very well be characterized as 'delusional,' or at the very least unrealistic, rather than as a tool for survival and as a proof of her resilience" (Bhuvaneswar and Shafer 115).[5] Although Ms. Weiss has the opportunity to be an advocate for Precious, her preconceived notions about Precious disallow her from treating Precious humanely. Therefore, Precious is little more than a scam artist trying to hoodwink the system, rather than a client in need of help who has the potential to outgrow social services. Ultimately, *Push* highlights traditional school systems and social services primarily as sites where discourses about Black pathology and respectability are cultivated and disseminated to the detriment of Precious, her peers, and women like her.

Nobody Want Me, Nobody Need Me

Push also links the repressive ideals of these social institutions and Precious's interactions with her despotic family to suggest that the two are perversely symbiotic units. Precious's father Carl is able to abuse her unchecked not only because of an extreme combination of alienation and isolation but also because of the ways in which he harnesses kyriocentric notions of respectability. Up until Precious's first pregnancy at age twelve, Carl seems to follow the pretense that the abuse is a secret, appearing to Precious at night when her mother is asleep. However, his interactions with Precious reveal that he is fully aware of his actions and that he views Precious as deserving of this behavior, particularly because of her body's responses. Later, when she climaxes during intercourse he justifies his abuse by exclaiming, "'*See*, you LIKE it! You jus' like your mama—you die for it!" (24; emphasis in original). Rather than regretting his abuse, Carl identifies Precious as sexually debased, an inherited trait from her mother, and as the antithesis of respectability. Carl obfuscates the issue of abuse in favor of foregrounding Precious's supposed pathology. Ironically, Carl relies on prevailing narratives of Black female sexual depravity even while he acts as an agent of abuse. That is, Carl identifies Precious as a sex-crazed jezebel, a sexual characterization of Black women rooted in the inequities of slavery that still influences the representation of Black women in the present. Patricia Hill Collins notes, "The institutionalized rape of enslaved Black women spawned the controlling image of the jezebel or wanton Black woman. This representation redefined Black women's bodies as sites of wild, unrestrained sexuality that could be tamed but never subdued" (*Black Sexual Politics* 56). Indeed, Collins suggests that this sentiment led to the conclusion that "jezebels couldn't be raped" (66). According to this logic, if Black women are jezebels then sexual assault is impossible. Precious's father Carl, not unlike slave masters who used sexist ideologies to support their violence, places the culpability of his actions on his victim rather than on himself. *Push*, then, allows us to connect Carl's incestuous actions with a larger history of the perpetration of violence against Black women, revealing the insidious effects of kyriarchy in a way that instead of lamenting the loss of Black masculinity indicts the sort of unchecked male privilege that Carl uses to justify his actions.

Like Carl, Mary Lee Johnston mobilizes notions of pathology and respectability to defend her abuse of Precious. Mary is perhaps the most fiendish literary mother in fiction, an abusive tyrant who verbally, physically, and sexually abuses her daughter. Though as a poor Black woman she has limited access to traditional institutions of power, she nonetheless recognizes the usefulness of dominant discourses of violence and authority and enacts tyrannical power in the only place she can: her home. As Janice Lee Liddell contends, "Mary Johnston appears to understand clearly that motherhood can be invoked as a symbol of power. . . . However, the power wielded by her is far from transformative. It is, in fact, destructive—violent, downgrading, and self-serving. Also, Mary's closed door policy renders this power nearly omnipotent within her household" (142). Mary's complete control of Precious for much of her daughter's life means that Precious is essentially a slave to her mother, a fact reinforced by their marked isolation: Mary rarely leaves the house, and the only visitors are the equally vicious and selfish Carl; Toosie, Precious's negligent maternal grandmother; and the occasional apathetic social services worker. There is no community actively fighting oppression that Precious can access, seemingly no escape or alternative from her natal home or Mary's control.[6] Instead, safety is a commodity controlled by the powerful and oppression flourishes unchecked within this family.[7] Precious's home life symbolizes the marginalization and erasure she experiences in the larger society, with her mother, alongside her father and the social institutions that fail her, as another agent enacting oppression. Thus *Push* invites readers to consider the ways in which women can also harness the power of kyriarchy to exact violence and repress others in ways that mirror the hegemonic oppression at the heart of the larger society.

Furthermore, Mary's destructive notions of family are rooted in sexual perversion and internalized notions of pathology and respectability. When Ms. Weiss asks Mary to talk about Carl's abuse of Precious, Mary's warped sense of reality is revealed. She recalls that at three years old, Precious shared the bed with both her parents and that Carl began to abuse the toddler in front of her:

> So he on me. Then he reach over to Precious! Start wif his finger between her legs. I say Carl what you doing! He say shut your big ass up! This is good for her! Then he git off me, take off her Pampers and try to stick his thing in Precious. You know what trip me out is it almost can go in Precious! I think she some kind freak baby then. I say stop Carl stop! I want him on *me*! I never wanted him to hurt her. I didn't want him doing *anything* to her. I wanted my man for myself. Sex me up, not my chile. So you cain't blame all that shit happen to Precious on *me*. I love Carl, I love him. He her daddy, but he was my man! (135–36; emphasis in original)

This graphic passage reveals the full extent of Mary's dysfunction. First, her primary orientation is toward her own pleasure and satisfaction, inasmuch as she imagines it will come from Carl through sexual gratification. Indeed, she allows Carl to "breastfeed" while Precious is bottle-fed because, according to Mary's spurious logic, "I bottle her, tittie him. Bottle more better for kidz. Sanitary" (135). Heterosexual desire and maternal care are presented as mutually exclusive, indeed, as competing discourses. Mary desires Carl's attention more than anything else, revealing an unhealthy notion of sexuality that revels in his male gaze. Moreover, to that end, Mary's objection to Carl's abuse is not an attempt to protect her child but rather anger and frustration that his attention has turned away from her. Sapphire's use of exclamation points and italics, in the phrase "I want him on *me*!," for example, conveys Mary's sense of urgency and selfish desperation, even in the face of her child's endangerment. In the declaration, "He her daddy, but he was my man!" *but* functions as a coordinating conjunction, foregrounding that, for Mary, Carl's status as Precious's father is no more important than his status as her lover. Indeed, Carl's status as her lover is even more important. Mary even goes so far as to hint that Precious herself is not only disreputable but also an aberration, "some sort of freak baby" who can apparently withstand intercourse at age three, ultimately rejecting any responsibility for Precious's years of uncontested molestation and unwanted pregnancies and proclaiming herself a victim and a spurned lover.[8]

Amazingly, despite her marked moral culpability, Mary also acts as a mouthpiece for skewed discourses of respectability. For example, she is particularly antagonistic toward Precious's efforts at self-improvement: "Mama say this new school ain' shit. Say you can't learn nuffin' writing in no book. Gotta git on that computer you want some money. When they gonna teach you how to do the computer" (65). Mary rejects Precious's attempts to gain basic literacy, not only arguing for Precious's intellectual incompetence (she frequently tells her daughter she is stupid and without value) but also contending that more technologically advanced knowledge is the only type worth learning since it can ostensibly garner more financial rewards, though she herself is computer illiterate. Likewise, her views on other African Americans reflect her own deep-seated self-loathing and are one of the novel's major examples of the devastating impact of internalized hatred, especially considering that Mary's behavior is a model for Precious. Seeing her teacher Blue Rain's dreadlocks on the first day of class sparks the following revelation from Precious: "My muver do not like niggers wear they hair like that! My muver say Farrakhan OK but he done gone too far" (40).[9] At first glance these two statements seem like disparate remarks: Precious reveals Mary's opinion first on a hairstyle and then on a political and religious leader. However, these two statements, when read together, form a larger picture of Mary's perspective, as dreadlocks and Louis Farrakhan are quite connected. Although simply a hairstyle to some, dreadlocks also signify particular religious and political leanings (Banks 172). Originally affiliated with the Rastafarian faith, dreadlocks within African American society and American society at large often signal that the wearer eschews more mainstream straightened hairstyles and perhaps more mainstream identity politics.[10] Likewise, the subsequent reference to Louis Farrakhan, leader of the Nation of Islam (NOI), conjures the specter of Black nationalism, another marker of politics outside the norm. Mary's critique of the latter's "going too far" seems to reflect the concern, not that his ideologies are anti-Semitic and homophobic, considering her own political failings, but rather that they are seemingly out of the mainstream, ironic given that Farrakhan's notions are, in fact, largely conservative. Thus, despite her own marked depravity in these instances, Mary's views on race and identity ironically mirror prevailing repressive notions of propriety and respectability. In that way, *Push* challenges the idea that such values are necessarily connected to the most upstanding morality, instead insisting that Mary's misuse of power and propensity for abuse couples well with such repressive notions of race and identity. In other words, *Push* reveals that respectability politics is often a major vehicle to perpetuate violence and repression, while masquerading under the pretense of moderation and family values.

Friends and Family

Precious reacts to the overwhelming antipathy she experiences in her family and community by initially believing in a rigid politics of respectability. Like the other examples of respectability politics this book has discussed, notions of respectability in *Push* replicate dominant ideals of family and identity based on conservative iterations of power, class, gender, and sexuality. Respectability politics in *Push* also emphasizes heteronormativity, nationalist political sentiment, a romanticized version of African heritage, and xenophobia. In particular, Precious adheres to an ethos of respectability couched in the conservative rhetoric of groups such as the Five Percenters and the NOI in an effort to make sense of her family life and the world.[11] Regarding NOI leader Louis Farrakhan, who becomes one of Precious's main role models, Manning Marable asserts:

> On issue after issue, Farrakhan's positions on major public policies are as reactionary as those of Newt Gingrich and his "Contract with America" Republican Congress. To this day, Farrakhan retains his belief in "racial purity" and opposes integration as a strategy for Black advancement. . . . On several occasions, he has expressed support for the death penalty as a punishment for many different "crimes," such as interracial sex. He has described homosexuality as "unnatural and sick." His economic philosophy, like that of Elijah Muhammad, is a version of Black entrepreneurial capitalism, the political economy of Booker T. Washington. From the vantage point of white extreme conservatism, Farrakhan's racial fundamentalism has unmistakable parallels with fascist and white racist ideologies and organizations. (176)

Ultimately, as Clarence Lusane insists, the NOI's "conservative cultural agenda, in which regressive gender politics is central," promotes a "politics of patriarchy" (183).

Considering the problematic nature of the historical Farrakhan's teachings, Precious's admiration for his philosophy and respectability politics is troubling. Precious muses: "First thing I see when I wake up is picture Farrakhan's face on the wall. I love him. He is against crack addicts and crackers. Crackers is the cause of everything bad. It why my father ack like he do. He has forgot he is the Original Man! So he fuck me, fuck me, beat me, have a chile by me" (34). This ideology enacts a type of violence by displacing the pain of Precious's abuse in favor of foregrounding Black men's loss of ancient patriarchal power, helping foster a sense of ambivalence toward her own suffering (68). Patricia Hill Collins has argued in *Black Sexual Politics* that this "strong woman/ weak man" thesis relies on a politics of respectability based on women's submission. Thus, while Farrakhan's argument might seem to some like a straightforward indictment of the destructiveness of white supremacy, his philosophy fails to identify the marginalizing effects of sexism. In fact, Farrakhan's philosophy seeks to reify kyriocentric structures in blackface, grounding his claims in a utopian vision of ancient Africa. By offering up whites as proverbial bogeymen, this ideology fails to underscore that whites are not the only ones who mobilize domination and hegemony and thus does little to validate Precious's experience with Carl and Mary. Consequently the respectability politics and rhetoric of this type of Black nationalist philosophy cannot ameliorate either Precious's condition or that of her ghetto community, a failure underscoring the limited usefulness of respectability politics in truly improving circumstances for African Americans in wide-reaching ways.

In addition to not offering any sustained solutions for her parents' abuse, the politics of respectability Precious adheres to operates under a heightened sense of heteronormativity that identifies queerness as a grave social sin. Much as this paradigm reductively characterizes whites as "crackers," it portrays LGBT folk as a destructive social presence because, as Roderick Ferguson suggests, "Black nationalist movements often intersected with sociological discourses and state aims by demanding the gendered and sexual regulation of African American nonheteronormative formations" (111). Thus for much of the novel Precious's brash, streetwise confessions are laced with antigay sentiment, and she frequently uses pejorative language to describe LGBT individuals. When Precious encounters Jermaine, a butch-identified lesbian, in her literacy class, she is outwardly disgusted and considers her "some kinda freak," echoing the same language Mary uses to describe Precious as a baby, suggesting that these two instances of discursive violence are linked (44). Like Ursa rejecting Cat in *Corregidora*, Precious does not want to lose her heterosexual privilege by being associated with Jermaine. She goes as far as moving her chair away from her classmate on the first day of class, asserting, "I don't want no one getting the wrong idea about *me*," as if Jermaine's sexuality were a contagion to be avoided (49; emphasis in original). Precious's pronounced homophobia and heterosexism echo notions about the supremacy of heterosexuality and reject the possibility of community, friendship, or intimacy with those who are not avowedly straight and cisgender. Precious has equally harsh words for drug addicts and immigrants, all in an effort to align herself with "norml pepul" and not the freaks in the margin (105).[12] These declarations reflect the ways in which Precious's attachment to a politics of respectability both reifies dominant notions about what constitutes pathology and forestalls the possibility not only of queer sexuality, but of intimacy and family more generally.

Despite her predilection for nationalist politics that advocate an apparent acceptance of Blackness, Precious's notions of beauty are notably regressive and ambivalent, a circumstance that underscores the politics' ultimate inefficacy. For example, she distrusts those who are dark-skinned, female, and fat, even though (and undoubtedly because) those very adjectives describe her. After seeing a "fat dark-skin woman" in the lobby of her new school, Precious muses, "She look OK I guess. I like light-skin people, they nice. I likes slim people too" (29). The latter statements shed light on what Precious really thinks about the woman's appearance: because she is neither fair nor slim, the woman's appearance is not ideal. Indeed, Precious wishes she were fair-skinned and thin so that boys would find her more attractive, clearly having internalized notions of colorism that identify light skin as beautiful (111). Moreover, she recognizes that her poverty and her Blackness contribute to body fictions that mark her as less than valuable according to both conventional logic and her family. This knowledge contextualizes how she understands the abuse she has endured: "My fahver don't see me really. If he did he would know I was like a white girl, a *real* person, inside" (32; emphasis in original). Precious tragically voices a dominant discourse that explicitly links humanity and whiteness: the notion that white people are real people, whereas Blacks, like herself, are socially invisible and without value. Again, such circumstances compel us to consider that respectability politics does little to instill notions of self-worth and self-esteem for those, like Precious, who have little chance of really adhering to its tenets.

Yet although Precious espouses these paradigms of respectability, she, unlike Mary, experiences the paradox of respectability, understanding and, most importantly, admitting that these narratives of respectability are largely exclusionary and that she herself is marginalized in them: "I big, I talk, I eats, I cooks, I laugh, watch TV, do what muver say. But can see when the picture come back that I don't exist. Don't nobody want me. Don't nobody need me. I know who I am. I know who they say I am—vampire sucking the system's blood. Ugly Black grease to be wipe away, punish, kilt, changed, finded a job for" (31). Precious recognizes that she is "out of the picture" of mainstream society, that according to the prevailing ideology and the predominant rhetoric of the Reagan era she is an unwanted drain on the system, a "vampire" sucking the economic lifeblood out of society, undeserving of the resources set aside for decent, law-abiding citizens. According to this ideology, Precious is destined to be a welfare queen, a pathological creature and modern-day jezebel who is unmarried, oversexed, and perpetually unemployed or underemployed. She has a gaggle of children in tow—fathered by several men—and has no intentions of having, or ability to have, a stable, nuclear family. Precious's nascent recognition of her marginalization prompts her to (begin to) reject her family's notions and the respectability politics of Black nationalism and to envision her life in new ways. *Push*, then, suggests that by employing a hermeneutics of suspicion toward dominant ideologies of Black identity and family as Precious begins to do, one can renegotiate the terms of engagement with, and move beyond the bounds of, damaging respectability politics.

Despite the ubiquity of hegemonic oppression, there are transgressive epistemologies of identity and community that are productive and nurturing for Precious, and this is exemplified in the Diasporic community of the Each One Teach One classroom.[13] Precious's classmates have had similar experiences of abuse, neglect, and abandonment, in addition to struggling with literacy. Like Sophie joining a sex phobia group in *Breath, Eyes, Memory*, Precious joins a Diasporic community of survivors that represents an ethic of community support and accountability as they move toward healing; her classmates are women of African descent from the United States, Puerto Rico, and Jamaica. It is not simply a coincidence that Precious's closest classmates are Black women from various parts of the Diaspora. This circumstance reflects the realities of migration and immigration for Blacks originally from the U.S. South and across the Caribbean who wind up in New York and who coexist in communities of color across the city. *Push*, however, like *Praisesong for the Widow* and *Breath, Eyes, Memory*, includes this Diasporic community in an effort not to collapse Black women's experiences but instead to illuminate the interconnectedness of Black women's traumas and healing. In other words, just as Black women experience trauma for being both Black and female, so too can they come together in dedicated healing spaces.

Precious's experiences with traditional schooling are dramatically juxtaposed to her experiences in the Diasporic community of the alternative school: while Precious is bullied by her peers and ignored by her teachers in the former space, the women from Each One Teach One express an ethic of care from the first day of class. During a class break, a simple act of kindness exemplifies the potential for connection and community in this classroom: "Rhonda say she goin' to the store, anybody want somethin'? I want somethin' but I ain' got no money. . . . Rhonda look me, say, I got you. I look up in her eye. She smile. I feel like I'm gonna cry again. Everybody gonna think I'm a punk, crying, crying. I'm not used to this. But this what I always want, some friendly niceness" (48). The recipient of years of disdain and disapprobation, Precious's first experience of "friendly niceness" becomes a pivotal moment that paves the way for further emotional intimacy among the women. This is not an isolated incident but a product of the women's pointed rejection of divisiveness. Precious muses, "These girlz is my friends. I been like the baby in a way 'cause I was only 16 first day I walk in. They visit at hospital when I had Abdul and take up a collection when Mama kick me out and bring stuff to ½way house for me—clothes, cassette player, tuna fish, and Cambull soup, and stuff. They and Ms Rain is my friends and family" (95). Precious's class is an example of fictive kin who exemplify an ethic of community support and accountability, sustaining and affirming each other with an egalitarian ethic of care. The women are kind to each other, extolling each other during lessons, and encouraging each other's scholastic endeavors. They also form pragmatic support systems, stepping in when Precious gives birth to Abdul (her mother Mary, on the other hand, never visits her at the hospital) and helping her create a comfortable space for her and her son at the halfway house.

This ethic of community support and accountability starkly contrasts to what Precious and her peers have experienced in their natal homes, debunking the notion of inherited pathology prevalent in normative discourses of "underclass" families. In fact, the women act in ways that reject the notion that the experiences they have with their biological family are the only ways to have intimate relationships. The relations among the Each One Teach One crew draw attention to the fact that healthy families are not necessarily contingent on biological ties or on the presence of paternal figures but are instead fostered through an intentional and pragmatic ethic of love, support, and care.

Precious's experiences within the Diasporic Each One Teach classroom community also help precipitate her experience of the paradox of respectability. It becomes increasingly difficult for Precious to maintain her narrow notions of propriety, personal appearance, sexuality, immigration status, and other matters when the very individuals who she is supposed to distrust—gays, immigrants, and former drug addicts, for example—are the main people who embrace her and treat her as family. Furthermore, these folk take her to task when she invokes problematic language and ideology. While reading *The Color Purple*, a novel that positively features a queer relationship, Precious identifies with the abused protagonist, Celie, but attempts to reject her queerness. In a rather transparent effort to assert her bruised heterosexual privilege, Precious says as much, hoping to have a receptive audience to her homophobic rants:

> But just when I go to break on that shit, go to tell class what Five Percenters 'n Farrakhan got to say about butches, Ms Rain tell me I don't like homosexuals she guess I don't like her 'cause she one. I was shocked as shit. Then I jus' shut up. Too bad about Farrakhan. I still believe allah and stuff. I guess I still believe everything. Ms Rain say homos not who rape me, not homos who let me sit up not learn for sixteen years, not homos who sell crack fuck Harlem. It's true. Ms Rain the one who put chalk in my hand, make me queen of the ABCs. (81)

This is a pivotal moment in Precious's development, for she begins to critically assess the information she has received about sexuality. The ambivalence of the statement "I guess I still believe everything" does, however, point to Precious's experience of the paradox of respectability. Precious has difficulty in dismissing the nationalist philosophy that has thus far been her only comfort, yet she is faced with the reality of the philosophy's marked shortcomings.

Thereafter, she must reconcile the indoctrination she has received with the lived experience of Ms. Rain's helpfulness and the lack of any decisive evidence that homosexuality has wrecked either her life or her community. Ms. Rain's commentary, as shared by Precious, attempts to contextualize Precious's circumstances within the larger condition of Harlem. Thus Ms. Rain places the responsibility for Precious's abuse and illiteracy on a nexus of poor parenting, racism, classism, and neglectful social services. Likewise, she implies that Harlem is crack-infested, not because of some nebulous queer threat, but because of more complicated circumstances, particularly neglect from the political establishment. Much of Precious's homophobia serves as an attempt to access the power of heterosexual privilege and as a mask to hide her own misgivings about her sexuality. Being a poor Black woman means she has very little access to social power; heterosexual privilege is something she can latch onto and leverage against others. Furthermore, the sexual abuse she has experienced from both parents has confused her sense of boundaries and ultimately what she thinks is appropriate. Precious falls in line with a conservative, misogynistic, and antigay respectability politics that offers comforting, albeit stultifying, borders of control, suggesting that respectability politics obfuscates serious issues, doing little more than creating the appearance of strong "family values" for someone like Precious.

Precious's evolving ideas about sexuality, though they are still clearly heterosexist, mark her narration with more ambivalence born of the paradox of respectability. For one, she forms a close bond with Jermaine, a woman who she recognizes has endured similar abuse and violence, much of it in reaction to her sexual orientation. Precious, like Avey and Sophie, is then able to link her own painful past to that of other oppressed groups. Furthermore, her recognition that Ms. Rain—the savior that made her the queen of the ABCs—is a lesbian, although, in Precious's words, "you can not tell it," causes her to begin to rethink her stance on gender identity (95). How can Ms. Rain be a "butch" but still be what the mainstream might consider cisgender and "feminine"? And, more importantly, how can she and Jermaine be gay and also be her advocates, mentors, and friends? Precious ultimately concludes that being gay may not be a grave sin.

While she still maintains respect for Farrakhan as a leader and her homophobia does not disappear completely (she later prays her son Abdul does not grow up to be a gay drug addict), Precious's rampant disdain for LGBT folk is mitigated by a more thoughtful, questioning spirit. Tellingly, she admits, "I forgets all that ol' shit lately—Five Percenters, Black Israelites, etc etc. . . . I never be butch like Celie but it don't make me happy—make me sad. Maybe I never find no love, nobody. At least when I look at girls I see *them* and when they look they see *ME*, not what I looks like. But it seems like boyz just see what you looks like" (95; emphasis in original). Over time, Precious begins to eschew her former disgust at queerness and identifies queer relationships as potentially viable and beautiful expressions of an ethic of community support and accountability. Indeed, she laments her lack of attraction to women, for she recognizes the level of connection and intimacy she feels with other women and fears that she cannot connect with men in the same way, a relevant concern considering the ways in which she has been abused, neglected, and harassed, and the woman-centered community she has found at her school. *Push* does not provide any easy answers to this dilemma of inti-macy and attachment, a situation that remains unresolved at the end of the novel. Precious's experience of an ethic of community support and accountability with queer women and her shifts in perspective are not a panacea for all of her problems. The novel does invite readers to consider, however, that these shifts allow Precious more agency and opportunities for growth, suggesting that an ethic of community support and account-ability is a practical method, though not necessarily a magical solution, for resisting or challenging dominant structures of power as they mani-fest among fictive kin and other family systems.

Push also depicts an ethic of community support and accountability coming out of the students' work on the Life Stories Project, illustrating that when marginalized people come together and speak truth to power, like Aunt Cuney, Jay, and Avey in *Praisesong*, Ma Chess in *Annie John*, or Sophie and Atie in *Breath*, there is the possibility to resist kyriarchy. In the Life Stories Project, Ms. Rain encourages her students to put their stories together to form a collaborative series of memoirs as their final assignment. While Precious's poems frame the stories, *Push* includes the narratives of Puerto Rican classmate Rita Romero, Jamaican classmate Rhonda Patrice Johnson, and African American classmate Jermaine Hicks. Although the Life Stories Project has been called a "lengthy postscript in which Precious' classmates tell the story of their lives and [where] we are treated to a recitation of crimes committed against women by men" (Kakutani C29), its presence and placement in the novel are compelling and integral parts of the novel's larger discussion of family.

While the placement of the life stories does make for an abrupt depar-ture from Precious's first-person narrative and could certainly have been integrated more seamlessly throughout the novel, their inclusion in this way purposefully underscores the women's shared experience of destructive family life. Rather than ending with the rather poetic scene of Precious reading to her son Abdul, in which she states, "In his beauty I see my own," the reader is jarred out of the Madonna and child sym-bolism to (re)consider the stark reality of all the women's lives (140). For one, including the life stories as a postscript acknowledges that while the women become literate and form a cohesive Diasporic community of fictive kin, their individual stories also reject respectability politics and affirm their unconventional family. The novel's depiction of the women's life stories is also a pointed reminder of the pervasiveness of racism, sex-ism, and homophobia in the women's lives and speaks to the fact that these factors still exert a powerful influence.

It is significant that the women's stories bear a striking resemblance to Precious's harrowing experience of familial abuse and institutional neglect. For example, Rita's life, like that of Precious, has been a spiral of degradations: "foster care, rape, drugs, prostitution, HIV, jail, rehab" (150). Moreover, Rita experiences all of this after witnessing her mother's murder by her racist father. Nonetheless, Rita refuses to define her life by only these tragic circumstances, spending most of her time discussing her mother, a dark-skinned Afro-Latina who made her living as a psychic medium. Her father identified as white and wanted Rita to reject her African heritage and speak only English. Rita nevertheless reveals, "I wanna be what Mami is, not what he is" (147). Not only does this statement honor her racial and ethnic heritages, it shows that Rita rejects the respectability politics, violence, and repression that her father represents and instead embraces the knowledge, self-awareness, and ethic of community support and accountability that her mother represents. Jermaine's life story focuses primarily on her childhood experience of her parents' abusive marriage and her ongoing persecution because of her sexuality. Even as a child, she is verbally and physically assaulted for her desire to transgress gender norms. Men in her life try to "school" her on proper female behavior: their curriculum is rape and assault, and the lessons to be learned are submission, humility, and conventional respectability. Despite these repeated abuses, Jermaine does not change her gender representation or connect the abuse with her sexuality, proclaiming, "Men did not make me this way. Nothing happened to make me this way. I was born butch!" (169). Jermaine rejects not only dissemblance but also the dominant discourse that her sexuality is a result of another's pathology. She describes her orientation as a sincere desire rather than as something unnatural and claims that her experiences with homophobia and violence are others' attempts to project their fear and loathing onto her body. Jermaine's life story, another refutation of the efficacy of respectability politics, invites readers to consider the possibility for attaining agency and self-worth by moving beyond the bounds of normative intimacies. Rhonda's memoir, like the traumatic stories of her classmates, details how sexism and classism can leave women vulnerable to exploitation and destitution. Rhonda is a Jamaican immigrant whose childhood was marked by family trauma. She arrived in the United States at age twelve but by then had already been out of school for several years. Her mother, who adhered to repressive notions about women's value, had concluded, "You almost grown so what's the use" and had kicked Rhonda out when she revealed she was a victim of incest (151). Rhonda asserts that her mother made a primarily economic decision, rather than a choice based on her daughter's welfare. Rhonda, like Precious, rejects dissemblance and respectability politics, breaking the taboo on incest and illuminating a mother indebted to sexist notions of who deserves to learn and be protected.

Unlike the revisionist history of the Black nationalist groups Precious has previously supported, the Each One Teach One crew actually reflects a supportive Diasporic community. Rather than idealizing a fabled African past where black men were strong patriarchs who protected submissive black women, the Diasporic members of Precious's Each One Teach One classroom community speak to the realities of kyriarchy in various places, underscoring that respectability politics is a flawed strategy for dealing with the various iterations of imperial power that Black people experience. The life stories of Precious's classmates reflect from various angles the pervasiveness of racism, classism, sexism, and homophobia and the intersection of these notions with experiences of family. Rita's life illustrates how racism and sexism, internalized and outwardly manifested, have the potential to literally kill; Rhonda's life details how sexism and classism can leave women vulnerable to abuse and poverty; Jermaine's experiences of homophobia and sexism detail the fear and retribution that women who reject normative notions of gender and sexuality can incite. Although the four women come from different backgrounds throughout the Diaspora, all face persecution within their families because their identities—gender, race, class, ethnic identity, and sexual orientation—mark them as social Others. The fact that all sorts of authorities—parents, social workers, family, friends, and so on—have acted as gatekeepers of race, gender, and sexuality circumscriptions, repeatedly trying to disabuse these women of their hopes for agency, integrity, and safety, has made the women reluctant to share their stories for fear of retribution. However, all of these women share a spirit of resilience, fostered by the intervention of progressive social institutions and a Diasporic community of positive fictive kin to subvert the earlier (and persistent) efforts to undermine their selfhoods. Not only do their stories create individual rejections of kyriarchy, hegemony, and respectability politics, but taken together in the Life Stories Project they illuminate the possibility of forming a unified piece of oppositional discourse among women that rewrites their histories, collectively foregrounding an ethic of community support and accountability and a rejection of respectability politics.

Precious Jones: Poet, Rapper

Besides Precious's experiences of an ethic of community support and accountability in the Diasporic Each One Teach One community, *Push* compels us to consider that, despite her tumultuous upbringing, Precious can enact this ethic with her biological children. Indeed, Precious's participation in alternative education and especially her move toward literacy catalyze her connection to her children, underscoring that an ethic of community support and accountability can encourage and produce multiple types of familial intimacy. For example, the first thing Precious writes in an in-class assignment is "li Mg o mi m (Little Mongo on my mind)" (61). While Precious rarely sees her daughter Mongo because the latter lives with her grandmother Toosie, this is a fact she laments: "I hardly have not seen my daughter since she was a little baby. I never stick my bresses in her mouth. My muver say what for? It's outta style. She say I never do you" (32). Precious both reveals her sadness and anger for being unable to have the choice to connect with her daughter through breastfeeding and reflects that this ambivalence and disconnection exists not simply between Precious and Mongo but between Precious and her mother as well. In this moment, Precious protests and bears witness to two personal injustices, lamenting her circumscribed ability to connect with Mongo and indicting two destructive and hateful mothers: her mother and her grandmother. Precious also calls their parenting styles into question with her desire to read and write. *Push*, then, like *Breath, Eyes, Memory* and other Black women's writing, asserts the role of literacy as a method of challenging a familial history of violence and neglect.

Literacy is a tool of an ethic of community support and accountability that is increasingly important to Precious's growth as a woman and a mother. Rather than relying on discourses of respectability as tools for social mobility, the dialogue journals and poetry in her schoolwork are tools of an ethic of community support and accountability that become platforms for Precious to exercise her voice and power, enabling her to negotiate the terms of Abdul's development in key ways. Just as she was left behind and her intellectual growth was stunted, not out of any deficiency of her own, but because of neglect, Precious recognizes that her own parenting must eschew the fatalistic anti-intellectualism her mother subscribes to. She contends, "I is learning. I'm gonna start going to Family Literacy class on Tuesday. Important to read to baby after it's born. Important to have colors hanging from the wall. Listen baby, I puts my hand on my stomach, breathe deep. Listen baby (I write in my note-book)" (65). Precious refutes the notion that computers trump traditional print literacy, as her mother would suggest. As Madhu Dubey comments, "Contrary to the claim that electronic technologies are sponsoring a plu-ralist culture that is more hospitable to minority groups than is its print counterpart, Sapphire's novel suggests that print literacy can offer these groups a sense of agency denied them in electronic culture" (85). Put another way, Precious underscores the centrality of print literacy, and while *Push* is not antitechnology it does not promote electronic culture as the saving grace of the so-called underclass. It is perhaps important to note the setting of the novel: the present-day action is in 1988, with flash-backs to Precious's childhood in the 1970s and early 1980s. While com-puters were clearly an important feature of 1980s technology, I would argue that the fact that Precious's narrative takes place before the rise of the Internet and the ubiquity of the personal computer and the smart phone adds to the efficacy of print literature, as Dubey argues.

While recovering from the birth of Abdul, Precious spends much of her time contemplating how to raise her child and asserts that education and literacy, and not violence, abuse, or regressive notions of respectabil-ity, will be the cornerstones of her mothering relationship to her son.[14] She bears witness to the atrocities of her own life, using these experi-ences as guideposts in her parenting: "I bet chu one thing, I bet chu my baby can read. Bet a mutherfucker that! Betcha he ain' gonna have no dumb muver" (63). Here Precious asserts not only her unborn child's intelligence (inasmuch as she equates intelligence with literacy) but also her own expanding education, citing herself as the opposite of a "dumb muver." To that end, Precious understands that education and literacy also are markers for support and love: "I love me. I ain' gonna let that big fat bitch [her mother] kick my ass 'n shout on me. And I ain' giving Abdul away. And I ain' gonna stop school" (78). This declaration reflects a revolutionary shift in her thinking. Precious and Abdul exist on the bottom of the social ladder, part of the so-called permanent underclass. Precious nevertheless refutes the logic of contemporary manifestations of respectability politics that identifies both herself and Abdul as unwor-thy or unable to be educated, or contends that they must first become respectable to be of value. Like Sophie Caco, Precious, in enacting an ethic of community support and accountability, declares her desire to break from the cycle of abuse and oppression she has endured, coura-geously asserting that she and Abdul are important and worthy. Her attitude resists notions of irreducible Black pathology, as she refuses to remain mired in misperceptions of her own history, signaling that progressive notions of education are one way of reconceptualizing urban working-class Blacks.

After finally learning the alphabet, sixteen-year-old Precious transcribes and annotates it, illuminating it as a palimpsest onto which she can map her own critical concerns regarding respectability and family:

> A is fr Afrc
> (for Africa)
> B is for u bae
> (you baby)
> C is cl w bk
> (colored we Black).   (65)

Just the first three letters of Precious's alphabet reveal her central concerns. Given her marked interest in nationalist politics, it is perhaps no surprise that "A" is Africa; this annotation signals Precious's Diasporic consciousness. (Indeed, later she denotes that "M" is "frknka rl m (*Farrakhan real man*)" (66). However, Precious's second entry, "B is for u bae (*you baby*)," reminds us that the first-person voice is addressing not simply the reader but Precious's unborn child as well; it is Precious's attempt to foreground the importance of literacy for her unborn child as part of an ethic of community support and accountability, rejecting narratives that would claim that Precious (and her offspring) cannot learn. Her recitation of the alphabet is prefaced by her own instructions to the yet-unborn Abdul, instructions that emphasize her invocation of an ethic of community support and accountability. First, she cautions him to listen, and after outlining the ABCs she implores, "Listen baby, Muver love you. Muver not dumb. Listen baby: ABCDEFGHIJKLMONPQ RSTUVWXYZ. Thas the alphabet. Twenty-six letters in all. Them letters make up words. Them words everything" (66). Precious revamps the dialogue journal for her own purposes, emphasizing the importance of exchange between two parties, rejecting notions of paternalistic parental power. At this point, the exchange is more figurative than literal because Precious's unborn baby is unable to respond. Nonetheless, in this moment Precious takes the tools she has gained from the alternative school and uses them with a practical application of an ethic of community support and accountability in her own life, suggesting that experiences of progressive education can have positive far-reaching effects.

After mastering basic literacy, Precious almost immediately begins writing poetry that reflects not only a Diasporic consciousness but also a move toward more transgressive interpersonal relationships. Precious's writing is connected to and inspired by Black writers, such as Lucille Clifton, Langston Hughes, and Alice Walker. Furthermore, like the storytelling and poetry in *Annie John* and *Breath, Eyes, Memory*, the poetry in *Push* is a Diasporic ritual rooted in Black experience. And like other Diasporic rituals seen in those books and in *Praisesong for the Widow*, poetry, whether it comes in traditional forms, spoken word, or hip-hop, becomes crucial to the ways in which Precious asserts her voice and rejects respectability politics. When asked to recite a poem for a class assignment, Precious tellingly chooses Langston Hughes's "Mother to Son," dedicating it to Abdul. Hughes's words become a poignant stand-in for Precious's life thus far and her intentions for Abdul. As in Precious's own narrative, the poem's first-person speaker testifies to her own difficult journey:

Life for me ain't been no crystal stair
It's had tacks in it,
And splinters,
And boards torn up,
And places with no carpet on the floor—
Bare. (112–13)

These words from Hughes's bluesy homage are a poetic illustration of Precious's own hardships—an ascent filled with pitfalls, human obstacles, and neglect. Nonetheless, both Precious and the poem's speaker share a sense of perseverance. The speaker urges her son to never turn back, sit down, or fall on the proverbial set of steps. Likewise, Precious is invested in a notion of persistence that she passes on through her parenting of Abdul. Using Hughes's words as her own testimony, Precious rejects the identity of "welfare queen" and "baby mama," bearing witness to social injustice while also emphasizing her own strength despite grave barriers and without falling back on a conservative respectability politics. Precious uses the discourse embedded in Hughes's poetry to reconfigure herself, not as a vampire sucking the system's blood, but as a fighter and the mother of a fighter. Her recitation of "Mother to Son," like Jay Johnson's recitation of the "The Negro Speaks of Rivers" in *Praisesong*, also illustrates a connection to Diasporic art. Precious aligns herself with an artistic tradition that provides for an ethic of community support and accountability but also nurtures her burgeoning creative pursuits, making her an artist with clear Diasporic influences.

Precious, like Sophie and Atie Caco, also segues into creating her own pieces. And just as the Cacos' art is rooted in Haitian folk traditions, so is Precious's work deeply connected to Diasporic cultural traditions in the United States. In particular, Precious's poetry reflects the significance of hip-hop as a cultural form. By *hip-hop*, I mean the cultural movement that began to take shape in the 1970s in New York, where Blacks and Latinos, many of whom were of Caribbean descent, created music, dance, art, and fashion that reflected the conditions of post–civil rights era urban life and that still exists today. Although hip-hop is often erroneously conflated with rap, it is actually an umbrella term that includes rapping, deejaying, dancing, graffiti art, dynamic sartorial styles, and, increasingly, literature.[15] While some have argued that *Push* employs primarily a blues aesthetics, my analysis of the novel concurs with discussions that recognize hip-hop as the basis for the driving cultural aesthetic of the novel.[16] *Push* is set in the mid-1980s, during what William Jelani Cobb has called hip-hop's "Golden Age," and as such hip-hop is an important backdrop to Precious's life (41).[17] The novel mentions Precious's admiration for artists such as Queen Latifah; however, as Brittney Cooper suggests, Precious not only listens to hip-hop music but also composes poetry with a distinct hip-hop aesthetic. Cooper defines a hip-hop aesthetic as having three main tenets: "First, it employs a kind of social alchemy that transforms lack into substance. . . . Second, hip-hop music and cultural expression privileges a well-honed facility for defiance. . . . Finally, hip-hop aesthetics privilege street consciousness and cultural literacy" (4–5). Precious's poetry demonstrates all three aspects of Cooper's definition. For one, Precious is certainly working with limited resources; essentially, she is using a pad, a pen, and her own mind. The poetry she creates also stands in opposition to the notion that she has limited intellectual capabilities, instead reflecting her artistry, intelligence, and skill, challenging both respectability politics and narratives that she is part of the so-called undeserving poor. Lastly, Precious's poetry and life writing underscore her street smarts and savvy, portraying a sophisticated understanding of the world and her place in it.

Additionally, because hip-hop has its roots in Diasporic cultural expressions, Precious's hip-hop aesthetic is a reaffirmation of the sensibilities of the Diasporic community of the Each One Teach One class. Indeed, hip-hop's Diasporic roots are integral to understanding Precious's hip-hop-inflected poetry.[18] Scholars such as Jeff Chang, K.

Maurice Jones, Gwendolyn D. Pough, and Guthrie Ramsey have argued for the connection between hip-hop culture's birth in the Bronx in the 1970s to cultural expressions in dance, music, and art from across the African Diaspora, signifying on a variety of traditions, from the musical styles of the griots of West Africa to the "toasting" coming out of Jamaica. Hip-hop and the poetry Precious produces that is inspired by and connected to it thus exist as forms of cultural expression rooted in African Diasporic practices, not unlike dance in *Praisesong for the Widow*, obeah in *Annie John*, folktales in *Breath, Eyes, Memory*, and the blues in *Corregidora* and *The Color Purple*. Contrary to many depictions of hip-hop culture that largely emphasize the exploitation and co-optation of rap or the prevalence of misogyny and homophobia in hip-hop, *Push* positions hip-hop as both a space connected to Diasporic sensibilities and one that gives Precious the leverage to exercise her creativity while speaking truth to power.

Much of Precious's hip-hop poetry reflects her ongoing concern about her ability to create a sustainable life for herself and her family. For example, after her diagnosis of HIV, she slips into a depression in which she tries, somewhat successfully, to reconcile her feelings through poetry in her journal. In a stream-of-consciousness-style poem, she reveals her anger at the state of her life:

> I was fine til HIV thing
> [Ms Rain] say i still fine
> but prblm not jus HIV it mama Dady
> BUT I was gon dem
> I escap dem like Harriet [Tubman]
> Ms Ran say we can nt escap the pass
> The way free is hard.   (101)

Precious is a young woman who has indeed escaped a sort of slavery and, like her formerly enslaved ancestors, must unlearn previous patterns of survival to thrive in a new, somewhat less oppressive environment.[19] Her intense emotions that range across anger, despair, and joy fill the pages of her notebook and begin to replace the self-destructive behavior, such as self-mutilation, and the self-destructive respectability politics she engaged in and was indebted to when she was captive to her parents.

Yet despite Precious's turn to poetry and her invocation of a hip-hop aesthetic, she remains markedly ambivalent toward her experience of family because of the enduring consequences of poverty, illness, and abuse in her life, and there are remnants of respectability politics in her poetry. The poem "untitled" ends both the Life Stories class project and the novel and, like much of her other poetry, and indeed much of her narrative, is a meditation on the meaning of her life and her family. She concludes:

> it's a prison days
> we live in
> at least me
> I'm not really free
> baby, Mama, HIV   (175)

Precious at first employs a hip-hop aesthetic in this piece, diagnosing society's ailments, finding the modern world fundamentally prison-like, and invoking a Diasporic sensibility in alluding to the lyrics of Bob Marley's reggae song "Concrete Jungle." Then she qualifies the statement to foreground her own sense of imprisonment, citing three factors. The memory of her mother lingers as an oppressive force in her life, although she is literally beyond her mother's grasp. Her HIV-positive status is also a constant worry. It is, however, important to note that Precious lists motherhood as another aspect of her life that hampers her freedom. Precious does not simply bask in the glow of her motherhood; rather, she is pointedly ambivalent about it, as she recognizes the personal sacrifices she has made to keep her son. Right after Abdul was born, she had the opportunity to give up him for adoption, and although she ultimately rejected this decision, she does not idealize her motherhood. Indeed, when she imagines her ideal self, she is not a mother. She reveals that although "so much of [her] heart is love for Abdul," she would rather not have been put in the situation to have children at twelve and sixteen, respectively (114). She rightfully recognizes that "to not have no kids means I woulda had a different life" (114). Precious does not mythologize motherhood or champion a sort of "super Black woman" ideology. She loves her children but also recognizes that their births, in many ways, curtail her life chances, and she testifies to her conflicted feelings of love, anger, disappointment, and hope and her desire for an experience of an ethic of community support and accountability that would help her cope with, though not necessarily reconcile, her competing desires.

"Untitled" also resonates with the words of prominent and influential Black thinkers; Precious takes those words as part of a palimpsest over which she inserts her own analysis, much as in hip-hop music's use of sampling.[20] Besides alluding to revolutionary Jamaican singer Bob Marley, this poem, like other parts of the novel, pays homage to *The Color*

Purple. Like Celie, Precious asserts that her children are alive, despite the abuse and neglect they have received from their family and from society. Moreover, Precious uses catchphrases by Langston Hughes ("HOLD FAST TO DREAMS"), Louis Farrakhan ("GET UP OFF YOUR KNEES"), and Alice Walker ("CHANGE") to underscore all the things she considers (177). The words of the Advancement House's housemother and Ms. Rain, two women Precious identifies as positive maternal figures, also punctuate her verses; both women urge her to think creatively about her situation, advising her to "PLAY THE HAND YOU GOT" (176) and "DON'T ALWAYS RHYME" (177). Nonetheless, while Precious honors others' words, she owns her voice and her own perspective:

> I can see
> I can read
> nobody can see now
> but I might be a poet, rapper.   (176)

The phrases "I can see" and "I can read" refute the idea of her "obvious intellectual limitations" (119). She knows that perhaps few can envision the goals she has, but she plans to make use of her talent for words as a rapper/poet. Precious's coming to voice, literacy, and subsequent testimony are a direct outgrowth of her status as a mother, her experience of an ethic of community support and accountability in her Diasporic Each One, Teach One community, and her desire to discontinue the legacy of violence and sexual abuse she has endured. Precious engages with and talks back to the inaccuracy of repressive ideologies, while still struggling to come up with an alternative epistemology that will replace the inadequate prevailing conventions. Ultimately, as Precious is a flawed and complicated figure, her story is not a straightforward triumph but rather a meditation on the difficulty of undermining prevailing narratives and claiming one's voice in the service of sustaining, rather than debilitating, discourse.

Like other texts analyzed in this book, Sapphire's *Push* underscores the destructive power of the paradox of respectability. While Precious's narrative is fraught with anxiety because she has internalized repressive doctrines about power and propriety, over the course of the novel Precious recognizes that these views are at best against her interests and at worst fundamentally threatening to any sort of positive existence or self-awareness. In *Push*, an ethic of community support and accountability is found not only through the reimagining of kinship but also through the radical reimagining of institutional structures such as education and medical care. *Push* draws attention to an existential crisis, as Precious's narration is infused with a profound ambivalence, a circumstance that is only partially resolved at the end of the novel. Yet like *Praisesong for the Widow, Annie John, Breath, Eyes, Memory*, and other texts in this tradition, *Push* does compel us to consider a transgressive reimagining of family, one that eschews racism, classism, homophobia, and other forms of domination, as the way to create truly sustainable Black families in the face of hostility, diminishing resources, and pervasive doubt.

Epilogue

There are signs everywhere reminding us of the importance of thinking energetically about Black families in the Caribbean and the United States. Take, for example, a recent experience I had. I spent a good part of the first week of July 2012 looking for the August edition of *Essence* magazine. My contact at *Essence* had informed me that the piece I was featured in because of my work with the scholar-activist group the Crunk Feminist Collective would be in the issue with actress Nia Long on the cover. I eventually got my hands on a copy (or two) and, after basking in the glow of my fifteen minutes of fame, took a closer look at the issue. On the cover was Nia Long, resplendent in a yellow taffeta gown, her two sons smiling next to her. The headline for her cover story was "Single, Satisfied, and Raising Her Boys." In the article, Long, who is of African American and Trinidadian descent, admitted, "Marriage is not a priority for me. . . . I'm not saying I'll never do it; it's just not where we are as a family. For some reason that disappoints people. I'll be at home with my man, having a perfectly loving time, and I'll see all these comments on some site about how wrong I am for not being married. I've never seen a marriage work, which makes me sad to say, and it's not just residual stuff from my childhood, this is among my peers. But I don't feel less loved or less loving because I'm not married" (hampton 96–97). Like the individuals featured in the *Harvard Magazine* article cited in the introduction to this book, Long is ambivalent about marriage but fully committed to creating and sustaining a loving family life. Certainly, as a wealthy, privileged celebrity, Long faces circumstances very different from those of the working poor eschewing traditional marriage in the *Harvard Magazine* article. Nevertheless, both pieces—published around the same time, albeit in starkly different venues—convey the sense that Black folk are exceedingly creative in fashioning intimate familial relations that serve their needs but do not necessarily affirm idealized social norms.

I was also intrigued by Long's pragmatic rejection of respectability politics and her decision to shape her family life on her own terms. Despite the public disapprobation she faces as an unmarried mother of two, Long asserts that rather than being guided by a set of rules that may not make sense for her own life, she would rather live by a different set of rules, even if that means facing censure. Although she and her partner, an athlete in the NBA, are not married, their commitment and the family life she describes echo the sentiment of an ethic of community support and accountability. After discussing how reconciling with her father prompted her to reassess her familial bonds, Long notes, "I made a real commitment to emotional maturity, to peace in my home" (97). Perhaps this article could simply be dismissed as a superficial piece that has little relevance to the lived experiences of Blacks in the United States and the Caribbean. Indeed, an article about an actress in a Black women's lifestyle magazine may not seem to signify much for a study of late twentieth-century Black women's literature. However, reading this article just I was finishing a draft of this manuscript really underscored what is at stake in my project. My study of the paradox of respectability, ambivalence, and an ethic of community support and accountability is not about lambasting heterosexual unions, traditional marriage, or nuclear families, but rather about illuminating and making sense of the various strategies Black women writers have portrayed as having the potential to improve Black people's lives and to create healthy, loving families. And as this project and even the recent *Essence* article attest, there is evidence of Black women's creativity in family life everywhere.

Throughout this book, I have aimed to illuminate not only the limitations of respectability politics and the destructiveness of the paradox it creates but also the Diasporic rituals and the progressive and transgressive ethics that Black women writers repeatedly insist are the ties that bind Black families of all sorts together across the Caribbean and the United States. In the literary tradition that I have outlined throughout this project, respectability politics are revealed to be, not just a social strategy aimed at ameliorating the conditions of Blacks in the Caribbean and the United States, but an insufficient response to the vectors of racism, sexism, and classism, a response that, in fact, often reifies the very institutions and behaviors that exist and serve to oppress Blacks and that disrupts the very familial connections that respectability politics purports to uphold. So in *Praisesong for the Widow* the investment in a narrow notion of the American Dream that rejects Diasporic cultural traditions in favor of capitalist individualism is exposed as the root cause of the Johnson family's strife. A reassessment of core values and a recommitment to sustaining family practices sets Avey and, presumably, the rest of her family on a path back to healing. In *Annie John*, transgressive obeah communities and Annie's girlhood comrades fretfully coexist with the combination of "young lady business" and an investment in a strictly defined manifestation of the nuclear family. This tension not only drives a wedge between Annie, her mother, and her natal community but also alienates Annie from her peers and incites dis-ease, circumstances that are not fully resolved at the end of the novel. In *Breath, Eyes, Memory*, the Caco women, by embracing a virginity cult and retooling folktales as forms of coercion and surveillance, collude with the fascist state to subjugate one another. Not until Sophie reclaims folktales within a holistic healing community do healthy family dynamics appear in the text. In *Push*, Precious attempts to reject her abusive family by falling in line with a particularly repressive brand of Black nationalism, one that promises respectability and stability in exchange for her unquestioning allegiance. Her participation in an alternative school and the Diasporic community she finds there, along with her own creative pursuits in hip-hop and poetry, provide her with the support she needs. Time and again, Black women writers in this tradition reveal respectability politics' fault lines while also underscoring the sundry ways in which Black folks negotiate how to live in affirming families and communities.

I would be remiss, however, if I claimed that the works studied in this book offer solutions to the challenges that face Blacks within families and communities. Indeed, it would be more apt to say that these works offer strategies, while also calling into question other strategies, such as respectability politics. For example, while all the texts included in this study reveal and emphasize the efficacy of an ethic of community support and accountability, this ethic is never shown to be a panacea for racism, homophobia, or other social ills. *Praisesong*'s Avey knows that her newfound message will not move all the upwardly mobile Blacks she will encounter; Annie in *Annie John* chooses to leave Antigua for England without reconciling with her family and community; Sophie in *Breath, Eyes, Memory* seems poised to move forward with the help of her immediate family and community, but her other female kin who lack her First World resources and heterosexual privilege have decidedly fewer options; and *Push* ends with a postscript that suggests that Precious's life will continue to be an uphill battle because of her HIV status and the increasingly limited resources at her disposal.

All of these works suggest that an ethic of community support and accountability in and of itself is not enough to support Black people as they navigate the hostile territory of life in the Caribbean and the United States. Indeed, it is repeatedly shown that an ethic of community support and accountability must be part of a larger institutional shift to move from having transgressive to revolutionary power for Blacks. More specifically, just as respectability politics is linked to kyriarchy's major institutions, Black women writers reveal that an ethic of community support and accountability must be linked to progressive social institutions that would have the power to truly ameliorate Black people's lives. For while respectability politics has attempted to grant Black people access to, and the ability to negotiate power in, patently imperfect systems, works by Black women writers written since the 1970s invite us to consider that fundamental changes to the systems we live in ultimately provide the most radical possibilities for social change for Caribbean and U.S. societies' historically marginalized subjects.

Because of the continued assault on Black families and the continued offering up of respectability politics in the public imaginary as the solution to what ails Black communities, not only is an ethic of community support and accountability a strategy of continuing importance into the twenty-first century for Blacks in the Caribbean and the United States, but so are other strategies aimed at reconfiguring the institutional apparatus that continues to oppress Black families. Recently, for example, the governor general of Jamaica Sir Patrick Allen "called on Jamaicans to strengthen the social structures to prevent further social decline, as seen in the growth of single-parent households, unattached and uneducated youth, and violent crime" ("Leaders Call"). During the 2012 U.S. presidential campaign, Republican primary candidate Michelle Bachmann sparked controversy when she signaled her participation in a conservative advocacy group that claimed, "Slavery had a disastrous impact on African-American families, yet sadly a child born into slavery in 1860 was more likely to be raised by his mother and father in a two-parent household than was an African-American baby born after the election of the USA's first African-American President" (Contee). These two statements from Jamaica and the United States are, unfortunately, rather commonplace examples of the rhetoric used to describe and, indeed, pathologize Black families and to justify harmful legislation and social practices aimed at Blacks. At the heart of both examples is the idea that respectability politics, and in particular heterosexual marriage, is the magic bullet that will eliminate what is seen as Black family dysfunction. Because of these unrelenting misrepresentations of Black families, an ethic of community support and accountability, along with revolutionary social strategies aimed at institutional inequities, is more necessary and important than ever.

Twenty-first-century conceptions of Black family life in the Caribbean and the United States are often still troubling, but as the adage "The garden holds both the poison and the cure" suggests, novels by Black women writers from the United States and the Caribbean compel us to consider that Blacks often already possess the cultural tools both to challenge the pervasive misrepresentation of Black families and to create and encourage cultural practices that affirm Black family life in all its manifold iterations, while also agitating for structural change. In the twenty-first century, Black women writers from the United States and the Caribbean such as Tayari Jones, Danielle Evans, Patricia Powell, and Dionne Brand continue to craft complicated portrayals of Black family life that challenge both respectability politics and prevailing discourses about Black families across the Diaspora, underscoring the ongoing significance of a hermeneutics of suspicion set forth in the works of U.S. and Caribbean Black women writers from the 1970s, '80s, and '90s. An ethic of community support and accountability is just one example of an epistemology and social practice that illustrates the power of African American and Black Caribbean people to shape discourse and challenge hegemony, a power that is not only enduring but increasingly necessary.

Notes

Introduction

1. Daniel Patrick Moynihan is most often associated with late twentieth-century discussions of Black family dysfunction in the United States. His 1965 treatise, *The Negro Family: The Case for National Action*, more commonly known as the Moynihan Report, contends that poor Black families are enmeshed in an unfortunate "tangle of pathology." He argues, "In essence, the Negro community has been forced into a matriarchal structure which, because it is out of line with the rest of the American society, seriously retards the progress of the group as a whole, and imposes a crushing burden on the Negro male and, in consequence, on a great many Negro women as well."

Because working-class African Americans deviate from mainstream norms, Moynihan argues that this seriously impedes their life chances. Moynihan is often singled out for his perspectives on Black familial pathology; however, he drew many of his conclusions from the work of prominent anthropologists, psychologists, and sociologists, some of whom were Black—sources such as Kenneth Clark, W. E. B. DuBois, Stanley Elkins, E. Franklin Frazier, Nathan Glazer, and Gunnar Myrdal. Taken together, their research on family generally concluded that unlike most white families, Black families, especially working-class Black families, were chaotic and unstable and that much of this could be traced to the deleterious effects of slavery and Jim Crow and could be rectified through marriage.

2. For a range of discussion around African Americans, marriage, and family, see Billingsley; Coontz; F. Foster; Frazier, *Negro Family* and *Black Bourgeoisie*; McAdoo; Moynihan; J. Patterson; and O. Patterson.

3. Smock and Manning note that many cohabitating adults "believe their money situation must be solid before they will feel ready for marriage" (133). Therefore, considering the deeply entrenched economic inequities in American society, it is safe to say that for many of these couples marriage is most certainly out of reach.

4. For a range of discussion around marriage, family, and Blacks in the Caribbean, see Barrow; Clarke; L. Douglass; Matthews; Rodman; Senior; Simey; Slater; and Smith.

5. Paravisini-Gebert contends that in the Caribbean "the standards familiar to the metropolis may have been closely imitated by the small enclaves of Europeanized white or light-skinned middle and upper-middle classes, but were frequently transformed by the masses of the people who wove new configurations out of the fabric of colonial mores" (5).

6. Regarding African Americans and marriage, Jenkins suggests that "heterosexual marriage is repeatedly fantasized . . . as the sacred space that can take human beings, unpredictable social subjects with potentially errant personal *and* political desires, and make them safe both publicly and privately" (188; italics in original). Similarly, in the case of family dynamics in contemporary Jamaica, for example, LaFont and Pruitt conclude, "The internalization of the ideal of the nuclear family has been nearly complete. Legal marriage, legitimate children, and monogamy are the stated but seldom realized ideals" (224). LaFont and Pruitt argue that despite the ways in which the real and ideal infrequently coexist or may even be perhaps incompatible, master narratives about what constitutes a "proper" family infiltrate all aspects of Jamaican society, even if these narratives are not or cannot be fully enacted for much of the population.

7. It is also important to note that ideas of what constitutes a traditional family are far from stable. See, for example, Smith and Coontz for discussion of the shifting dynamics within family systems in the Caribbean and the United States respectively.

8. Smith highlights the propensity for scholars, politicians, pundits, and laypeople alike to "assert the value—or the absolute necessity—of 'traditional' family values, which means a traditional nuclear family with a male breadwinner and a female 'homemaker,'" despite the seeming liberalization of social mores (3).

9. I have chosen to capitalize the word *Diaspora* throughout my work when discussing the African Diaspora. Not unlike the move to capitalize the word *Black* in African American studies more generally, this choice reflects my understanding of *Diaspora* as a politicized term and is aimed at centering the significance of the African Diaspora as a complicated site of tradition and cultural practice in literary study.

10. See Brodber; Cliff, *Abeng* and *No Telephone to Heaven*; Naylor, *Women of Brewster Place*; and Walker.

11. Fictive kin, as opposed to consanguineal kin, or relatives related by blood, are individuals who are considered family but who are not connected to one another biologically or through marriage. This form of kinship has been a sustained practice across the African Diaspora. See, for example, Senior and Collins, *Black Feminist Thought*, for more analysis of this phenomenon.

12. Higginbotham specifically coined the phrase *politics of respectability* in her seminal study *Righteous Discontent*. I use the term *respectability politics* (in addition to *politics of respectability*) to denote the plurality and wide range of respectability discourses.

13. Higginbotham contends, "Duty-bound to teach the value of religion, education, and hard work, the women of the Black Baptist church adhered to a politics of respectability that equated public behavior with individual self-respect and with the advancement of African Americans as a group" (14). While Higginbotham notes that these church leaders rallied together to support their communities and combat racism, their often conservative class politics undermined some of their effectiveness: "The Baptist

women's preoccupation with respectability reflected a bourgeois vision that vacillated between an attack on the failure of America to live up to its liberal ideals of equality and justice and an attack on the values and lifestyles of those Blacks who transgressed white middle-class propriety" (15).

14. Wilson asserts, "Respectability holds a society together around a stratified class structure with standards of moral worth and judgment emanating from the upper class or overseas and imposed on the lower strata" (229). Reputation, on the other hand, is a set of behaviors that are a reaction to the constraints of respectability; they prize "in particular those talents and skills which bolster a self-image by putting down, undermining, and ridiculing respectability" (224).

15. It is important to note that the dialectics of respectability and reputation are gendered, with women most often being interpellated by the lures of respectability that (often falsely) promise security, stability, and increased social status.

16. More specifically, Wilson suggests, "Reputation is a standard of value that comes out of involvement with the world of relationships rather than out of individualistic standards of respectability" (227). Thus one can have a reputation for being a "good singer, a poor fisherman, a mediocre stud, a kind father, and a silly drunkard" all at once (227).

17. For more studies of respectability politics in the United States and the Caribbean, see, for example, Barnes; Carolyn Cooper, *Noises in the Blood* and *Sound Clash*; Frazier, *Black Bourgeoisie*; Thomas; and White.

18. Respectability politics is even more complex in that the Caribbean is not a unified conglomerate of nations but a diverse region filled with interrelated yet distinct cultures. Therefore, the interplay of respectability and reputation will not necessarily look the same in Jamaica as it does in Haiti or Antigua.

19. M. Jacqui Alexander notes, "The memory of slavery has receded in the lived experience of Caribbean people; colonization has greater force. The memory of colonization has receded in the lived experience of African American people; it is slavery that has carried historical weight. There is a cost to this polarized forgetting in the kinds of psychic distortions that both thought systems have produced: the hierarchies of inferiority and superiority and their internalizations; and the internecine struggles in a gendered, racialized political economy of global capital with its intrepid mobilization of race, gender, and nation as it manages crisis in this late stage of its evolution" (*Pedagogies of Crossing* 271).

20. Grewal and Kaplan define "scattered hegemonies" as institutions such as "global economic structures, patriarchal nationalisms, 'authentic' forms of tradition, local structures of domination and legal-juridical oppression on multiple levels" that are useful to analyze comparatively across cultures in reference to transnational feminisms (17).

21. See, for example, Alexander-Floyd; S. Alexander; Edmondson; Brody; Jenkins; Renk; and Thompson.

22. My concept of an "ethic of community support and accountability" echoes Collins's delineation of the "ethics of caring" and the "ethic of personal accountability" that characterize Black feminist epistemology (*Black Feminist Thought* 262–66). In using the term in this project, I am largely interested in how such an ethic challenges prevailing notions of respectability. Furthermore, my use of the word *community* is a deliberate choice that seeks to emphasize the importance of both biological and fictive kin.

23. Take, for instance, the institution of marriage in the United States. Collins notes that "the rules that regulate love relationships in the United States pivot on varying combinations of choosing partners who are the same and/or different from oneself. One fundamental rule governs all others—marry a partner of the same race and different gender" (*Black Sexual Politics* 248).

24. As Coontz advises: "Families have always been in flux, and many different family arrangements and values have worked for various groups at different times. . . . But it is also true that families have always been fragile, vulnerable to economic stress, and needful of practical and emotional support from beyond the nuclear family. And new opportunities for individuals and families to succeed have also brought new ways for them to fail" (46).

25. M. Jacqui Alexander has called this use of Diasporic ritual and traditions "healing work" and has suggested that this "healing work is the antidote to oppression" ("Keynote Address").

26. Renk notes that the mythical family "consisted of the moral and intellectual father, the angelic, asexual mother, and the dutiful child whose character has been shaped by the moral strength of his parents" (8).

27. As M. Jacqui Alexander suggests, "Neither of us African American nor Caribbean people created those earlier conditions of colonialism and Atlantic slavery. Yet we continue to live through them in a state of selective forgetting, setting up an artificial antipathy between them in their earlier incarnation, behaving now as if they have ceased to be first cousins" (*Pedagogies of Crossing* 273). See that book for further in-depth discussion of the complicated history of relations between Blacks from the Caribbean and the United States.

1 / A Wide Confraternity

1. Indeed, Lorn S. Foster argues that the "Jackson campaign was an extension of the civil rights movement and can best be understood in that context" (203). Foster further insists that many, including Jackson himself, believed him to be "an inheritor of King's vision of a United States where social justice would be a reality for everyone" (207). For more on the significance of Jesse Jackson's 1984 presidential campaign, see Barker and Walter; L. Morris.

2. See Noguera for a thorough discussion of the political climate in Grenada in the second half of the twentieth century.

3. By the 1980s, several Caribbean nations had achieved a measure of independence from colonial powers, including Antigua and Barbuda (1981), Barbados (1966), Grenada and Carriacou (1974), Jamaica (1962), and Trinidad and Tobago (1962).

4. Although published in 1983, *Praisesong* is set in the late 1970s, before the U.S. military invasion of Grenada.

5. See Braxton; Bryant; and Morrison, "Rootedness," for further discussion of the role of the ancestor in Black women's literature.

6. For more on the trope of flying Africans in Marshall's text and more generally, see Wilentz, *Binding Cultures* and "If You Surrender"; Storey; and Georgia Writers' Project.

7. Several scholars, including John and Wilentz ("If You Surrender"), have explored the significance of Marshall's depiction of the Ibo Landing tale. Rather than restating what has already been masterfully discussed, I focus in this section on the ring

shout and what this ritual illuminates about an ethic of community support and accountability.

8. Marshall further describes the ring shout as a "curious gliding shuffle which did not permit the soles of the heavy work shoes they had on to ever lift from the floor," although participants clapped their hand and moved their bodies in "dazzling syncopated rhythm" and loudly sang spirituals (34). Avey is so captivated by the scene "that under cover of darkness she performed in place the little rhythmic trudge. She joined in the singing under her breath: '*Got your life in my hands / Well well well . . .*'" (35; emphasis in original).

9. For more on the ring shout and dance more generally in the novel, see Cartwright; Courlander; and Stuckey.

10. Marshall identifies this connection as a mutual exchange and not simply a connection from Avey to the others: "Then it would seem to [Avey] that she had it all wrong and the threads didn't come from her, but from them, from everyone on the pier, including the rowdies, issuing out of their navels and hearts to stream into her. . . . She visualized the threads as being silken, like those used in the embroidery on a summer dress, and of a hundred different colors. And although they were thin to the point of invisibility, they felt as strong entering her as the lifelines of woven hemp that trailed out into the water at Coney Island" (191).

11. Benjamin asserts that there is another Diasporic allusion to these threads: that the threads are also a part of Aunt Nancy (or Anancy's) web. Aunt Nancy/Anancy is a West African trickster figure that in the United States becomes a female figure who is a "healer, master mediator, and revolutionary life force" (51). In this moment on the pier, Benjamin suggests there are traces of Aunt Nancy's web of connectivity that "acknowledges the need for Black Americans to make connections globally, form relationships locally, and acknowledge intra-cultural diversity" (51).

12. While this is a nostalgic moment in the text, it is not overly romanticized, especially considering the discussion of the fight that ensues among a few passengers. Rather than collapse the differences among these groups, this passage emphasizes their coexistence in all their multiplicity or, as Pollard observes, "The unexpressed implication is that wherever slave ships went, connection is likely to exist, worked over though it might be by the superstrate of the master culture" (296).

13. Aunt Cuney's influence, for example, remains with Avey well into adulthood: "In instilling the story of the Ibos in her child's mind, the old woman had entrusted her with a mission she couldn't even name yet had felt duty-bound to fulfill" (42). When Avey marries Jay, he too believes the legend of the Ibos: "I'm with your aunt Cuney and the old woman you were named for. I believe it, Avey. Every word" (115).

14. See, for example, Davis for a detailed analysis of the ways in which the blues has functioned as a form or method of social critique.

15. See duCille for a discussion of early Black women novelists' strategies of dissemblance around issues of sexuality. See also Hines on respectability discourses regarding Black women and sexuality.

16. Marshall's works, from *Brown Girl, Brownstones* to *The Chosen Place, the Timeless People, Daughters,* and *The Fisher King,* all emphasize Diasporic connections and movement.

17. Busia defines a traditional praisesong as a "particular kind of traditional heroic poem. Sung in various communities over the entire continent, praisesongs embrace all

manner of elaborate poetic form, but are always specifically ceremonial social poems, intended to be recited or sung in public at anniversaries and other celebrations, including the funerals of the great" (198). Nonetheless, Busia avers that Marshall's use of the term *praisesong* is appropriate because praisesongs "can also be sung to mark social transition" such as the novel describes (198).

18. Pettis notes, "Halsey Street becomes a metaphor for hundreds of similar streets in hundreds of cities where economic deprivation dominates; where underfed, poorly clothed children live; and where hopelessness and defeat threaten to complete the ravaging of the Black psyche" (123).

19. The novel also illustrates that the nuclear family Jay and Avey have formed does not offer the full range of support they both need in order to survive and thrive on Halsey Street, for Avey rails, "She was somebody who was used to the City. Everybody she knew was there. She couldn't even get to see or talk to her mother" (103–04). In other words, their isolation, and Avey's isolation in particular, exacerbates their marital tensions.

20. Marshall writes: "The last time, with Annawilda, it had taken three people—Jay, the doctor and the ambulance driver—to maneuver her unwieldy body down five flights. . . . This time she might not even make it down to the street and the waiting ambulance. This time when her water broke, Jay might be at work or—and she trembled with rage at the thought—lying somewhere with the woman's legs locked around him. She would have to send Sis to ask a neighbor to go to the candy store up on Broadway and call the ambulance. But by the time all this was done and the ambulance arrived it might be too late. The head might present itself even as they were bringing her down the stairs. She would find herself giving birth on one of the dim landings, with her screams and curses echoing from the top floor to the street, terrifying the children" (102). It is this anticipation of a horrific birthing experience that helps prompt Avey's fury on the fateful Tuesday night.

21. Avey muses on Jay's final words, deciding that, "like someone unable to recover from a childhood trauma—hunger, injury, abuse, a parent suddenly and inexplicably gone—Jerome Johnson never got over Halsey Street. Whereas she had long purged her thoughts and feelings of the place, and had come to regard the years there as having been lived by someone other than herself, it had continued to haunt him, and to figure in some way in nearly everything he did" (88). For Jay, Halsey Street, and the narrative that grows out of it, is the defining feature of his life.

22. The sexual intimacy they once shared also diminishes: "Jay's touch increasingly became that of a man whose thoughts were elsewhere, and whose body, even while merged with hers, felt impatient to leave and join them. . . . Love [became] like a burden he wanted rid of. Like a leg-iron which slowed him in the course he had set for himself" (129).

23. This means Jay vocally rejects any association with the cultural identifiers of Blackness and, rather than acknowledging the impact of institutional racism, blames African Americans for their disadvantages. He exclaims, "That's the trouble with half these Negroes you see out here. Always looking for the white man to give them something instead of getting out and doing for themselves" (131) and "If it was left to me I'd close every dancehall in Harlem and burn every drum! That's the only way these Negroes out here'll begin making any progress" (132). Kubitschek observes that "[Jay's] own suffering makes him vengeful towards those unwilling to pay with their lifeblood

for upward mobility" (55). Jay's skewed pronouncements reify racist notions of Black pathology, placing the full onus of poverty and underachievement on apparently carefree and lazy Blacks. Whereas Jay once identified and sympathized with fellow African Americans, his appropriation of a conservative ethos of respectability engenders a conflict between personal and communal politics and ultimately the denial of communal obligation. *Praisesong* thus shows that this hostility toward race- and class-based affinity engendered by respectability politics reflects a desire, not to somehow "transcend" race, but rather to dismiss the obligations of group solidarity out of shame and fear. This illustration, then, underscores the ways in which respectability politics supports a fundamentally destructive and divisive worldview.

24. Kubitschek notes that "in order to focus her energies on the economic struggle, Avey has censored her own voice. While settled in this pattern, she uses silence as a weapon, hiding her bad faith by indicating that others are simply impolite for bringing up difficult topics" (58). Also see Elia for an extended discussion of the use of silence as a trope in *Praisesong*.

25. However, despite her desire to ignore these moments, Avey is actually unable to remove Marion's objections from her mind: "'Versailles...' Marion had echoed despairingly when Avey had made mention once of the name. 'Do you know how many treaties were signed there, in that infamous Hall of Mirrors divvying up India, the West Indies, the world? Versailles'—repeating it with a hopeless shake of her head" (47; emphasis in original).

26. The Poor People's March was led by Martin Luther King Jr. and the Southern Christian Leadership Conference in order to protest low wages for sanitation workers in 1968.

27. This is a recurrent theme in Black women's literature. For example, Morrison in *The Bluest Eye* (1970) describes this as a fear about the "eruption of funk," or a breakdown of appropriate social behavior that might pejoratively mark one as a working-class Black person.

28. My use of the term *dis-ease* is culled from Christian and from Wilentz, *Healing Narratives*.

29. Marshall writes, "When [Avey] mentioned it [i.e., her self-misrecognition] to her doctor he had laughed; a sure sign, he had said, of money in the bank" (49). Although Avey's doctor is dismissive, his diagnosis is not entirely untrue, for it is her obsession with money and class status that has caused this psychic schism.

30. This realization also brings the dream of Aunt Cuney into sharp relief, for as Sandiford contends, Aunt Cuney "did not call [Avey] to renounce her right to the White Plains myth. . . . Rather Cuney was inviting her grand-niece to possess White Plains materiality without being possessed by it" (389).

31. These rituals include leaving roasted corn as an offering and pouring libations to welcome ancestral spirits.

32. Collier contends: "Although Marshall never states this explicitly, it is obvious that Lebert Joseph is the incarnation of the African deity Legba—trickster, guardian of the crossroads where all ways meet. Like Lebert Joseph, Legba is a lame old man in ragged clothes. Intensely personal and beloved, Legba is the liaison between man and the gods. He is vital to numerous rituals, both in West Africa and in the New World. Thus Lebert Joseph, in his implied role of Legba, contains many linkages: Africa and the Diaspora; the carnate and the spirit worlds; the present generation, the ancestors,

and the yet unborn" (312). However, both Benjamin and McNeil argue that Lebert Joseph is an allusion to another West African trickster figure, Anancy. See also Busia for more on Lebert's role in the novel and Gates for more on Legba's connection to the African trickster figure Esu-Elegbara.

33. Upon disembarking from the *Bianca Pride*, the Carriacouans on their way to the Excursion treat Avey not as a stranger or a tourist but rather as an insider, a participant in the festivities. Through this repeated "recognition," Marshall suggests a sort of transnational kinship between Avey and the out-islanders.

34. Janice Lee Liddell also asserts that Avey's trip to the most eastern part of the Caribbean—the islands closest to the continent of Africa—marks "Avey's essential reversal of the journey her African ancestors took as they trekked across the Atlantic from Africa to the New World" (39).

35. On the *Emmanuel C*, Lebert places Avey in a seat of distinction, next to the elders of the Carriacouan community. Like other aspects of her trip, these women again bring her back to her childhood and remind her of the "presiding mothers of Mount Olivet Baptist (her own mother's church long ago)—the Mother Caldwells and Mother Powes and Mother Greens, all those whose great age and long service to the church had earned them a title even more distinguished than 'sister' and a place of honor in the pews up front" (194).

36. Moreover, like the presiding mothers at Mount Olivet, these Carriacou matrons preside over Avey's sickness in another way: "Their lips close to her ears they spoke to her, soothing, low-pitched words which not only sought to comfort and reassure her, but which from their tone even seemed to approve of what was happening" (205). Every time Avey retches, the presiding mothers of the *Emmanuel C* murmur "*Bon*" or "Good," somehow knowing that Avey is not just regurgitating food but also eliminating the toxic elements of her life that have literally sickened her. While they are not sermonizing, their words are an exhortation of sorts that encourages the backslidden Avey toward her own salvation.

37. Avey sees the Beg Pardon enacted: "A small band of supplicants endlessly repeated the few lines that comprised the [song], pleading and petitioning not only for themselves and for their friends and neighbors present in the yard, but for all their far flung kin as well—the sons and daughters, grands and great-grands in Trinidad, Toronto, New York, London" (236). This praisesong both honors the raw power of the ancestors and is a sort of lamentation for those unable to participate. Though Avey cannot call her nation, with her presence at the Excursion she ceases to be part of the countless outside the yard's circle. That is, her very presence signals a participation in an ethic of community support and accountability that recognizes both the fragmented history of Blacks across the Diaspora and the ways in which Black folk have come together to form sustaining bonds of family and community.

38. Marshall frequently depicts celebratory rituals that reflect Diasporic culture. This scene is not unlike that of the marchers during carnival in her second novel, *The Chosen Place, the Timeless People*.

39. Thorsson contends that in this moment "Marshall, while acknowledging African retentions in the creole dances, is not arguing for a long-held set of African practices, but for a shared culture of yearning, of 'longing' for the very connection that these dances provide. The memory that sates this longing is not of others' experiences, but of one's own life" (649).

40. Marion's term of endearment is an allusion to Gwendolyn Brooks's poem "The Children of the Poor."

41. Likewise, Bröck asserts, "*Praisesong* is a novel clearly connected with the late seventies and eighties, operating, as it does, within a Black middle-class setting, a context that has become much more relevant for American society in the past few years than it was before, in terms of sheer numbers, politics, and the social status of Afro-Americans. My point is that Marshall, while on the one hand using this context as a backdrop, does so without uncritically dramatizing a protagonist's tragic defeat in isolated spaces" (88).

2 / Sins of the Mother?

1. H. Adlai Murdoch contends that despite the "concatenation of sex and race, geography and culture" that would "cause the novel to diverge somewhat from the white, male, European tradition," *Annie John* should be classified primarily as a bildungsroman because of the novel's preoccupation with coming of age and understanding the world (326). Murdoch and other scholars have celebrated *Annie John* as an important Caribbean bildungsroman, akin to such landmark texts such as Merle Hodge's *Crick Crack Monkey* and George Lamming's *In the Castle of My Skin*.

2. I refer to Mrs. Annie John, mother of Annie and wife of Alexander, as Mrs. John, except when discussing her premotherhood past, in which case she is referred to as Annie Senior. I refer to her daughter as Annie.

3. Patricia Ismond, in reference to the portrayal of childhood in *Annie John*, argues: "*Annie John* traces the various stages of [Annie's] progress from childhood to adolescence in terms of this relationship with her mother. It began with the fullness of maternal love, care and nurturing in infancy. The experience of being 'weaned,' a sundering between herself and her mother, marked the passage to girlhood. So that growing up and beginning to fend for herself meant an experience of increasing disfavor with her mother, presaging a silent opposition and undeclared war between them" (338). Ismond uses psychoanalytic discourse to outline the intensity of both the bonding and the separation that Annie and Mrs. John experience, concluding that Mrs. John's change in behavior is the catalyzing factor for the novel's central conflicts and Annie's increasing estrangement from her community. Ismond's analysis is typical not only of contemporary readings of Kincaid's work but also of the criticism written twenty years after the publication of Kincaid's first novel. See, for example, Covi; Niesen de Abruña; and Dutton.

4. Bouson describes Kincaid's works as almost completely autobiographical and sees Kincaid as thoroughly engaged in an ongoing project of both self-representation and confrontation with the specter of her own mother. She describes Kincaid's voice as an "effective way to talk back to her mother, allowing her to get the final word in her ongoing, internal dispute with her mother" (26). Indeed, for Bouson, much of Kincaid's work aims to bring a formerly silenced daughter to voice. See also Braziel and Gilmore for more on the role of autobiography in *Annie John* and throughout Kincaid's oeuvre.

5. Nevertheless, in the same interview Kincaid also reveals that her acclaimed daughterly voice is inseparable from and, indeed, built upon the voice of her mother: "My second book, *Annie John*, is about a girl's relationship with her mother because the fertile soil of my creative life is my mother. When I write, in some things I use

my mother's voice, because I like my mother's voice. I like the way she sees things" ("Jamaica Kincaid" [Cudjoe] 402). Thus Kincaid herself troubles the notion that the maternal is always an antagonistic force, revealing a much more complicated tension between her incessant rewriting of her familial history and her unabashed admiration for her mother's worldview.

6. Evelyn O' Callaghan suggests, "Annie John's disenchantment with the myopia of her colonized mother . . . suggests Antigua's disenchantment with colonial ideology" (*Woman Version* 7). O'Callaghan interprets Mrs. John as an allegorical figure who signifies betrayal and repression. Like the psychoanalytical and autobiographical criticism of the novel, this postcolonial reading underscores the mother as the exemplification of hypocrisy and conflict. For more on this critical perspective, see S. Alexander; M. Ferguson; and O'Callaghan, *Woman Version*.

7. More specifically, Thomas insists that Kincaid replays a problematic mother-daughter narrative throughout her body of work: "In Kincaid, who is too often read alone, apart from other Black and Caribbean writers, it is the sexual crisis of a Black mother's daughter in the context of British colonization which drives the discourse, not in just one or two texts but in her lifework as a whole" (126). Indeed, Greg Thomas has suggested that Kincaid's body of work becomes increasingly "politically conservative" and heterosexist over the years (105).

8. Thomas notes: "The girl-child is totally enraptured by the woman, who turns out to be irreplaceable in the passionate psyche of adolescence and adulthood. When this same love administers a new order of body relations, determined specifically by British colonial relations, the loving child is nothing short of crushed. As she strives to turn her bitterness into hatred in order to cope with this loss of childhood romance, she escapes into a world of fantasy supplied by the colonizer. The daughter is quick to surpass the mother in her adoption of alien norms" (126). This passage essentially describes the plot of every Kincaid novel thus far. "Girl," the opening chapter of Kincaid's first book, a collection of short stories entitled *At the Bottom of the River*, is a caustic diatribe in which a mother admonishes a silent daughter against behaviors that would make her the "slut [she is] so bent on becoming." The collection's other stories are largely repeated longings for eroticized mother-daughter spaces. In addition to *Annie John*, Kincaid's subsequent offerings such as *Lucy*, *The Autobiography of my Mother*, even *My Brother* and *Mr. Potter*, texts ostensibly about men, incessantly rework similar mother-daughter themes.

9. While I use Thomas's analysis as a point of departure, my analysis of Kincaid differs from his in crucial ways. His argument seeks to debunk Kincaid's centrality in some feminist discourse on family and identity. My goal in this chapter is to add nuance to critical studies of *Annie John* without dismissing the novel completely.

10. At the start of the novel, Annie is ten, Mrs. John is forty, and Mr. John is seventy-five. As a bildungsroman, the novel is unsurprisingly focused on growing older. However, Annie's aging is not the only concern. In the last chapter, Annie reveals, "My mother's name is Annie also. My father's name is Alexander, and he is thirty-five years older than my mother. Two of his children are four and six years older than she is" (130).

11. Interestingly, the Johns live in a nuclear family seemingly without extended kinship networks nearby, in what is somewhat of an anomaly for a Black Caribbean family of their class.

12. While the "young lady business" may have indeed changed the tone of Annie and her mother's relationship during Annie's puberty, it is an indication of a larger institutional impetus, one whose roots are very deep. Even as a child, Annie did not simply observe her mother every day while basking in a pre-Oedipal union. All throughout childhood, she was already being groomed for "ladyhood." Accompanying her mother shopping, assisting her in the kitchen, and sharing in other activities with her mother have deep meaning; unbeknownst to Annie, the childhood "play" of these activities is a dress rehearsal for the role of wife and mother she is expected to fulfill eventually. While Kincaid's narrative emphasizes Annie's discomfiture at the changes in her mother's attention, it also reveals that the "young lady business" did not begin at puberty—it began almost at birth. Thus there is no "true" pre-Oedipal space in the novel; indoctrination with the ideals of respectability is not a marker of adolescence (though certainly it gathers speed during this time), but rather a marker of appropriate female socialization in colonial society.

13. For example, Mrs. John is extremely disdainful of the "unladylike" Mrs. Catherine, who is in a nonmonogamous partnership with their local fishermen, Mr. Nigel and Mr. Earl (122). Mrs. Catherine is decidedly a woman and not a lady.

14. Simone A. James Alexander notes that, "subsumed by colonialist beliefs, Mrs. John's vision is colored, perhaps by a generation of similar experiences" (53).

15. Likewise, when Annie is six years old Mrs. John helps her open a savings account and, to instill thriftiness, does not allow her to "withdraw even a farthing from [the] bank account until just a few weeks" before her departure to England (141).

16. These are not simple reminiscences; rather, as MacDonald-Smythe argues, "These stories speak of the mother's desire to establish a personal history, the recording of her life and the establishment of her identity as woman and mother, albeit an identity which participates in the power of an enveloping folk world, albeit one which has been partially co-opted into heterosexual servitude" (62).

17. Mrs. John's influence also prompts Annie to make another conclusion, this time with regard to a white classmate named Ruth: "Ruth had come all the way from England. Perhaps she did not want to be in the West Indies at all. Perhaps she wanted to be in England, where no one would remind her constantly of the terrible things her ancestors had done; perhaps she had felt even worse when her father was a missionary in Africa. I could see how Ruth felt from looking at her face. Her ancestors had been the masters, while ours had been the slaves. She had such a lot to be ashamed of, and by being with us every day she was always being reminded" (76). Rather than seeing herself as bearing the stigma of having enslaved ancestors, Annie places the stigma on the descendants of the enslavers.

18. Olmos and Paravisini-Gebert define obeah as a "belief system divided into two broad categories. The first involves the casting of spells for various purposes, both good and evil: protecting oneself, property, family, or loved ones; harming real or perceived enemies; bringing fortune in love, employment, personal or business pursuits. The second involves healing through the application of knowledge of herbal and animal medicinal properties. Obeah, thus conceived, is not a religion as such but a system of beliefs grounded in spirituality and an acknowledgment of the supernatural and involving aspects of witchcraft, sorcery, magic, spells, and healing" (286). See their book and Simpson for more on obeah.

19. Annie reflects: "I was afraid of the dead, as was everyone I knew. We were afraid

of the dead because we never could tell when they might show up again. Sometimes they showed up in a dream, but that wasn't so bad, because they usually only brought a warning, and in any case you wake up from a dream. But sometimes they would show up standing under a tree just as you were passing by. Then they might follow you home, and even though they might not be able to come into your house, they might wait for you and follow you wherever you went; in that case, they would never give up until you joined them. My mother knew of many people who had died in such a way. My mother knew of many people who had died, including her own brother" (4). Here Kincaid describes a world where death is not the end of interaction with the living and where the dead hold a great power over their living counterparts.

20. However, in showing that Mr. John's former lovers also wield obeah, albeit for more destructive purposes, the novel reveals that obeah has the potential to also be used malevolently.

21. Of Annie's depression-like illness, Kincaid writes, "I looked inside my head. A black thing was lying down there, and it shut out all my memory of the things that had happened to me. I knew that in my fifteen years a lot of things had happened, but now I couldn't put my finger on a single thing. As I fell asleep, I had no feeling in any part of my body except the back of my skull, which felt as if it would split open and spew out huge red flames" (112).

22. Tiffin rightfully argues, "Western medical constructions of the body are challenged by competing curative systems, symbolized by the ordering and reordering of medicines in the cabinet during Annie's illness: the first in accord with the more eclectic philosophies of Annie's mother and Ma Jolie; the second by Annie's father (who is more deeply entrenched within Western constructions of the body and with medical science's exclusionist philosophy)" (912).

23. Ma Chess takes medicinal obeah baths only "in water in which things animal and vegetable had been boiled for a long time. Before she took this bath, she first swam in the sea" (124). For Ma Chess, bathing is not simply an act that removes dirt from the skin; this cleansing goes beyond the outer surface.

24. When Ma Chess first observes Annie on her sickbed, she pronounces to Mrs. John: "Not like Johnnie. Not like Johnnie at all" (124). This statement has a multivalent meaning. Ma Chess is referring to her only son, Johnnie, who was presumably killed by an obeah curse. The statement refers to the hallowed position the long-dead Johnnie occupies in the Chess family imaginary (Kincaid writes that the women in the Chess family "worshipped" Johnnie while he was both alive and dead). Thus Annie could never be like her uncle Johnnie. However, notwithstanding Ma Chess's veneration of her son, the text follows this declaration with a detailed account of Ma Chess's loving care of her granddaughter without the use of obeah. Therefore, the pronouncement that Annie is "not like Johnnie at all" also refers to Ma Chess's diagnosis of Annie's illness. An obeah curse did not injure Annie.

25. Indeed, Ma Chess "regretted that [Mrs. John] didn't show more of an interest in obeah things," meaning she lamented the fact that Mrs. John did not want to be an obeah woman (123).

26. Interestingly, Mr. John does seem to be using obeah cures at the end of the novel, when Annie reveals that her father drinks teas made from herbs and bark rather than the medicines his doctor prescribes. It seems that the belief in obeah cures wins out in the end.

27. Annie describes the Red Girl as a "beautiful thing": "She had big, broad, flat feet, and they were naked to the bare ground; her dress was dirty, the skirt and blouse tearing away from each other at one side; the red hair . . . was matted and tangled; her hands were big and fat, and her fingernails held at least ten anthills of dirt under them. And on top of that, she had such an unbelievable, wonderful smell, as if she had never taken a bath in her whole life" (57).

28. See O'Callaghan, "Compulsory Heterosexuality," and Thomas for a detailed discussion of queer sexuality in *Annie John*.

29. It is important to note that Annie keeps what she sees as her mother's disapproval to herself: "Except for the ordinary things that naturally came up, I never told her about my changed feeling for my mother. I could see in what high regard Gwen held me, and I couldn't bear for her to see the great thing I had had once and then lost without an explanation" (48).

30. Likewise, MacDonald-Smythe argues: "Annie's desire for autonomy repeats her mother's earlier departure from an autocratic father and imitates Ma Chess's willful emancipation from the confines of domesticity. Each female is in fact seeking a space within which to articulate her selfhood. Annie hopes to find freedom in a trunk, Ma Chess finds it outside the house, a domestic space that had muted her voice and the authority of her Black magic. Her daughter, Annie Sr., on the other hand, uses the domestic as a secular stage upon which she plays out the magic of her good mothering" (49).

31. After describing how everything around her was built or made by her mother and father, Annie concludes: "When I look at things in a certain way, I suppose I should say that the two of them made me with their own hands" (132–33). The realization that she is a "product" of her parents is partly what prompts Annie to venture out in a world where she can (re)create herself.

3 / Daughters of This Land

1. Liberation theology is a form of Christian ideology, originally developed by South American Roman Catholics, that has become both international and interdenominational and is of particular importance for Blacks across the Americas. This doctrine emphasizes social and political liberation in the teachings of Jesus Christ. See, for example, the work of Brazilian education reformer Paulo Freire and of African American theologian James Cone.

2. That is not to say that Aristide is flawless. In fact, he has faced accusations of corruption and human rights abuses. Danticat is ambivalent herself about Aristide. When asked in 2003 to assess Aristide, Danticat claims, "My view still is that he was voted in power. I can't really gauge how much change there's been since 1990. I know he has his supporters and detractors. I will quote Brecht: 'I'm on the side of the people.' Whatever the people decide about him, I will follow. Life's hard in Haiti right now. And the hardest thing is that the future does not lie with one person. A lot of the focus is often put on him. He can't save Haiti. No one individual can. He can't pull the strings and make everything better. It all becomes a personality cult: Can one person save Haiti?" (Barsamian).

3. Although *matriarchy* often has a negative connotation in African American and Black Caribbean social discourse, Danticat uses the term loosely to denote a family filled primarily with women. That is, Danticat is not referring to a social system where

women occupy seats of institutional power or where they emasculate men. Indeed, the novel describes a family where, although men are largely absent, kyriocentric thinking and behavior are very prevalent.

4. When asked in an interview, "Do you think that the mothers' concern with their daughters' sexuality, the concern for virginity as expressed in the book, is something that is particularly and singularly Haitian?," Danticat avers, "Oh no. *Not at all.* The 'testing' in the book . . . goes back to the Virgin Mary. If you look at the apocryphal gospels, after the Virgin Mary gives birth to the Christ child, a midwife comes and tries to test her virginity by insertion, if you can imagine. The family in the book was never meant to be a 'typical' Haitian family, if there is ever a typical family in any culture" ("Author Q and A," emphasis in original). Indeed, after charges that she was suggesting that testing was a nationwide cultural practice across Haiti, Danticat appended an afterword to the novel where she writes a letter to Sophie that "cautions readers not to take a narrowly allegorical or sociological approach to the novel" (Francis, "Uncovered Stories" 73). Danticat writes, "Tired of protesting, I feel I must explain. Of course, not all Haitian mothers are like your mother. Not all Haitian daughters are tested, as you have been" (*Breath* 236).

5. Debra Walker King defines body fictions as the "externally defined identities and representations as bodies" that can overdetermine how we understand Black women's lives (vii).

6. Historian David Nicholls defines *noirisme* as the "most active and influential protest movement of the post [American] occupation years" (167). The philosophy was an offshoot of the philosophy of Jean Price-Mars and other Haitian ethnologists. Nicholls goes to argue that "these *noiristes* of the 1930s emphasized Haiti's African past, believing that as Haitians were basically African in their genetic composition their culture and social structure should be allowed to mirror this fact" (167).

7. In the *vodou* pantheon, the *Marassas* are a powerful cult of twins, known to be demanding and capricious. Alfred Metraux writes: "Twins (marassa), living and dead, are endowed with supernatural power which makes them exceptional beings. In the Voodoo pantheon they hold a privileged position beside the *grands mystères.* Some people would even claim that they are more powerful than the *loa.* They are invoked and saluted at the beginning of a ceremony immediately after Legba in some regions. . . . They even come before him" (146). In addition to Metraux, see Desmangles and Laguerre for more detailed discussions of the *Marassa* figures in *vodou.*

8. Martine's desire to control Sophie is exhibited in more subtle ways as well. When Sophie first arrives at her mother's home, Martine introduces her to a "tall well-dressed doll . . . caramel-colored with a fine pointy nose" (44). After unbraiding the doll's hair and putting pajamas on it, Martine reveals, "She is like a friend to me. She kept me company while we were apart" (45). It is clear that her fair-skinned doll has been a proxy for her absent daughter, and I would argue that the doll symbolizes even more about Martine's mothering: it also reflects Martine's desire to infantilize Sophie, which is connected to her desire for them to be *Marassas.* Martine's doll ultimately indicates her willingness to subsume Sophie's identity to one she has the control to fully shape.

9. Oshun, alternately spelled Ochun and Osun, is an orisha strongly identified with love, sensuality, beauty, and rivers. Although not a mother goddess per se like her fellow orisha Yemoja, Oshun is, nonetheless, the "divinity of fertility and feminine

essence. Women appeal to her for child-bearing and for the alleviation of female disorders. She is fond of babies and is sought if a baby becomes ill" (Karade 26). When Yoruban religion was brought to the Americas (during slavery), Oshun and other orishas experienced name changes and/or became syncretized with Christian saints. Erzulie, the mother/fertility goddess of Haitian *vodou* cosmology, who is also syncretized with the Virgin Mary and is an important figure in *Breath*, has aspects of Oshun.

10. Likewise, in another part of Oshun's mythography, the goddess is again understood as a powerful and underestimated force: "Once when the seventeen odu came down from heaven, they comprised sixteen men plus a woman. Once on earth the men neglected the seventeenth who was Oshun. They snubbed her because she was a woman. And Oshun sat down, and watched them, and *laughed*. Instantly their luck turned. Instantly people shivered with a first attack of fever. Semen dried up and men became impotent. Things got worse and, not making the right conclusion, the sixteen odu returned to heaven to ask God's advice. 'How many are you' God asked. *Sixteen*. 'How many were you when you left heaven?' *Seventeen*. 'Well, then, you left someone behind and that is the source of the problem.' Oshun's water was drowning their fire. The only solution was direct and immediate sacrifice to Oshun lest she destroy the world with her hidden power of the night. The sixteen odu begged and begged her, sacrificed and sacrificed, and finally she relented and the world began to move again" (Thompson 252).

11. While Tante Atie is technically Sophie's aunt, she acts as a surrogate mother, or what Collins has articulated as an "othermother," a woman who assists or in some cases supplants a biological mother in her maternal duties (*Black Feminist Thought* 178).

12. The novel opens with Atie rejecting a Mother's Day card from Sophie, claiming that the card "is for a mother, your mother. . . . When it is Aunt's Day, you can make me one" (9). Atie reifies the primacy of biological motherhood in this moment.

13. Atie takes great pride in their family name and heritage, despite their marginalized social standing: when she and Sophie walk by their family's burial plot, Atie advises Sophie to "walk straight, you are in the presence of family" and reverently identifies the names of the deceased buried there. This brief moment signals the immense respect Atie has for her ancestors and also her commitment to upholding their memories. Atie goes on to explain the origin of their surname: "Our family name, Caco, it is the name of a scarlet bird. A bird so crimson, it makes the reddest hibiscus or the brightest flame trees seem white. The Caco bird, when it dies, there is always a rush of blood that rises to its neck and the wings, they look so bright, you would think them on fire" (150). The Caco bird, especially with its fiery death imagery, brings to mind the mythical phoenix that ceremoniously burns itself on a funeral pyre only to triumphantly reemerge from its own ashes. This phoenix imagery is redolent of the possibilities of rebirth and transformation, themes at the center of Atie's, and eventually Sophie's, stories. The name Caco also has several other meanings. It clearly resonates with the word *cacao*, a crop important to the local economy in Haiti. Additionally, Caco refers to the "Caco Wars" fought in Haiti during the first quarter of the twentieth century. In each of these wars Haitians, especially those from the countryside, formed militias and guerrilla groups against an imposed American military presence for control of their government. The Cacos are in many ways a symbol of Haitian nationalism, independence, and revolutionary spirit. (See historian Mary

Renda's *Taking Haiti* for a more detailed discussion of the Caco Wars). However, there is also a darker side to the Caco Wars. During this insurrection, women's bodies were targets for war (Francis, "Silences" 78). Not only were members of the U.S. forces routinely and systematically assaulting Haitian women, but also official Haitian histories of the Caco War often elide the memory of women's suffering. Thus the Caco women are connected to the flora and fauna of Haiti, its cacao and the caco bird, and Haiti's complicated history of revolution and war. Through the use of a surname with such multivalent meanings, *Breath* signifies on the variety of stories the Caco women are endowed to tell.

14. In this interview, Danticat also connects her conclusions about coming to voice in written and oral forms with Paule Marshall's discussion of her literary influences in the "From the Poets in the Kitchen." See Danticat, "Interview," for more connections between Marshall and Danticat.

15. Danticat uses sensual, romantic imagery to describe Atie and Louise's relationship. For example, after reading a poem, Atie "and Louise strolled into the night, like silhouettes on a picture postcard" (135). In another instance, Danticat writes that while the two women were comforting each other, "Louise buried her head in Tante Atie's shoulder. Their faces were so close that their lips could meet if they both turned at the same time" (138). Thus, while Danticat never outright describes their relationship as sexual, sexual imagery abounds.

16. Martine asserts to Sophie: "The old girl [Atie] lost her nerve. She lost her fight. You should have seen us when we were young. We always dreamt of becoming important women. We were going to be the first women doctors from my mother's village. We would not stop at being doctors either. We were going to be engineers too. Imagine our surprise when we found out we had limits" (*Breath* 43).

17. Chancy contends that "the line Danticat leaves untranslated suggests the interconnectedness of like spirits: she speaks my voice, thus, she is my voice. And since Atie's tongue is creole, it can never be entirely translated, nor does her love attempt that transmutation" (131).

18. This reclamation is signaled by Atie's recitation of Sophie's Mother's Day poem (108) and her declaration that it a precious memory (120).

19. Sophie becomes Martine's *Marassa*, a twin to her pain, rather than just experiencing a deep, unfathomable love for her mother: "Even though she had forced it on me, of her sudden will, we were now even more than friends. We were twins, in spirit. *Marassas*" (200).

20. Nonetheless, despite the depiction of Joseph as Sophie's supportive partner, the novel reveals that the couple have sexual problems not simply because of Sophie's traumatic sexual past: there are also limitations in Joseph's understanding of Sophie's pain, in that he says Sophie "seem[s] to enjoy [sex]" despite her claims to the contrary (196). See also Green for further discussion on Joseph and Sophie's marriage.

21. Martine also shares this Diasporic kinship. She admits, "I feel like I could have been Southern African-American" and then speaks of her experiences in the Afro-Protestant church and her affinity for spirituals (214). Tellingly, her favorite spiritual is "Sometimes I Feel Like a Motherless Child." This exchange underscores that though there are distinct cultural differences there are also unifying rituals that can positively connect African Americans and Blacks of Caribbean descent.

22. Mardorossian observes, "The novel encourages us to see African American

culture within the context of a worldwide Black ethos rather than as a sign of a larger intermixed and hybridized (North) America. It constructs a diasporic Black identity based on a common link to Africa and the history of slavery and opposes this inclusive notion of Blackness to white America's racist and purist ways" (133).

23. Griffin suggests that in this tradition healing denotes "the way in which the body, literally and discursively scarred, ripped, and mutilated, has to learn to love itself, to function in the world with other bodies and often in opposition to those persons and things that seek to destroy it. Of course, the body never can return to a pre-scarred state. It is not a matter of getting back to a 'truer' self, but instead of claiming the body, scars and all—in a narrative of love and care. As such healing does not deny the construction of bodies, but instead suggests that they can be constructed differently, for different ends" (524).

24. The other members of Sophie's therapy group are Chicana and Ethiopian, respectively. Francis rightfully argues that "Danticat is not content to leave Sophie's trauma as an individual experience or a peculiarly Haitian problem; instead she makes evident that sexual traumas are a collective plight shared by postcolonial women" ("Silences" 85).

25. Danticat alludes to the importance of *Santería* by mentioning that Rena, Sophie's therapist, is a *Santería* priestess. See Olmos and Paravisini-Gebert for a larger discussion of *Santería*.

26. Sophie notes that Erzulie was "our goddess of love who doubled for us as the Virgin Mother" (113). Hewett identifies Danticat's use of the word *double* here as a play on words, whereby Sophie recognizes the syncretism not only as a sort of "doubling" she and other Haitians have employed but as a way to differentiate Erzulie from her Christian counterpart (132).

27. Erzulie Freda is described alternately as a white woman. See Karen McCarthy Brown for more on Erzulie's various manifestations.

28. In *Mama Lola*, Karen McCarthy Brown writes, "Ezili Dantò is above all else the mother, the one who bears children. . . . It is well known that Ezili Dantò has not married any of the spirits who are her sexual partners. Being a single mother who raises children on her own is an important part of her identity" (228).

29. That is not to say that the novel fails to critique the *vodou* pantheon, however. See Chancy for an extended look at the novel's critique of Erzulie (124–26). *Breath* nonetheless does portray the goddess's narrative as one that has the potential to empower women.

30. See Rody for an extended discussion of the trope of the "magical daughter" who returns to engage painful histories.

4 / The Language of Family

1. For more on the 1996 Welfare Reform Act, see, for example, Hartman and Reed.

2. The social changes of the 1960s and 1970s, fueled by the civil rights and Black Power movements, the women's rights movement, the gay liberation movement, and other movements for radical social change, not only brought us to what some might argue is a more egalitarian society but also sparked the "culture wars" of the 1980s and '90s. During these times, and indeed into the present, conservative social policies and practices have attempted to erode and undermine much of the progress of the civil rights era. In these subsequent culture wars, narratives about Black pathology

have been employed frequently to justify remaining and increasing marginalization and disenfranchisement. According to these arguments, Blacks are simply unable to function within mainstream society because of broken families, predilections toward crime, innate dysfunction, and a whole host of other supposed deviations. Popular discourse indebted to flawed paradigms of the Moynihan Report and other ideologies has portrayed Blacks, and in particular Black families, as entrenched in pathology, so much so that it is doubtful they could ever, as a group, arrive at any sort of "normalcy." See Alexander-Floyd; Bell; D'Souza; Herrnstein and Murray; Kelley; Sowell; and West for further reading, from various political perspectives, on the culture wars.

3. The most extended critique of *Push* comes in the form of Percival Everett's biting satirical novel *Erasure*, which lampoons both Sapphire and *Push*, as well as Alice Walker's *The Color Purple* and Richard Wright's *Native Son*. In *Erasure*, *Push* becomes the best-selling novel *We's Lives in Da Ghetto*. Everett's narrator, the aptly named Thelonious "Monk" Ellison, is, rather like Everett, a writer whose critically acclaimed, though somewhat obscure, texts are sometimes overlooked in bookstores, overshadowed by more titillating urban fiction. Ellison's work languishes because it is not considered "Black enough" (43). Ellison is driven to paroxysms of rage after seeing the success of *We's Lives in Da Ghetto* and thereafter writes his own "ghetto novel," *My Pafology* (later renamed *Fuck*), a text that is a clear reworking of *Native Son*. What is perhaps most compelling about Everett's text with regard to *Push* is its delineation of the publishing industry's insatiable demands for sensationalist fiction featuring "authentic" Black vernacular. More particularly, Everett blasts Sapphire as an opportunist who received a $500,000 advance for her first novel, rather than as a literacy activist (her own self-description) who makes space for the silenced.

4. Kelley further contends that this behavioral analysis falls apart when applied to wealthier folk "who are presumed to be 'functional' and 'normative'" but who may in fact engage in "risky" or irresponsible behaviors similar to those cited as endemic to poor Blacks (19). The difference, Kelley insists, is that public discourse depicts poor urban Blacks often monolithically, either as passive victims of circumstance or as willful, destructive agents, with little desire to consider the diversity of Black lived experience. For more on the critical debates regarding the underclass, see Auletta; Katz; Kelley; and Lawson.

5. Ms. Weiss's further rationale for the latter assumption comes from the fact that the Each One Teach One program focuses on language acquisition rather than seemingly more practical job-readiness skill building. In Precious's file, Weiss writes, "Ms Rain places great emphasis on writing and reading books. Little work is done with computers or the variety of multiple choice pre-G.E.D. and G.E.D. workbooks available at low cost to JPTA programs" (119). Interestingly, Weiss's words echo Mary's declaration that computers trump any sort of print literacy. Weiss asserts that, with what she identifies as Precious's "obvious intellectual limitations," the "time and resources it would require for this young woman to get a G.E.D. or into college would be considerable" (119). The implication is not only that this is economically unfeasible but that Precious is clearly undeserving of such resources. Precious, then, should aim to attain, not a rigorous liberal arts education, but rather a more practical and indeed minimalist vocational education.

6. Precious remembers Miz West as a neighbor whom she ran errands for as a child

and who offered her kindness on occasion. However, most of the individuals Precious encounters are either openly hostile or apathetic.

7. In addition to frequently assaulting and abusing Precious, Mary expects her daughter to perform all the housework and household errands: "Why Mama never do anything? One time I ax her, when I get up from her knocking me down, she say, That's what you here for" (22).

8. Mary does not reveal her own sexual abuse of Precious in this therapy session; nonetheless, Precious has been frequently sexually dominated by not only Carl but Mary as well, and she frequently remembers these traumatic violations. Like Carl, Mary beats her daughter if she resists or complains. Thus Mary not only allows and enables Precious's abuse by Carl but also exerts a similar brand of sexual tyranny, underscoring the notion that Precious's body is not to be protected but instead to be always open to exploitation and another's sexual satisfaction.

9. Interestingly, Precious responds to her mother's claims with ambivalence, foreshadowing the eventual break with her mother's thinking she will experience: "Too far where I wanna ax. I don't know how I feel about people with hair like that" (40; emphasis in original).

10. See, for example, Banks and Rooks for detailed discussions surrounding the identity politics of Black hair.

11. Lusane notes, "The NOI has been attractive to many African Americans for the work that the organization does in communities around issues such as drug trafficking, AIDS, youth gangs, and security in inner-city housing projects. While other Black organizations have little visible presence at the street level in the Black community, the highly visible NOI—with its distinct persona of clean-shaven, bow-tie wearing, and pressed dress suit-sporting men—is ubiquitous as it provides security services, operates small businesses, and sells its newspaper, *The Final Call*. The complete abandonment by the state of any responsibility for the wretched and oppressive life that poor African Americans struggle with on a daily basis is further reason for the often positive reception that the NOI receives from the Black community" (182–83).

12. Regarding heroin addicts, Precious muses: "There eyez is like far away space ships. they don see you, only smell pepul go buy for money. They money dogs. If they sniff money they will try to take it. I guess. Thas whut I always here. We hate dope addicts. We, me, norml pepul" (105).

13. According to Doane and Hodges, "Sapphire allows Precious to push about as far as she can. The community of nurturing women Precious discovers are all clients and employees of a welfare system that is itself threatened. Yet compassionate and well-intentioned individuals use its resources to push for alternatives that suggest a different more cooperative social order" (130).

14. Daly rightfully contends that "although childbirth is usually regarded as an interruption in one's education, Precious transforms it into a chapter in her schooling . . . [reflecting] on the relationship between the history of slavery and her own rape." *Push* does not gloss over the fact that giving birth to her second child, Abdul, could very well mean the end of Precious's formal schooling (it includes a protracted debate between Precious and Ms. Rain about the virtues of adoption and whether Precious will be able to care for both herself and an infant), but it underscores that Precious is being shaped by both formal schooling and her own ongoing interpretation and analysis of the master narratives that have shaped her life.

15. Take, for example, the rise of hip-hop literature or "street lit." While this genre is certainly indebted to the ghetto tales of authors such as Donald Goines and Iceberg Slim, its current iterations are largely novels written by black women. Rapper and activist Sista Souljah's 1999 debut novel *The Coldest Winter Ever* is often considered the inaugural text in the increasingly popular genre, which often features salacious stories of urban blacks surviving and thriving on mean streets across the United States.

16. Rountree and Michlin have both argued that *Push* employs a blues aesthetic. However, my reading is more aligned with Brittney Cooper's reading of the novel, which suggests that "*Push* actively resists a singular reading through the blues tradition, because it is the social concerns of the hip-hop generation that primarily inform the protagonist's negotiation of age-old questions about motherhood, sexuality, family, and racism" (4).

17. Referencing the years 1984–92, Cobb argues that what made the era "worthy of the term golden—an adjective gleaned from that longest glorified of precious metals in hip hop—was the sheer number of stylistic innovations that came into existence," citing a range of artists such as 2 Live Crew, Big Daddy Kane, Doug E. Fresh, KRS-One, MC Lyte, NWA, Queen Latifah, Rakim, and Slick Rick (47).

18. See Chang; K. Jones; Pough; and Ramsey for more on hip-hop's Diasporic origins.

19. Precious's road to literacy also has another connection to slavery in that it mirrors the desire to read and write and the trope of literacy as freedom seen in such slave narratives such as Frederick Douglass's.

20. See Brittney Cooper for more on the role of sampling in the novel.

Works Cited

Administration for Children and Families. "Fact Sheet: The Personal Responsibility and Work Opportunity Reconciliation Act of 1996." 1996. www.gpo.gov/fdsys/pkg/PLAW-104publ193/html/PLAW-104publ193.htm. 1 Oct. 2012.

Alexander, M. Jacqui. "Keynote Address: Black Women and the Practice of Freedom." Transnational Feminisms and Women in the Diaspora Symposium. University of Alabama. 20 Oct. 2011.

——. *Pedagogies of Crossing: Meditations on Feminism, Sexual Politics, Memory, and the Sacred.* Durham: Duke University Press, 2006.

Alexander, Simone A. James. *Mother Imagery in the Novels of Afro-Caribbean Women.* Columbia: University of Missouri Press, 2001.

Alexander-Floyd, Nikol G. *Gender, Race, and Nationalism in Contemporary Black Politics.* New York: Palgrave Macmillan, 2007.

Auletta, Ken. *The Underclass.* New York: Overlook, 1999.

Bambara, Toni Cade. *The Salt Eaters.* New York: Vintage, 1992.

Banks, Ingrid. *Hair Matters: Beauty, Power, and Black Women's Consciousness.* New York: New York University Press, 2000.

Barker, Lucius J., and Ronald W. Walter, eds. *Jesse Jackson's 1984 Presidential Campaign: Challenge and Change in American Politics.* Urbana: University of Illinois University Press, 1989.

Barnes, Natasha. *Cultural Conundrums: Gender, Race, Nation, and the Making of Caribbean Cultural Politics.* Ann Arbor: University of Michigan Press, 2006.

Barrow, Christine. *Family in the Caribbean: Themes and Perspectives.* Kingston: Ian Randle, 1996.

Bell, Derrick. *Faces at the Bottom of the Well: The Permanence of Racism*. New York: Basic Books, 1993.

Benjamin, Shanna Greene. "Weaving the Web of Reintegration: Locating Aunt Nancy in *Praisesong for the Widow*." *MELUS* 30.1 (2005): 49–67.

Bhuvaneswar, Chaya, and Audrey Shafer. "Survivor of That Time, That Place: Clinical Uses of Violence Survivors' Narratives." *Journal of Medical Humanities* 25.2 (2004): 109–27.

Billingsley, Andrew. *Climbing Jacob's Ladder: The Enduring Legacy of African American Families*. New York: Simon and Schuster, 1992.

Bouson, J. Brooks. *Jamaica Kincaid: Writing Memory, Writing Back to the Mother*. Albany: State University of New York Press, 2005.

Braxton, Joanne. "Ancestral Presence: The Outraged Mother Figure in Contemporary Afra-American Writing." *Wild Women in the Whirlwind: Afro-American Culture and the Contemporary Literary Renaissance*. Ed. Joanne Braxton and Andrée McLaughlin. New Brunswick: Rutgers University Press, 1990.

Braziel, Jana Evans. *Caribbean Genesis: Jamaica Kincaid and the Writing of New Worlds*. Albany: State University of New York Press, 2009.

Bröck, Sabine. "'Transcending the Loophole of Retreat': Paule Marshall's Placing of Female Generations." *Callaloo* no. 30 (Winter 1987): 79–80.

Brodber, Erna. *Jane and Louisa Soon Come Home*. London: New Beacon Books, 1981.

Brody, Jennifer DeVere. *Impossible Purities: Blackness, Femininity, and Victorian Culture*. Durham: Duke University Press, 1998.

Brown, Karen McCarthy. *Mama Lola: A Vodou Priestess in Brooklyn*. Berkeley: University of California Press, 1991.

Brown, Kimberly Nichelle. *Writing the Black Revolutionary Diva: Women's Subjectivity and the Decolonizing Text*. Bloomington: Indiana University Press, 2010.

Bryant, Jacqueline K. *The Foremother Figure in Early Black Women's Literature*. New York: Garland, 1999.

Busia, Abena P. A. "What Is Your Nation? Reconnecting Africa and Her Diaspora through Paule Marshall's *Praisesong for the Widow*." *Changing Our Own Words: Essays on Criticism, Theory, and Writing by Black Women*. Ed. Cheryl A. Wall New Brunswick: Rutgers University Press, 1989.

Carney, Vaughn A. "Publishing's Ugly Obsession." *Wall Street Journal*. 17 June 1996: A14.

Cartwright, Keith. "Notes toward a Voodoo Hermeneutics: Soul Rhythms, Marvelous Transitions, and Passages to the Creole Saints in *Praisesong for the Widow*." *Southern Quarterly* 41.4 (2003): 127–43.

Chancy, Myriam J. A. *Framing Silence: Revolutionary Novels by Haitian Women*. New Brunswick: Rutgers University Press, 1997.

Chang, Jeff. *Can't Stop, Won't Stop: A History of the Hip-Hop Generation.* New York: Picador, 2005.

Christian, Barbara T. "Ritualistic Process and the Structure of Paule Marshall's *Praisesong for the Widow*." *Callaloo* no. 18 (Spring-Summer 1983): 74–84.

Clarke, Edith. *My Mother Who Fathered Me: A Study of the Families in Three Selected Communities of Jamaica.* Kingston: University of the West Indies Press, 2002.

Cliff, Michelle. *Abeng.* Trumansburg, NY: Crossing Press, 1984.

———. *No Telephone to Heaven.* New York: Dutton, 1987.

Cobb, William Jelani. *To the Break of Dawn: A Freestyle on the Hip Hop Aesthetic.* New York: New York University Press, 2008.

Collier, Eugenia. "The Closing of the Circle: Movement from Division to Wholeness in Paule Marshall's Fiction." *Black Women Writers (1950–1980): A Critical Evaluation.* Ed. Mari Evans. New York: Doubleday, 1984. 295–315.

Collins, Patricia Hill. *Black Feminist Thought: Knowledge, Consciousness, and the Politics of Empowerment.* 2nd ed. New York: Routledge, 2000.

———. *Black Sexual Politics: African Americans, Gender, and the New Racism.* New York: Routledge, 2005.

Contee, Cheryl. "Michelle Bachmann Signs Pledge That Says Black Children Better Off During Slavery." *Jack and Jill Politics.* 8 July 2011. www.blackyouthproject.com/2011/07/michelle-bachmann-signs-pledge-that-says-black-children-better-off-during-slavery/. 8 July 2011.

Coontz, Stephanie. *The Way We Never Were: American Families and the Nostalgia Trap.* New York: Basic Books, 1992.

Cooper, Brittney. "Maybe I'll Be a Poet, Rapper: Hip-Hop Feminism and Literary Aesthetics in Sapphire's *Push*." *African American Review.* Forthcoming.

Cooper, Carolyn. *Sound Clash: Jamaican Dancehall Culture at Large.* New York: Palgrave Macmillan, 2004.

Courlander, Harold. *Negro Folk Music.* New York: Columbia University Press, 1963.

Covi, Giovanna. *Jamaica Kincaid's Prismatic Subjects: Making Sense of Being in the World.* London: Mango, 2003.

Daly, Brenda. "Seeds of Shame or Seeds of Change? When Daughters Give Birth to Their Fathers' Children." *This Giving Birth: Pregnancy and Childbirth in American Women's Writing.* Ed. Julie Tharp and Susan MacCullum-Whitcomb. Bowling Green: Bowling Green State University Popular Press, 2000. 103–23.

Danticat, Edwidge. *Breath, Eyes, Memory.* New York: Vintage Contemporaries, 1998.

———. "Author Q and A." Interview. n.d. www.randomhouse.com/acmart/catalog/display.pperl?isbn=9780375705045&view=qa. 5 Sept. 2013.

———. "An Interview with Edwidge Danticat." Interview by Bonnie M. Lyons. *Contemporary Literature* 44.2 (2003): 183–98.

———. "Edwidge Danticat Interview." Interview with David Barsamian. *Progressive*. Oct. 2003. http://progressive.org/mag_intvdanticat. 29 Aug. 2013.

Davies, Carole Boyce. "Black Woman's Journey into Self: A Womanist Reading of Paule Marshall's *Praisesong for the Widow*." *Matatu* 1.1 (1987): 19–34.

———. *Black Women, Writing and Identity: Migrations of the Subject*. New York: Routledge, 1994.

Davies, Carole Boyce, and Elaine Savory Fido, eds. *Out of the Kumbla: Caribbean Women and Literature*. Trenton, NJ: Africa World Press, 1990.

Davis, Angela Y. *Blues Legacies and Black Feminism: Gertrude "Ma" Rainey, Bessie Smith, and Billie Holiday*. New York: Pantheon, 1998.

Desmangles, Leslie G. *The Faces of the Gods: Vodou and Roman Catholicism in Haiti*. Chapel Hill: University of North Carolina Press, 1992.

Doane, Janice, and Devon Hodges. *Telling Incest: Narratives of Dangerous Remembering from Stein to Sapphire*. Ann Arbor: University of Michigan Press, 2001.

Donnell, Alison. *Twentieth-Century Caribbean Literature: Critical Moments in Anglophone Literary History*. London: Routledge, 2006.

Douglass, Frederick. *Narrative of the Life of Frederick Douglass, an American Slave, Written by Himself*. Ed. William L. Andrews and William S. McFeely. New York: W. W. Norton, 1997.

Douglass, Lisa. *The Power of Sentiment: Love, Hierarchy, and the Jamaican Family Elite*. Boulder, CO: Westview Press, 1992.

D'Souza, Dinesh. *The End of Racism: Principles for a Multiracial Society*. New York: Free Press, 1995.

Dubey, Madhu. *Signs and Cities: Black Literary Postmodernism*. Chicago: University of Chicago Press, 2003.

duCille, Ann. *The Coupling Convention: Sex, Text, and Tradition in Black Women's Fiction*. New York: Oxford University Press, 1993.

Dutton, Wendy. "Merge and Separate: Jamaica Kincaid's Fiction." *World Literature Today* 63 (1989): 406–10.

Edmondson, Belinda. *Making Men: Gender, Literary Authority, and Women's Writing in Caribbean Narrative*. Durham: Duke University Press, 1999.

Elia, Nada. *Trances, Dances, and Vociferations: Agency and Resistance in Africana Women's Narratives*. New York: Garland, 2001.

Everett, Percival. *Erasure*. Hanover: University Press of New England, 2001.

Ferguson, Moira. *Jamaica Kincaid: Where the Land Meets the Body*. Charlottesville: University Press of Virginia, 1994.

Ferguson, Roderick A. *Aberrations in Black: Toward a Queer of Color Critique*. Minneapolis: University of Minnesota Press, 2004.

Fiorenza, Elisabeth Schüssler. *Wisdom Ways: Introducing Feminist Biblical Interpretation*. Maryknoll, NY: Orbis Books, 2001.

Foster, Frances Smith. *'Til Death or Distance Do Us Part: Love and Marriage in African America*. Oxford: Oxford University Press, 2010.

Foster, Lorn S. "Avenues for Black Political Mobilization: The Presidential Campaign of Reverend Jesse Jackson." *The Social and Political Implications of the Jesse Jackson Presidential Campaign*. Ed. Lorenzo Morris. New York: Praeger, 1990.

Francis, Donette A. "'Silences Too Horrific to Disturb': Writing Sexual Histories in Edwidge Danticat's *Breath, Eyes, Memory*." *Research in African Literatures* 35.2 (2004): 75–90.

———. "Uncovered Stories: Politicizing Sexual Histories in Third Wave Caribbean Women's Writing." *Black Renaissance Noire* 6.1 (2004): 61–81.

Frazier, E. Franklin. *Black Bourgeoisie*. New York: Free Press, 1997.

———. *The Negro Family in the United States*. New York: Dryden Press, 1951.

Fulton, DoVeanna S. *Speaking Power: Black Feminist Orality in Women's Narratives of Slavery*. Albany: State University of New York Press, 2006.

Gadsey, Meredith. *Sucking Salt: Caribbean Women Writers, Migration, and Survival*. Columbia: University of Missouri Press, 2006.

Gates, Henry Louis. *The Signifying Monkey: A Theory of African-American Literary Criticism*. New York: Oxford University Press, 1988.

Georgia Writers' Project. *Drums and Shadows: Survival Studies among the Georgia Coastal Negroes*. Athens: University of Georgia Press, 1986.

Gerber, Nancy. *Portrait of the Mother-Artist: Class and Creativity in Contemporary American Fiction*. Lanham, MD: Lexington Books, 2003.

Gilmore, Leigh. *The Limits of Autobiography: Trauma and Testimony*. Ithaca: Cornell University Press, 2001.

Green, Tara T. "'When Women Tell Stories': Healing in Edwidge Danticat's *Breath, Eyes, Memory*." *Contemporary African American Fiction: New Critical Essays*. Ed. Dana A. Williams. Columbus: Ohio State University Press, 2009.

Grewal, Inderpal, and Caren Kaplan, eds. *Scattered Hegemonies: Postmodernity and Transnational Feminist Practices*. Minneapolis: University of Minnesota Press, 1994.

Griffin, Farah Jasmine. "Textual Healing: Claiming Black Women's Bodies, the Erotic and Resistance in Contemporary Novels of Slavery." *Callaloo* 19.2 (1996): 519–36.

hampton, dream. "Nia Long's Pride and Joy." *Essence* Aug. 2012: 92+.

Harbawi, Semia. "Against All Odds: The Experience of Trauma and the Economy of Survival in Edwidge Danticat's *Breath, Eyes, Memory*." *Wasafiri* 23.1 (2008): 38–44.

Harnett, Kevin. "When Having Babies Beats Marriage." *Harvard Magazine* July-Aug. 2012: 11+.

Hartman, Chester W., ed. *Challenges to Equality: Poverty and Race in America*. New York: M. E. Sharpe, 2001.

Herrnstein, Richard J., and Charles Murray. *The Bell Curve: Intelligence and Class Structure in American Life*. New York: Free Press, 1996.

Hewett, Heather. "Mothering across Borders: Narratives of Immigrant Mothers in the United States." *Women's Studies Quarterly* 37.3–4 (2009): 121–39.

Higginbotham, Evelyn Brooks. *Righteous Discontent: The Women's Movement in the Black Baptist Church, 1880–1920.* Cambridge, MA: Harvard University Press, 1993.

Hines, Darlene Clark. "Rape and the Inner Lives of Black Women in the Middle West: Preliminary Thoughts on the Culture of Dissemblance." *Words of Fire: An Anthology of African-American Feminist Thought.* Ed. Beverly Guy-Sheftall. New York: New Press, 1995.

Hodge, Merle. *Crick Crack Monkey.* Oxford: Heinemann, 1970.

Ismond, Patricia. "Jamaica Kincaid: 'First They Must Be Children.'" *World Literature Written in English* 28.2 (1988): 336–41.

Jenkins, Candice M. *Private Lives, Proper Relations: Regulating Black Intimacy.* Minneapolis: University of Minneapolis Press, 2007.

John, Catherine A. *Clear Word and Third Sight: Folk Groundings and Diasporic Consciousness in African Caribbean Writing.* Durham: Duke University Press, 2003.

Jones, Gayl. *Corregidora.* Boston: Beacon Press, 1986.

Jones, K. Maurice. *Say It Loud: The Story of Rap Music.* Brookfield, CT: Millbrook, 1999.

Kakutani, Michiko. "A Cruel World, Endless until a Teacher Steps In." *New York Times* 14 June 1996: C29.

Karade, Baba Ifa. *The Handbook of Yoruba Religious Concepts.* Boston: Weiser Books, 1994.

Katz, Michael B., ed. *The "Underclass" Debate: Views from History.* Princeton: Princeton University Press, 1992.

Kelley, Robin D. G. *Yo' Mama's Disfunktional! Fighting the Culture Wars in Urban America.* Boston: Beacon Press, 1997.

Kincaid, Jamaica. *Annie John.* New York: Farrar, Straus and Giroux, 1997.

———. *At the Bottom of the River.* New York: Farrar, Straus and Giroux, 2000.

———. "Jamaica Kincaid and the Modernist Project: An Interview." Interview by Selwyn R. Cudjoe. *Callaloo* 39 (1989): 396–411.

———. "Jamaica Kincaid Hates Happy Endings." Interview by Marilyn Berlin Snell. *Mother Jones* Sept.–Oct. 1997. www.motherjones.com/politics/1997/09/jamaica-kincaid-hates-happy-endings.

King, Debra Walker. "Introduction: Body Fictions." *Body Politics and the Fictional Double.* Ed. Debra Walker King. Bloomington: Indiana University Press, 2000.

Kubitschek, Missy Dehn. "Paule Marshall's Women on Quest." *Black American Literature Forum* 21. 1–2 (1987): 43–60.

LaFont, Suzanne, and Deborah Pruitt. "The Colonial Legacy: Gendered Laws in Jamaica." *Daughters of Caliban: Caribbean Women in the Twentieth Century.* Ed. Consuelo López Springfield. Bloomington: Indiana University Press.

Laguerre, Michel S. *Voodoo Heritage*. Beverly Hills, CA: Sage Publications, 1980.

Lawson, Bill, ed. *The Underclass Question*. Philadelphia: Temple University Press, 1992.

"Leaders Call for Focus on Family, Unity at Independence." *Jamaica Observer*. 6 Aug. 2011. www.jamaicaobserver.com/news/ Leaders-call-for-focus-on-family--unity-at-Independence 9384687.

Liddell, Janice Lee. "Agents of Pain and Redemption in Sapphire's *Push.*" *Arms Akimbo: Africana Women in Contemporary Literature*. Ed. Janice Lee Liddell and Yakini Belinda Kemp. Gainesville: University Press of Florida, 1999.

Loichot, Valérie. "Edwidge Danticat's Kitchen History." *Meridians: feminism, race, transnationalism* 5.1 (2004): 92–116.

Lusane, Clarence. *Race in the Global Era: African Americans at the Millennium*. Boston: South End Press, 1999.

MacDonald-Smythe, Antonia. *Making Homes in the West/Indies: Constructions of Subjectivity in the Writings of Michelle Cliff and Jamaica Kincaid*. New York: Garland, 2001.

Mahoney, Rosemary. "'Don't Nobody Want Me. Don't Nobody Need Me.'" *New York Times* 7 July 1996: BR9.

Marable, Manning. *Black Leadership*. New York: Columbia University Press, 1998.

Mardorossian, Carine M. *Reclaiming Difference: Caribbean Women Rewrite Postcolonialism*. Charlottesville: University Press of Virginia, 2005.

Marshall, Paule. *The Chosen Place, the Timeless People*. New York: Vintage, 1984.

———. "From the Poets in the Kitchen." *Callaloo* 18 (1983): 22–30.

———. *Praisesong for the Widow*. New York: Plume, 1983.

Matthews, Dom Basil. *Crisis of the West Indian Family*. Westport, CT: Greenwood Press, 1971.

McAdoo, Harriette Pipes, ed. *Black Families*. 4th ed. Thousand Oaks, CA: Sage Publications, 2007.

McNeil, Elizabeth. "The Gullah Seeker's Journey in Paule Marshall's *Praisesong for the Widow.*" *MELUS* 34.1 (2009): 185–209.

Metraux, Alfred. *Voodo in Haiti*. New York: Schocken Books, 1972.

Michlin, Monica. "Narrative as Empowerment: Push and the Signifying on Prior African American Novels on Incest." *Etudes Anglaises* 59.2 (2006): 170–85.

Mohanty, Chandra. *Feminism without Borders: Decolonizing Theory, Practicing Solidarity*. Durham: Duke University Press, 2003.

Morris, Ann R., and Margaret Dunn. "'The Bloodstream of Our Inheritance': Female Identity and the Caribbean Mothers'-Land." *Motherlands: Black Women's Writing from the Africa, the Caribbean, and South Asia*. Ed. Susheila Nasta. New Brunswick: Rutgers University Press, 1992.

Morris, Lorenzo, ed. *The Social and Political Implications of the Jesse Jackson Presidential Campaign*. New York: Praeger, 1990.

Morrison, Toni. *The Bluest Eye*. New York: Vintage, 2007.

———. *Paradise*. New York: Plume, 1999.

———. "Rootedness: The Ancestor as Foundation." *Toni Morrison: What Moves at the Margin*. Ed. Carolyn C. Denard. Jackson: University Press of Missouri, 2008.

———. *Sula*. New York: Vintage, 2004.

Moynihan, Daniel Patrick. *The Negro Family: The Case for National Action*. Office of Planning and Research, Department of Labor. March 1965. www.dol.gov/oasam/programs/history/webid-meynihan.htm. 18 June 2008.

Murdoch, H. Adlai. "Severing the (M)other Connection: The Representation of Cultural Identity in Jamaica Kincaid's *Annie John*." *Callaloo* 13.2 (1990): 325–40.

Naylor, Gloria. *Mama Day*. New York: Vintage, 1989.

———. *The Women of Brewster Place*. New York: Penguin, 1983.

Nicholls, David. *From Dessalines to Duvalier: Race, Colour and National Independence in Haiti*. New Brunswick: Rutgers University Press, 1996.

Niesen de Abruña, Laura. "Family Connection: Mother Country in the Fiction of Jean Rhys and Jamaica Kincaid." *Motherlands: Black Women's Writing from Africa, the Caribbean and South Asia*. Ed. Susheila Nasta. London: Women's Press, 1991.

Noguera, Pedro A. *The Imperatives of Power: Political Change and the Social Basis of Regime Support in Grenada from 1951–1991*. New York: Peter Lang, 1997.

O'Callaghan, Evelyn. "Compulsory Heterosexuality and Textual/Sexual Alternatives in Selected Texts by West Indian Writers." *Caribbean Portraits: Essays on Gender Ideologies and Identities*. Ed. Christine Barrow. Kingston: Ian Randle Publications, 1998. 294–319.

———. *Woman Version: Theoretical Approaches to West Indian Fiction by Women*. London: Macmillan Caribbean, 1993.

Olmos, Margarite Fernández, and Lizabeth Paravisini-Gebert. *Sacred Possessions: Vodou, Santería, Obeah, and the Caribbean*. New Brunswick: Rutgers University Press, 1997.

Olupona, Jacob Kehinde. Foreword. *Women in the Yoruba Religious Sphere*. By Oyeronke Olajubu. Albany: State University of New York Press, 2003.

Paravisini-Gebert, Lizabeth. "Decolonizing Feminism: The Home Grown Roots of Caribbean Women's Movements." *Daughters of Caliban: Caribbean Women in the Twentieth Century*. Ed. Consuelo López Springfield. Bloomington: Indiana University Press, 1997.

Patterson, James T. *Freedom Is Not Enough: The Moynihan Report and America's Struggle over Black Family Life from LBJ to Obama*. New York: Basic Books, 2010.

Patterson, Orlando. *Rituals of Blood: Consequences of Slavery in Two American Centuries*. Washington, DC: Civitas Counterpoint, 1998.

Perry, Donna. "Initiation in Jamaica Kincaid's *Annie John*." *Caribbean Women Writers: Essays from the First International Conference*. Ed. Selwyn R. Cudjoe. Wellesley: Calaloux Publications, 1990. 245–53.

Pettis, Joyce. *Towards Wholeness in Paule Marshall's Fiction*. Charlottesville: University Press of Virginia, 1995.

Pollard, Velma. "Cultural Connections in Paule Marshall's *Praise Song for the Widow*." *World Literature Written in English* 25.2 (1985): 285–98.

Pough, Gwendolyn D. *Check It While I Wreck It: Black Womanhood, Hip-Hop Culture, and the Public Sphere*. Boston: Northeastern University Press, 2004.

Powell, Patricia. *Me Dying Trial: A Novel*. Boston: Bluestreak, 2003.

Pyne-Timothy, Helen. "Adolescent Rebellion and Gender Relations in *At the Bottom of the River* and *Annie John*." *Caribbean Women Writers: Essays from the First International Conference*. Ed. Selwyn R. Cudjoe. Wellesley: Calaloux Publications, 1990. 233–42.

Ramsey, Guthrie P. *Race Music: Black Cultures from Bebop to Hip-Hop*. Berkeley: University of California Press, 2003.

Reed, Adolph, Jr., ed. *Without Justice for All: The New Liberalism and Our Retreat from Racial Equality*. New York: Westview Press, 2001.

Renda, Mary A. *Taking Haiti: Military Occupation and the Culture of U.S. Imperialism, 1915–1940*. Chapel Hill: University of North Carolina Press, 2001.

Renk, Kathleen J. *Caribbean Shadows and Victorian Ghosts: Women's Writing and Decolonization*. Charlottesville: University Press of Virginia, 1999.

Rodman, Hyman. *Lower-Class Families: The Culture of Poverty in Negro Trinidad*. New York: Oxford University Press, 1971.

Rody, Caroline. *The Daughter's Return: African-American and Caribbean Women's Fictions of History*. Oxford: Oxford University Press, 2001.

Rooks, Noliwe M. *Hair Raising: Beauty, Culture, and African American Women*. New Brunswick: Rutgers University Press, 1996.

Rossi, Jennifer C. "'Let the words bring wings to our feet': Negotiating Exile and Trauma through Narrative in Danticat's *Breath, Eyes, Memory*." *Obsidian III* 6, no. 7 (2005–06): 147–58. Web. 23 July 2010.

Rountree, Wendy A. "Overcoming Violence: Blues Expression in Sapphire's *Push*." *Atenea* 24.1 (2004): 133–43.

Sandiford, Keith A. "Paule Marshall's *Praisesong for the Widow*: The Reluctant Heiress, or Whose Life Is It Anyway." *Black American Literature Forum* 20.4 (1986): 371–92.

Sapphire. "Artist with a Mission: A Conversation with Sapphire." Interview by Owen Keehnen. 1996. www.glbtq.com/sfeatures/interviewsapphire.html. 9 June 2008.

———. *Push*. New York: Vintage, 1996.

———. "Sapphire's Big Push." Interview by Mark Marvel. 1996. www.findarticles.com/p/articles/mi_m1285/is_n6_v26/ai_18450196. 19 June 2008.

Senior, Olive. *Working Miracles: Women's Lives in the English-Speaking Caribbean*. London: James Curry, 1991.

Simey, T. S. *Welfare and Planning in the West Indies*. Oxford: Clarendon Press, 1946.

Simmons, Diane. *Jamaica Kincaid*. New York: Twayne, 1994.

Simpson, George Eaton. *Black Religions in the New World*. New York: Columbia University Press, 1978.

Slater, Mariam K. *The Caribbean Family: Legitimacy in Martinique*. New York: St. Martin's Press, 1977.

Smith, Raymond T. *The Matrifocal Family: Power, Pluralism, and Politics*. New York: Routledge, 1996.

Smock, Pamela, and Wendy Manning. "New Couples, New Families: The Cohabitation Revolution in the United States." *Families as They Really Are*. Ed. Barbara J. Risman. New York: W. W. Norton, 2010.

Sowell, Thomas. *The Vision of the Anointed: Self-Congratulation as a Basis for Social Policy*. New York: Basic Books, 1996.

Stapleton, Laurie. "Toward a New Learning System: A Freirean Reading of Sapphire's *Push*." *Women's Studies Quarterly* 1.2 (2004): 213–23.

Stevenson, Pascha A. "Dreaming in Color: Race and the Spectacular in *The Agüero Sisters* and *Praisesong for the Widow*." *Frontiers: A Journal of Women's Studies*. 28.3 (2007): 141–59.

Storey, Olivia Smith. "Flying Words: Contests of Orality and Literacy in the Trope of the Flying Africans." *Journal of Colonialism and Colonial History* 5.3 (2004):

Stuckey, Sterling. *Slave Culture: Nationalist Theory and the Foundations of Black America*. New York: Oxford University Press, 1987.

Thomas, Greg. *The Sexual Demon of Colonial Power: Pan-African Embodiment and Erotic Schemes of Power*. Bloomington: Indiana University Press, 2007.

Thompson, Lisa B. *Beyond the Black Lady: Sexuality and the New African American Middle Class*. Urbana-Champaign: University of Illinois Press, 2009.

Thorsson, Courtney. "Dancing Up a Nation: Paule Marshall's *Praisesong for the Widow*." *Callaloo* 30.2 (2007): 644–52.

Tiffin, Helen. "Cold Hearts and (Foreign) Tongues: Recitation and Reclamation of the Female Body in the Works of Erna Brodber and Jamaica Kincaid." *Callaloo* 16.3 (1993): 909–21.

Walker, Alice. *The Color Purple*. New York: Harcourt, 2003.

Wall, Cheryl A. *Worrying the Line: Black Women Writers, Lineage, and Literary Tradition*. Chapel Hill: University of North Carolina Press, 2005.

West, Cornel. *Race Matters*. New York: Beacon Press, 2001.

White, E. Frances. *Dark Continent of Our Bodies: Black Feminism and the Politics of Respectability*. Philadelphia: Temple University Press, 2001.

Wilentz, Gay. *Binding Cultures: Black Women Writers in Africa and the Diaspora*. Bloomington: Indiana University Press, 1992.

———. *Healing Narratives: Women Writers Curing Cultural Disease.* New Brunswick: Rutgers University Press, 2000.

———. "If You Surrender to the Air: Folk Legends of Flight and Resistance in African American Literature." *MELUS* 16.1 (Spring 1989–90): 21–32.

Wilson, Peter J. *Crab Antics: The Social Anthropology of English-Speaking Negro Societies of the Caribbean.* New Haven: Yale University Press, 1973.

Index

3/26/14